W9-BPS-295

Rousseau's *Social Contract*

ROUSSEAU'S
SOCIAL CONTRACT

AN INTERPRETIVE ESSAY

LESTER G. CROCKER

THE PRESS OF CASE WESTERN RESERVE UNIVERSITY
CLEVELAND   1968

For Jean Fabre,
erudito praeclaro, amico dilecto

Preface

WHAT makes Rousseau a truly challenging figure, an inexhaustibly intriguing one, is that his message, like those of other seminal figures, is still subject to debate, not only as to its validity, but as to its meaning and import as well. We are still learning how to read Rousseau—even as some claim that we are only beginning to read Marx and Freud. And it is true that there is much in Rousseau that we have not learned to read. Continuing reinterpretations of his works are a witness to this fact.[1] Rousseau himself twice stated that he could not be understood by his own time, and continuing diversity of opinion would lead one to question whether he has been understood in ours.

Two facts are of concern to us: first, the existence, since Rousseau's time, of analogical ways of thinking about a fundamental reorganization of society and the treatment of its individual components; second, the ability which our own historical experience gives us to penetrate the meaning of his thought and to assess its significance to us. Some will object, on grounds of principle, to categorizing and judging Rousseau's political theory in the light of quite different times. To this it may be replied that if the *interpretation* of his theories is carried out on the basis of his own thought, and if we admit that they, or analogical theories, have continued to influence men's minds continuously from his time to ours, then an *evaluation* of his thought and of its implications can legitimately be made from the perspective of our own judgments and experience. The refusal of comparison and of judgment is not acceptable to the humanistically inclined

writer. Yet it must be made quite clear at the outset that it is
never my thought to hold Rousseau accountable for later historical developments (such as the existence, philosophy, or form of
totalitarian societies). It is my purpose to interpret the meaning
and the inherent tendencies of his vision of the good society.

One obstacle to a "complete" reading of Rousseau has been his
vocabulary—i.e., his using words in senses peculiar to himself.
In another context he warned Mme. d'Epinay about this. "Learn
my own dictionary better, my good friend, if you want us to
understand each other. Realize that my terms rarely have their
usual meaning." [2] The result has been that his interpreters have
often taken his words (such as "liberty") in the sense in which
they themselves used them, or in the sense they expected them to
have, or wished them to have, instead of in the sense which he
gave them. In fact, Rousseau was well aware of the power of
words—not only as a master rhetorician himself, but as one who
had denounced language for its corrupting effect on truthful
communication. I think that he would have subscribed to Susanne Langer's remark:

> Because our moral life is negotiated so largely by symbols, it is
> more oppressive than the morality of animals. . . . animals react
> only to deed that is done or is actually imminent; . . . whereas
> we control each other's merely incipient behavior with fantasies
> of force. . . . the power of symbols enables us not only to limit
> each other's actions, but to command them; not only to *restrain* one
> another, but to *constrain*. . . . The story of man's martyrdom is a
> sequel to the story of his intelligence, his power of symbolical en-
> visagement.[3]

A second obstacle in reading Rousseau is the emotions which,
as a person and a thinker, he has consistently aroused since his
own time. It seems that one has to be "for" him or "against" him,
to condemn him or to idolize him, in either case to the point of
fanaticism. Since many who entitle themselves "defenders" of
Rousseau are partisans of the liberal democratic tradition and
have interpreted his thought as belonging to the substance of
that tradition, it is inevitable that they become emotionally
aroused by those who consider Rousseau to be the genius and

innovator of the totalitarian democratic tradition (though let us say again, he is by no means its sole author!) and that they call such writers "enemies" of Rousseau—as if the situation might not well be reversed if they stood in the other camp. The real "enemy" of Rousseau, in my opinion, is not one who seeks the truth objectively, but one who seeks to use Rousseau's writings to support his own preformed viewpoint.

If the second obstacle is to impose aprioristically a given view, the third lies in the failure to consider adequately the totality of Rousseau's writings and their relation to each other. Literary scholars frequently slight the philosophical substance, while political philosophers tend to neglect the apparently non-political writings. Both groups are in error. Rousseau himself tells us in the *Confessions* that in the last analysis everything is reducible to politics or is a part of it. In the larger sense of the word—the sense in which he used it—*La Nouvelle Héloïse* and *Emile* are quite as much political works as *Du Contrat social* (the *Social Contract*).

The *Social Contract* is, of course, Rousseau's principal theoretical treatise, though it by no means contains all of his ideas. The divergent interpretations of that work stem from apparently contradictory or ambiguous statements, some of which are given greater weight than others, according to the inclination of the commentators. For the most part, the "contradictions" and ambiguities are not real, but a result of Rousseau's peculiar interpretations of words or ideas. It follows that we need more light with which to read the *Social Contract*, and that light must come from without—from his other writings, and also from his personality, which expressed itself in them in a most extraordinary way. We must provide a context for the *Social Contract* by reconstructing to some degree the type of mind that conceived it and the kind of society in which that mind dreamed of living.[4] For this purpose I shall in the first chapter examine pertinent aspects of Rousseau's other writings in chronological order. References to his personality will necessarily be brief. The problems raised by a detailed consideration of his character and experience and of their relation to his philosophy are so complex that to treat them in depth would require the writing of a different kind of book. This I have in fact done, at least for the first part of Rousseau's life, and the interested reader may wish to turn to that volume.[5]

Following a study of the context, we shall hopefully be in a position to interpret Rousseau's meanings and intentions in the *Social Contract*. We shall approach it not as an isolated unit but as one segment of a total enterprise which he has left for us to put together, having never completed it as he conceived it in his mind.

A third chapter, which will follow the fortunes of Rousseau's ideas, is intended to be suggestive, not exhaustive. In it we are primarily concerned not with determining historical influence, but rather with suggesting certain meaningful identities in ways of thinking. A consideration of three twentieth-century utopias (or anti-utopias) will provide fruitful analogies and will focus on the implications of a philosophy and the later reverberations of a concept which has had its own fortunes, regardless of Rousseau's influence. These additional perspectives will enable us in the final chapter to postulate the idea of a political archetype and to draw other conclusions.

It is not the purpose of this essay to review the extensive literature in the controversy over Rousseau's politics. (For a good review, see J. W. Chapman's *Rousseau—Totalitarian or Liberal?*) Nor is it my intention to enter into debate and propose systematic refutations of opposing critiques. My purpose is expressed in the subtitle. I shall feel free to bring in other accounts when I find it useful to do so. Consequently, the bibliography is not intended to be exhaustive, and I have not deemed it necessary to cite all the works I have read.

Within the text itself my method of citation has been to refer to those works of Rousseau's which have been translated into English first by their original French titles and thereafter in English. Works which have not been translated are referred to by their French titles throughout, with the exception of *Projet de constitution pour la Corse* (*Project of a Constitution for Corsica*) and *Considérations sur le gouvernement de Pologne* (*Considerations on the Government of Poland*). Since both are frequently referred to by the English equivalents of the French titles, I have used the English titles though no translations presently exist.

I wish to thank the following publishers for allowing me to include copyrighted material: Brandt & Brandt, for permission to reprint passages from *Nineteen Eighty-Four*, by George Orwell, copyright 1949, by Harcourt, Brace and World; and The Macmillan Company, for permission to reproduce quotations from *Walden Two*, by B. F. Skinner, copyright 1948, by B. F. Skinner.

To Professors Gregor Sebba and Leland Thielemann, and to Mr. Howard Webber, Director of the Press of Case Western Reserve University, I express my gratitude for their valuable criticisms and suggestions. Needless to say, they are not responsible for any of the opinions in this essay.

January 1, 1968

Notes

[1] See, for instance, my article "Julie, ou la nouvelle duplicité," *Annales de la Société Jean-Jacques Rousseau*, XXXVI (1963–65), 105–52. (*Annales de la Société Jean-Jacques Rousseau* hereinafter will be abbreviated *AJJR*.)

[2] *Correspondance*, ed. R. A. Leigh (Geneva, 1965 *et seq.*), III, 295–96. Letter dated 12 March 1756. The older edition of Rousseau's correspondence, entitled *Correspondance générale*, is by Dufour-Plan.

[3] S. Langer, *Philosophy in a New Key* (Cambridge, 1942), p. 286.

[4] The *Social Contract*, according to O. Vossler, is fragmentary and does not "bear its meaning explicitly enclosed in itself." (W. Hempel, review of O. Vossler, *Rousseaus Freiheitslehre*, in *AJJR*, XXXVI [1967], 313.)

[5] See my biography, *Jean-Jacques Rousseau: The Quest* (1712–1758), New York, 1968; but the problem will be approached specifically in the second (as yet uncompleted) volume. Several ideas and developments in the first chapter of this essay are also expressed in the aforementioned book, which is addressed to a more general audience; they are necessary to an understanding of the second chapter.

Contents

Rousseau's *Social Contract*

1. The Context

In a little known piece, "Projet pour l'éducation de M. de Sainte-Marie," written in 1740 during an unhappy experience as tutor to a fractious child, Rousseau gives us the first sign of his intellectual orientation in the matter of interpersonal relations.[1] The tutor, he declares, must control the child's behavior. He must form his charge early "in the mold of obedience and docility." Overt coercion or punishment, however, is the wrong way of doing this. Instead, Rousseau proposes a strategy of deceptive tactics and stage settings. Rewards and punishment are the necessary stimuli. But they must *seem* to be the mechanical consequences of proper or improper conduct—like the rewards and punishments used today to condition animals in laboratory experiments—rather than evidence of *personal* approval or disapproval on the part of the figure in authority. Thus the father grants rewards only when secretly prompted by the tutor. Rousseau goes so far as to set up a secret system of signals, such as the tutor's touching certain buttons on his coat (like the third-base coach in a baseball game), so that the father should pretend to have in mind the particular attitude which the tutor wishes him to take. The child, then, unaware of the manipulation to which he is being submitted, has the impression of a necessary concatenation of cause and effect. The end to which this system of training is a means is, we are told, "to know how to catch [men] by their virtues and their weak points, so as to use them for [one's] own purpose." The other significant idea in the "Projet" is that reason, in Rousseau's opinion, was given to us to combat nature. These are, of course, initial tendencies, the import of which is as yet minor. Inasmuch as they will develop into a major strategy, however, they give us a key to the interpretation of Rousseau's great systems.

Nine years after the "Projet," in 1749, came the famous "Illumination of Vincennes." Rousseau had not succeeded in finding a role or identity in Parisian society. There is no doubt that he had done everything he could to win the recognition and fame that were necessary to an identity which he could accept as his own and which would enable him to overcome his powerful feelings of inferiority. Had he been able to accomplish this, there would have been no "crisis of Vincennes." But this hope, for reasons that would take us too far afield to analyze, was from the beginning an impossible one. It is enough to remember that his reply to the question of "Whether the renascence of the sciences and the arts has contributed to the improvement of morals," posed by the Academy of Dijon in its prize contest, was determined ultimately by psychological factors which produced an intellectual conviction.

The story of his rapturous revelation on the road to Vincennes is too well known to warrant retelling. He had found a great idea, but more significant was the emotional release it brought to him. His great inspiration was more than a new intellectual outlook; it was a deliverance. He had found the way to free himself from the bondage of dependence on the approbation of a world that would not recognize his worth and in which he could not feel at home, a world in which he suffered the stings of inferiority, failure, and rejection, but which he felt was inferior to him. This was the way of proving his superior worth, the way of independence. In reality, it was another way of forcing recognition—a disguised dependence.

But all these emotional factors were bound up in an intellectual concept. The question in the *Mercure de France* had unlocked the door to a dazzling vision of a different kind of world. As yet the vision was only of the past, of a world in which men did not devour each other, or live an artificial life of false appearances and dissimulation, or rival for wealth, prestige, and importance in order to feel and proclaim their superiority and to have that feeling confirmed by others.

The *Discours sur les sciences et les arts* (*Discourse on the Sciences and the Arts*, 1750; hereafter referred to as the first *Discourse*) contains the beginnings of Rousseau's social criticism. The arts and sciences are both a sign and a cause of the moral vileness and the artificiality and falsehood that characterize social life. Another psychological factor is already in evidence. Beneath Rousseau's revolt against the established order and value system lies a deep-seated *need* for order, that is, for a rigid value system; and this need will express itself in his philosophy.[2] Again we are involved with the basic makeup of his personality, with the overdeveloped sense of right and mission that is an essential element of the obsessional state of mind which characterizes him. If we understand the paradoxical connection that can occur between opposites in certain types of human personality, the persistent ambivalence that may be present in them, we shall not be surprised that he is both an individualist, or rebel, and an authoritarian—one who will go so far as to demand total control of the individual and the reshaping of his personality. We shall find that, on the one hand, he will defend nature and condemn society; on the other hand, society will find in him its most extreme defender, and nature its most cruel repressor. It is well known that fantasy and projection into ideal worlds were an outstanding feature of Rousseau's personality; and, indeed, they always characterize the obsessionist. The ideal worlds we shall watch him constructing in his writings were a way of finding a home (and to a large extent he was aware of it) for his ideal self, for Jean-Jacques as he consciously or unconsciously wished to be. This "home" we shall find to be, above all else, one of order—i.e., of rigid values.

In the first *Discourse* we encounter for the first time Rousseau's persistent admiration for Spartans, and for certain other primitive peoples. The qualities he admires in them are explicit: their scorn for intellectual and aesthetic activities, their discipline of the individual ego as evidenced in the military virtues, and, in general, a spirit of devotion to and unlimited sacrifice for the collectivity. "Zeal" would be the proper word. This spirit is what he will call "virtue." Sparta, as we know, was a totalitarian society, militaristic, egalitarian, and willfully obscurantist. Obscurantism was a means to discipline of the ego; we must realize that it was in this light that Rousseau understood and approved it. He also admired Sparta's puritanism, and indeed his own puritanism has not been adequately emphasized by scholars.

We see already the germ of Rousseau's undeveloped political philosophy when he tells us: "It is easier to guide people than to enlighten them," easier "to force them to do good than to induce them to do it of their own free will." [3] His citizens, as we shall see, will be regimented, trained from earliest childhood to place community above self, and, most important, to do this not intellectually, but reflexively. As for the arts and sciences, perhaps they are not entirely avoidable. However, they too can be controlled and directed, utilized by the collectivity for its chosen ends instead of being allowed, as in the present societies of anarchic individualists, to promote disintegration of the social fabric.

Rousseau's romantic outcries against social chains, against the chains of opinion that bind the individual and deprive him of his autonomy of judgment, are manifestations of an almost anarchistic wish for independence. But we must take these outbursts as modes of reaction against the world he knew. Fundamentally, his own longing is for a happy dependence, and dependence will inform his ideal societies. Rousseau's abiding belief, his central tenet, is that dependence on other *men* (as individuals or partial groups) is inherently and irremediably pernicious. It forces men "to be tyrants or slaves, to become envious, dishonest and treacherous." [4] This fact leads us to see the real consistency of his work, beneath the apparent contradictions. Always, he will support independence in this sense. But there is another road, and it is the chosen way of his idealized intellectual and emotional fantasies. There is another kind of dependence, one that men have not known since Sparta—the *impersonal* dependence on the collective will. There was no other way, he was convinced, to a just and happy society; and this, it should never be forgotten, was his sole aim. Thus his individualism is a confrontation with existing societies; but the condemnation of individualism, of free thought and action, of unguided pluralism, is already hatched in the first *Discourse*. Rousseau (as he himself was to say about self-styled cosmopolitans) did not love men; but he loved Mankind.[5] As he wrote in the *Confessions*, he loved men when he was far away from them. This kind of abstract love, let us note in passing, is the harbinger of fanaticisms which justify the imposition of cruelty and oppression in the name of an abstract welfare or an eventual utopia.

Now at last Rousseau had found the identity he had been seeking—as guide, teacher, prophet to mankind: a role which implies a kind of fanaticism. He had a passion for justice which, like that of Don Quixote, could not brook the compromises and imperfections that are part of the human condition. Hence his millennial vision and his tone bear the mark of the prophet.[6]

Another powerful thrust followed, in the Preface to his play *Narcisse* (1753). Here his thinking becomes both sharper and harder. He proposes two firm reasons for condemning existing societies: they make men dependent on other individuals or on what we would call power groups; and they are competitive, not co-operative. It is impossible for men to coexist in a competitive society without "deceiving each other, betraying each other, destroying each other." There is a simple reason for this necessity: our personal interests set us in opposition to each other and to the general welfare as well. Thus he rejects, and he will continue to reject, the prevailing philosophy of enlightened self-interest as an exercise in futility and self-delusion, or a trap for dupes—so it is, at least, in competitive societies.

One other point, and I shall make it only once, though it is recurrent in Rousseau's writings: the people cannot be trusted by the statesman. Men are evil in society, which has awakened their *amour-propre*. This, he will explain, is an aggressive and destructive form of pride. The people are too stupid to know the general interest or too selfish to follow it. Here is a key sentence in the Preface to *Narcisse:* "For customs are the morality of the common people; as soon as they stop respecting them, they have no other rule except their passions, no brake except the laws, *which can sometimes contain the wicked but never make them good."* [7] The phrase I have italicized foreshadows the future lines of Rousseau's social planning. In a contemporaneous letter he writes: "We must reason with the wise, but never with the public. The common herd has long been compared to a flock of sheep." [8]

Rousseau's critique of society reached its culmination in the *Discours sur l'origine de l'inégalité* (*Discourse on the Origin of Inequality,* 1755; hereafter referred to as the second *Discourse*). Although it is still essentially negative, the second *Discourse,* in its very criticisms, contains by implication the principles he will develop in his positive writings. Understanding this, we are no longer troubled by the apparent contradiction between the two phases, and we are able to take the second *Discourse* as the groundwork for his program for a controlled collectivity. Its indictment of society bares the evils which Rousseau will make it his business to avoid or overcome. In every human relationship inequality, oppression, and domination are inevitable. Men are corrupted in society because society rests on power and exploitation, rather than on law and co-operation.[9] Because natural self-love is perverted to *amour-propre,* which is a comparative need for prestige and superiority, they "no longer seek to satisfy themselves by their real good, but by hurting others." [10] Freedom is lost by material and spiritual dependency. The former compels men to seek wealth and power at any price, the latter compels them to dominate others in order to obtain recognition (or the satisfactions of "opinion").[11] "What can we think," he asks, "of a relationship in which each individual's reason dictates maxims directly contrary to those which the public reason preaches to the social body, and in which he finds his own benefit in the misfortune of others?" [12] We at once see the connection with the *Social Contract,* in the first version of which (meditated on at about this time and written shortly after) Rousseau will say that unity requires "a universal motive that makes each part act for a common end relative to the whole." [13] In a statement such as this we can also grasp a notion that is basic to his thinking, although it is generally overlooked. If he maintains in the second *Discourse* that men are not naturally social, it is because, as he understands the expression, being "naturally social" would require them *naturally* to put the general interest above their individual welfare. They would be dependent, *naturally,* on a collective whole. The purpose of his positive, ideal reconstructions, as the sentence we have quoted already indicates, will be precisely this: to show the way in which culture can effectuate that which nature has failed to do. In various shapes and contexts they will tell us how to make men social beings, i.e., virtuous beings subjected to order, in the way that nature would have done it (were not human societies, by their very essence, an alienation from nature)—that is, by giving to men reflexive social behavior having the certainty, as he puts it in *Emile,* of behavior determined by physical laws. But none of this can ever come about "naturally," that is, in the unguided course of history. As one scholar comments, men cannot save themselves or by themselves escape from the horrors of history; they require a leader, guide, or master. [14]

In this light, Rousseau's condemnation in the second *Discourse* of free competition, private rights (such as property), and inequality takes on added meaning from the eventual conclusion. Other *dicta* reveal ways of thinking that are typical of a pattern which psychologists and sociologists now call "the authoritarian mind." He approves of the Spartan practice of exposing children and eliminating the weak. (The fact that he was one of the weak makes the affirmation all the more typical.) Women he defines as the sex that should obey. As in the first *Discourse,* Lycurgus is his hero and model; but now the reason becomes clearer. Lycurgus was the great Legislator, in Rousseau's mind, because he "gave a people morals." What Rousseau means (he goes on to explain) is that in Sparta, and in Sparta alone, the law was concerned not with direct, or *overt,* regulation of its citizens' behavior, but with indirect control through what he calls "education." [15] Now it will become perfectly clear in

Rousseau's later works that for him "education" is something different from our understanding of the word. It is, in fact, a process of training, or indoctrination, for what he will call "docility"—a process of making people manageable and determining their behavior.[16] Lycurgus' greatness, then, lay in imposing mores which made laws almost unnecessary: "Laws, generally weaker than passions, contain men without changing them."

I have referred in passing to another fundamental notion that haunted Rousseau's mind, man's alienation—from nature, from other men, and (through what he calls bondage to "opinion"[17]) from himself. There is an interesting historical analogy in the fact that all twentieth-century totalitarian movements, as well as the earlier Marxist philosophy, arose as antidotes to alienation. Rousseau, like Fourier and Marx, writes one Marxist scholar, "understood that it is insane to seek happiness in the struggle against others, in domination and oppression; it can be found only in the reconciliation of mankind."[18]

It is precisely in this direction that Rousseau makes his next move. If culture is to repair the work of nature, which failed to make man a social being, it must create a new, superior "self" that will surpass, absorb, and unite the separated individuals, for each of whom his own little self is the center of the world. This is the central philosophical theme of the important article which Rousseau wrote, also in 1755, for the *Encyclopédie*, entitled "Economie politique" ("Political Economy").

"Political Economy" proclaims that the solution to the human problem lies in finding ways to give to the collective or "general" interest a *natural force*—that is, one that is reflexive and does not depend on a process of rational reflection—as, for example, in the unsocialized individual self-interest is a natural force. This, we recall, is what Sparta exemplified. Accomplishing this end involves the artificial conversion of the social or political body into an analogue of an organic body: "an organized, living body, similar to that of man." What is the defining character of such a body? It is fusion, or unity—the opposite of that of existing societies, which are in a relation of juxtaposition. In the truly social body, as in the natural, "the life of both is the self which is common to the whole, the reciprocal sensitivity and the internal harmony of all the parts." It follows that "the political body is also, then, a moral being, which has a will." [19] We can see why this must be so in Rousseau's grand design. Were it otherwise, the individual conscience might at times be morally superior to the law, or at least consider itself as such. And then we could bid adieu to the collective, organic unity of the political body. Consequently, Rousseau declares that "nothing which the law commands can be illegitimate." By definition, the law is just, or to put it differently, law is prior to justice. [20] It follows, too, that there is no limit in what is called "natural rights" to the properly exercised power of the State (a boundary that will be explicated in the *Social Contract*). The new collective State replaces nature and is the highest, the sole authority. The new artificially created "self," for which Rousseau has had to coin a phrase, *"le moi commun"* ("the collective self"), and its will, which he denominates *"la volonté générale"* ("the general will"), must achieve unquestioned precedence over their antitheses and deadly, eternal foes, called by Rousseau *"le moi humain"* ("the human [i.e., natural] self") and *"la volonté particulière"* ("the private will"). There is no longer an ethical problem, inasmuch as this kind of political subjection *is* essentially ethical, for the collective self is the highest moral value and the chief ethical agency. "The morality of the individual and that of the City," affirms Burgelin, "are really only one." [21] The reduction of the ethical and the political to equivalence inevitably results in the absorption of the ethical by the political. And this is precisely what Rousseau intended when he wrote in the *Confessions* that ultimately everything is part of politics, the art of governing men. He repeated the idea in *Emile,* affirming that "those who try to treat morals and politics separately will never understand anything about either one of them." [22]

Private wills are not only those of atomistic individuals. They include smaller general wills—what we denote as "group interests." These are "private" by virtue of their distinctness from the true general will, that of the *moi commun*, which is obviously always one and universal, since a "self" does not have contradictory wills. Private wills, whether individual or those of special groups, are, according to Rousseau, inevitably opposed to the general will—we may assume, by definition. It follows—and this is a point of maximum importance—that Rousseau has no trust in the unguided individual, whose *natural* egocentrism is the critical obstacle to be overcome. He understands, then, that the work of culture is to alienate the individual ego from the dynamics of instinct, to impose renunciation and limitations. What distinguishes his thought is his intent: to carry this process to its utmost possible limits, and at the same time, to do it in such a way that the individual will not feel that there has been any renunciation or sacrifice. He will seek ways to produce a reflexive behavior and a complete emotional identification, such as nature produces in the family, with a collective self that the individual will consider as his own self.[23] This will constitute the originality and peculiar genius of Rousseau's thought.

At this point he introduces another of his great inventions. In his mind, as we have just seen, the question is one of constraint and freedom. Is it possible to constrain behavior, to shape it (to "yoke" it, he would say) to the general will without destroying freedom? Rousseau's brilliant reply is that this is precisely what law does: "it subjects men in order to make them free." Under law, each obeys and no one commands; each serves, yet has no master, since all are equal under it. Law is "that celestial voice which dictates to each citizen the precepts of public reason, and teaches him to act according to the maxims of his own judgment, and not to be in contradiction with himself." [24]

The unwary reader will be misled into an enthusiastic acceptance of a concept that seems perfectly straightforward and liberal. Only if we peer closely into the last sentence will we realize the real measure of Rousseau's intent. His concept of submission to law reaches far beyond overt action, reaches into the mind and personality. It sets up for each citizen a "true" judgment and a "true" self which he must accept as his own, even if he does not really experience them as such—though Rousseau's prime intent is to *make* him experience them as such. Accepting them as his own, he will forgo, *ipso facto*, any possibility of opposition.

With dissent and pluralism thus eliminated, the *moi commun* can be forged—but only *if* they are first eliminated. It is scarcely necessary to underscore the difference between Rousseau's concept of law and liberty and that which obtains in all liberal or "open" societies. In these, obedience to the general judgment or will (i.e., law) does not involve acceptance of them by an individual as his own, except in the special and quite different sense that he has agreed to obey the law. (In the *Social Contract* Rousseau will deliberately confuse the two senses.) The difference is that we keep our own judgment and will intact; even though we do not attempt to effectuate them directly, we may still try to do so by legal means if we choose. In a word, there is a distance safeguarded between the individual will and the general will, not a fusion of them, and no renunciation is required beyond that of action.

What Rousseau has actually done is to redefine freedom in terms of an "ought," which is obedience, willing or compelled, to the "collective self" rather than to the "human self," to "culture" rather than to nature. We must, however, be aware of his motive and goal. He does not wish to exploit men, but on the contrary, to put an end to their exploitation by powerful, aggressive individuals and groups. He aims only at making men happy by substituting community and harmony for competition and alienation. It is clear to him that there is no way to reach this millennial, utopian goal other than to submit all, equally, to the one overriding will of the State, as formulated in law. A new kind of dependency, rational but total, on the Whole, must be substituted for the evil kind of dependency that has developed historically. The self-sufficiency of the state of nature is thus recovered, by transferring it to the Whole.

Whether this plan was for Rousseau a dream and a fantasy rather than a program of action matters little. All utopias are dreams until someone attempts to make them come true. He saw with perfect clarity that the end he sought in this logical, consistent system he was building for his ideal society required the deepest control of minds and wills. Is it not nature herself that he is planning to outwit and to reconstruct? Though an imbecile can punish crimes, he says, "the true statesman knows how to forestall them; he extends his respectable empire over will even more than over actions." [25] Rousseau is being quite consistent with what he has written elsewhere, and he will never depart from this crucial proposition. To it we must add another, one that is equally crucial. No one, Rousseau recognizes, wants to give up his natural freedom. Therefore, "the greatest talent of leaders is to disguise their power to make it less odious, and to lead the State so peaceably that it seems not to need leaders." This statement reintroduces his favorite technique of *la main cachée*, or the hidden hand, which, strangely, his commentators seem scarcely to have noticed. [26] It is curious to see it reappear in a letter to Mme. d'Epinay (March 1756) in which he discusses her problems with her children. He warns her that her purpose must be to "tame" them, to bring about their complete "submissiveness" ("docility" will be a favorite word). But she will never accomplish this end by relying on rational persuasion or overt constraint. "Act in this fashion," he concludes, "but keep the secret well." Rousseau's motto was "To risk one's life for the truth"; but one of those truths was the usefulness, the necessity, of duplicity and "illusion."

In statements like these we see what is really important, and novel, in Rousseau's doctrine. It is not only the purpose or the institutions, but the techniques of action on the individual. To speak of collective unity or the rule of the general will is inadequate, indeed utterly futile, unless we take the final step, the one that counts. To think that laws, or obedience to laws, can achieve this end is self-delusion. Success or failure hinges almost entirely on what we do to men, on what Rousseau calls "forming citizens":

> If it is good to know how to use men such as they are [the limit of Machiavellian politics, which Rousseau now surpasses], it is much better yet to make them such as you need them to be. The most absolute authority is that which penetrates inside of man and works on the will no less than on actions. Form men, then, if you want to command men. If you want men to obey the laws, make them love them; and if you want them to do what they should,

let it be enough for it to occur to them that they should do it. . . .
But our modern governments . . . do not imagine that it is necessary, or even possible, to go that far.²⁷

It is clear beyond dispute that what Rousseau has in mind is
what we should call the conditioning of men to reflexive behavior, a notion for which, as he understood, his time was not
ready.

We must not forget that no one is naturally a citizen. To make
a citizen—that is, a person who will put the general welfare and
will above his own, or rather consider them as his own—is the
most difficult of all projects.

> Now, to form citizens is not the work of a day; and to have them
> such when they are men, you have to teach them when they are
> children. . . . If, for example, they are taught early enough to
> consider themselves only in their relationship to the Body of the
> State, and to perceive, so to speak, their own existence only as a
> part of its existence, [then they can] love it with that exquisite
> feeling that every man has for himself alone.²⁸

When that comes about, their natural egocentric impulses will
be transformed into *virtue*, their indestructible passions guided
into beneficent channels. "It is too late to draw us out of ourselves once the *moi humain* [contrasted with the *moi commun*],
concentrated in our hearts, has acquired that despicable activity
which absorbs all virtue. . . ." ²⁹

Although Rousseau does not plan to discuss the education of
children here, he makes it clear that they will be raised in
common, so that they will learn "to cherish each other as broth-
ers, never to want anything except what society wants." The
aim, again, is to bring self-interest, "which isolates individuals"
and sets them against each other, under control. To understand
fully this last point, which lies at the base of the whole theoretical construction, let us turn to Rousseau's most vigorous statement on the subject, which we find in a Fragment he did not
publish:

> What makes humanity unhappy is the contradiction between our
> condition and our desires, between our duties and our inclination,

between nature and social institutions, between the man and the citizen. Make man one, and you will make him as happy as he can be. Give him all to the State, or leave him all to himself. But if you divide his heart, you tear him in two. . . . For being nothing except by the Republic, they will be nothing except for it; it will have all they have and will be all they are. To the force of coercion you have added that of will. . . . In another system, there will always be in the State something that does not belong to the State, were it only the will of its members.[30]

The statement is sharper, but the thought is no different: the shift from private person to citizen involves a shift in orientation from self to community, from pleasure to duty, which can be brought about only by "denaturing" and "reshaping" the personality (the terms are Rousseau's), never merely by the constraint of laws. To form the true social "body," that organic, harmonious unity, an end to the disorder or anarchy we now call "freedom" is required.

This brings us back to the crucial question: will people be willing to give up their freedom? Such a sacrifice is not contemplated. Even as men are to be transformed, so must the very meaning of freedom be, so that they will think they are free in obeying, or so that they will freely do whatever is required of them. Each of these somewhat different concepts will be developed by Rousseau, but particularly the second. The first is more rational, though it depends on the emotional identification we have seen. The second involves his creation of what behaviorists now call "human engineering," "behavioral engineering," or "cultural engineering"—systems of control such as those used in some twentieth-century totalitarian societies. What Rousseau calls "liberty," then, will have to be something compatible with the idea of complete control by carefully hidden conditioning and indoctrination.[31]

In these early writings Rousseau has adumbrated an idea he will consistently carry forward—that in a good society (a real society) men are made to be citizens, necessarily virtuous and happy. Whereas Voltaire, Diderot, and others were working to enlarge the sphere of individual self-expression and personal freedom within the existing political framework, we may expect that Rousseau, who believed that such a course would lead to enhancing the anarchy of egocentric, anti-social tendencies, will devise political institutions which favor behavioral control while maintaining a form or concept of political liberty.

We come now to what may be called the middle section of Rousseau's writings. The *Social Contract* is only one of a constellation of four works, all of which were written within a brief span of a few years (1758–62) and reflect the same attitudes and ideas. We must expect, then, that an examination of the other three will illuminate the *Social Contract*.

First, however, we must mention the inspiration which was the fountainhead of three of these works, and which, in retrospect, seems an inevitable part of Rousseau's pattern of thought. Not long after writing "Political Economy," and while he was enjoying his new residence at L'Ermitage (consequently, in the spring or summer of 1756), he conceived the idea of a work to be called *La Morale sensitive, ou le matérialisme du sage*. Self-observation, he tells us in the *Confessions* (Book IX), had led him to the conclusion that if the causes of the changes in men's characters could be determined, we should be able to control men. "It is incontrovertibly more difficult for a good man to resist fully formed desires that he must conquer, than to forestall, change or modify those same desires in their sources, if he could reach back into them." Following Condillac, Rousseau concludes that our states depend on "prior impressions of external objects" which unconsciously fashion our ideas, feelings, and acts. Could we not, he asks, construct an "external regimen," using these "physical principles" to maintain the soul "in the state most favorable to virtue"? We now see Rousseau on the way to his great invention of "human engineering." At this early stage, it is only self-manipulation.

How many errors we should spare reason, how many vices we should stifle before their birth, if we were able to force the animal

economy to favor the moral order it so upsets. . . . everything
acts on our machine and consequently in our soul; everything
offers us a thousand sure holds to govern at their start the feelings
that control us.[32]

Rousseau never wrote this work. I suspect he discovered that
the same person cannot do the manipulating, by reflective
thought, and be at the same time the passive subject who is to
develop spontaneous, reflexive reactions. He will recognize that a
"guide" (Wolmar, Emile's tutor, or the Legislator) is needed to
perform the operations on a subject who is unaware of what is
being done to him. We shall see how Rousseau develops his
peculiar method, which is described symbolically in a remarkable
chapter of *La Nouvelle Héloïse* [33] as *"la main cachée du jardi-
nier"* (the hidden hand of the gardener).

The works that flow from the genial inspiration of *La Morale
sensitive* will make evident Rousseau's abiding belief that an
autonomous moral force, possessing the certainty of natural laws,
cannot be autonomously acquired. The individual's moral freedom, in which Rousseau firmly believed, is what makes his
political freedom intolerable, since he will use it for egoistic or
anti-social ends. As the heroine of *La Nouvelle Héloïse* will say,
"We could never have become virtuous by our own strength." In
his famous letter to Voltaire of August 18, 1756, Rousseau
declares that only nature "is able to compare ends and means
exactly, and to measure force according to resistance." This is
precisely what his plan of "behavioral engineering" involves.

The minor work in the major constellation is the *Lettre à M.
d'Alembert sur les spectacles* (*Letter to d'Alembert on the Theater, 1758*). The fierce attack which Rousseau launches against
the theater rests on the same idea that forms the vertebral column
of the earlier writings, hatred for an ego-centered, competitive
society. But there is a new emphasis on puritanism. Filling out
his social philosophy, he now insists that amusements should be
reduced to a bare minimum. Every amusement that does not
serve a useful social purpose is an outright evil, he argues. Most
dangerous, and most essentially a matter for governmental
control, are sexual mores and activities. In the second *Discourse,*

he had already shown how sex is at the core of aggressive competitiveness. Now he asserts that it directs to egocentric pleasure (*le
moi humain*) the emotional energy that should be reserved for
"virtue" (that is, devotion to the collective whole). Again Sparta
is proposed as model, with its "frugal and laborious life, its pure
and severe mores." Control of sex means one thing: control of
women. This inferior sex, he declares, born to serve men, must
be kept to its domestic duties, confined to female quarters, and
rarely permitted to mingle in men's company.

The methods of manipulation and deception are so powerfully
present in Rousseau's mind that they come out even here. Without their help it would not be possible, he evidently believed, to
maintain that *order* (just and moral) which was one of his
highest values and which men, left to their own contrivings, had
never attained and could never attain. "Do you want to make a
people active and hard-working? Give them public festivals,
offer them amusements that make them love their condition, and
prevent them from enjoying a more pleasant one." [34] If theater
there must be, then what he euphemistically calls "public opinion" should control it and guide it in a useful direction. Since
men are motivated by pleasure, nothing can corrupt a society
more surely, nothing can be better utilized for shaping the
citizens, than their entertainments. [35]

"Public opinion" means that in small towns (Rousseau never
ceases to cry out his abomination of capitals) people can watch
over each other, and the police can watch over all. In Plato's time
and in early Rome, he comments approvingly, "citizens, watch-
ing over each other, accused each other publicly out of zeal for
justice." We have witnessed such practices since Rousseau's
time. "How can the government control morals? I reply that it is
through public opinion. . . . When we do not live within ourselves, but in others, it is their judgments that rule everything." [36]
Without thought control, there is no way of achieving complete
dependence of the individual on the whole. "*Neither reason,
nor virtue nor laws will conquer public opinion as long as we do
not find the art of changing it.*"

Thus far has Rousseau gone in the *Letter to d'Alembert.* The

works that follow will be devoted to the development of methodology, to putting theory into practice. His great novel, *La Nouvelle Héloïse* (1760), is on the surface a story of seduction *via*
virtue, and of redemption. I have shown elsewhere that the
entire work is transfused with duplicity, and that its main subject is the socialization of the refractory individual.[37] What had
been an abstract idea now becomes an intellectual experiment in
the technique and consequences of human engineering. The
premise has been that the ego (*"amour-propre"*) is the enemy of
society; the conclusion, that it must be restructured and re-
oriented toward the collective whole. It remained to him to fill
the gap, by finding out and demonstrating how this could be
done.

The experiment, or demonstration, unfolds on two distinct
levels, but the techniques are basically the same. There are the
plebes, or servants, and there is the ruling elite. The question is
whether the romantic protagonist, Saint-Preux, who is the rebellious and unreconstructed individualist (or the "natural man" in
society) can be made fit for admission into the elite; and whether
Julie (Saint-Preux's former mistress and now the wife of the
master, Wolmar) can really "hold up" and survive under the
stresses which this process involves for her. I shall not attempt to
describe here how Saint-Preux's personality is broken down and
reduced to an infantile *docility* and dependence, or how Wolmar
nonetheless fails to achieve his ultimate goal with him or with
Julie.[38] The elite manipulate the *plebes,* for the benefit of the
collectivity (but principally for their own benefit). The elite, in
turn, are manipulated and controlled by Wolmar, who is the
model of the godlike leader, or "guide," or Legislator, the man
who knows how to "form," to "denature," to "remake" other men
(all Rousseau's terms).[39]

The techniques by which personality is transformed are quite
remarkable. Among them are the building of new associations to
replace old, and the use of what is now called "operant
conditioning." [40] Wolmar is a "penetrating eye," a "living eye,"
who sees and controls the inner lives of his subjects, until they
become his psychological prisoners. His function is (to borrow a

word from the *Social Contract*) to "inform"—that is, to indoctrinate, to manipulate, and to reshape men in the desired image—as Rousseau had urged in "Political Economy." [41]

The various techniques used by Wolmar involve a constant factor: duplicity. It will be Rousseau's continuing belief that overt coercion is self-defeating, that the subjects of manipulation must believe they are acting freely. In several works he will repeat that they must be brought to will "freely" what the guide (or tutor) wants them to will. This becomes quite explicit during the long description of the social and economic organization of Wolmar's domain. By a skillful blend of coercion and duplicity the workers are manipulated, regimented, exploited, without ever realizing what is being done to them. Instead of trying to eliminate the competitive instincts, which he had so vehemently condemned, Rousseau, realizing their depth and their power, harnesses them in various ways to the service of the community. Similarly, self-interest and even the fatal *amour propre* are put to work by various stratagems. "I have never seen any government in which self-interest is so wisely manipulated and in which it notwithstanding has less influence than here. Everything is done with eagerness." [42] The aim, as ever, is to develop reflexive behavior, thus eliminating the need for rational choice of the virtuous course—which Rousseau, aware of men's natural egocentricity, never expected, never relied on. (Rejecting this, he rejected the philosophy of the Enlightenment.) "Never have I seen a household in which everyone served better and was less aware of serving." Wolmar's domain is a microcosm of the great society, his household a model of the organic society of the *moi commun* into which the *moi humain* has been absorbed. Here, says Saint-Preux, "the state of war no longer exists." [43] Instead, "order, peace and innocence" reign. On this level, Rousseau's purpose is achieved. Moral laws have been given that *necessity* of physical laws which he says we must give them. The individual belongs to the collectivity (as in the *Social Contract*) without reservation. The guide, he writes, "had authority over actions only; now he gives himself authority over will." The French vocabulary here suggests the training of animals. We see, then, that Rousseau is carrying out the great precept he announced in "Political Economy," when he spoke of the leader in a state. We are about to see that it will not be otherwise in *Emile.* We shall not be surprised then, to find the same precept in the *Social Contract.*[44]

Because the manipulation is hidden, an inflexible "yoke" is imposed in a way that leaves the illusion of voluntary commitment. Rousseau puts it in plain words: "The art of the master is to conceal restraints under the veil of pleasure and self-interest, so that [the people] think they want everything they are being made to do. . . . Without ever showing it, you establish habits more powerful than authority itself." [45]

In Wolmar's domain, too, festivals are organized as one way of fomenting a spirit of "spontaneous" unanimity. Women—in accordance with Rousseau's announced principle—are kept separate, and sexual activities rigorously repressed and controlled. Here again, the manipulation is indirect and hidden.

> To forestall a dangerous familiarity between the two sexes, we do not hinder them by positive laws which they would be tempted to violate secretly; but, *without seeming to be thinking about the matter,* we establish customs more powerful than authority itself. We do not forbid them to see each other, but we arrange things so that they have neither the opportunity nor the desire. We manage it by giving them entirely different occupations, habits, tastes, pleasures. . . .[46]

Thus the basic human relations and drives are to be altered by re-conditioning. And again, sheer trickery may be called on: "We shall have to invent some ingenious kinds of lots which the less worthy may draw on each occasion of our bringing them together, and then they will accuse their own ill luck and not the rulers." A system of mutual spying, informing, and denunciation is a vigorous adjunct to the other techniques of control, and Rousseau goes to some pains to argue that these practices are justified by the end they serve. We can only conclude that although he writes in this work that man should never be treated as a means (V,2), his own book belies the statement.[47]

Although there are differences between the situations set up in *La Nouvelle Héloïse* and in the *Social Contract,* the principles, purposes, and methodology are the same. As Burgelin puts it, Clarens is really a small fatherland, rather than a large family. It is without doubt a totalitarian institution.[48]

Since Rousseau has told us in "Political Economy" that we must catch children young if we want to make them into what we desire them to be, we may expect methodology to follow principle on this score, too. The method of forming children in *La Nouvelle Héloïse* leans heavily on artifice and on deception. Punishments and rewards must seem to be impersonal and mechanically necessary (as in the "Projet pour l'éducation de M. de Sainte-Marie"); and this end can be achieved only by following the method of *la main cachée.* Spying is used to check on the success of the manipulative process. "In this way, [the children] being free to follow the inclinations of their hearts, without disguise or alteration, we can study their natural movements in their most secret sources."[49] Such a statement is essentially the same as that of Helvétius in *De l'Esprit:* "In order to direct the movements of the human puppet, we should need to know the strings that actuate it." The analogy with the *Social Contract* is most striking when Wolmar expresses a quite remarkable and significant paradox. His purpose, he explains, is to make the child at once "free and docile." The paradox reaffirms the peculiar meaning Rousseau gave to the word *"liberté."* It can be explained only as a more subtle, complex, and complete process of control that captures the will itself. Like the citizen, or the worker, the child will do *freely* what the guide thinks he should do.

The impressive feature of Rousseau's thought is its consistency. That is why it is so astonishing that *Emile*—a work in which he says, echoing the fragment we quoted earlier, "it is not good to shape our species halfway"—should be generally understood as a pedagogy whose aim is freedom. Of course Rousseau again claims this; but by now we are well prepared to realize that his *"liberté"* is not our "liberty."

Emile goes beyond *La Nouvelle Héloïse,* not only in scope, but in depth and ingenuity. The tactics Rousseau devises to manipulate Emile are so complex and devious, at times, as to bear the mark of an abnormal mind. The consistency lies in the aim of bringing the child to choose "freely" what the tutor has decided in advance that he shall choose. *Emile* is a second, more complete manual of human engineering, an experiment in capturing hearts, minds, and wills. Is it duplicity, or self-duplicity, when Rousseau tells us that his Emile is free because he is dependent only on impersonal things or forces? (This is another recurrent idea, one which must be given greater weight than scholars have given to it.) Shall we overlook the fact that the things and forces are always under the very personal control of the tutor-guide, who manipulates them secretly in such fashion as to control his subject as he wishes? Is there any doubt that the "impersonality" is usually a false front, a calculated illusion, even at times outright trickery? The child, we are told, must be "bent to the most absolute obedience," but without the tutor's seeming to impose any personal intervention; subject only to "necessary" limits, he will still feel free. This is what Rousseau calls "guided freedom" (*"la liberté bien réglée"*)—a term that might also be applied to his political thought.

> Let him think that he is always the master, but be sure that you are always the master. There is no subjection so complete as that which keeps the appearance of freedom; that is the way to capture the will itself. Isn't the poor child . . . at your mercy? . . . His work, his games, his pleasures, his pains—isn't all that in your hands without his knowing it? Of course he should only do what he wants; but he should want to do only what you want him to do.[50]

I do not know how any statement could be clearer, more incontrovertible, or more significant.[51]

All the other ideas are there, too. The consistency is overwhelming. The tutor is "to spy on him [Emile] ceaselessly and, *without his being aware of it,* to intuit his feelings in advance and forestall those he is not to have." [52] We encounter the same overriding fear of sex throughout. The tutor goes to unimaginable lengths and devious stratagems to blunt Emile's sexual drives. He is supposed to be unaware of them until he is twenty. He will be married a virgin. The youth must not be let out of sight, day or night, not allowed to go to bed until he is in a state of exhaustion. Even then the tutor should share his bed. Interpreting the word "natural," as he usually does, according to his own preferences, Rousseau assures us that sexual desire is not a genuine physical need; it is the work of the imagination, which can be controlled. By delaying sexuality, he reiterates, we shall be following nature. The rationale for this procedure is explicit: "After twenty, continence is a moral duty; it is necessary in order to learn to rule over oneself and to remain the master of one's appetites." [53] Self-indulgence and egocentric pleasure must be overcome.

Toward the end Emile, now a married adult, will say to his tutor: "I want to obey your laws, I shall always want to. . . . Make me free by protecting me against my passions; force me to be my own master by obedience to my reason, not to my senses." The book closes with these words of Emile: "But remain the master of the young masters. Advise us, govern us; we shall be docile. As long as I live, I shall need you." In spite of all that Rousseau says, then, Emile will never achieve true independence or maturity. He will always need the "guide"—as the break-up of his marriage after the tutor's departure will prove (*Emile et Sophie*).

In sum, then, Rousseau's method has been to avoid overt interference with free self-expression, but to control Emile's behavior on every occasion. True spontaneity is inevitably lost, and behavior becomes, as Rousseau desires, certain or automatic, and predictable. The appearance or illusion of freedom must, however, be carefully maintained as a necessary element in the process of control. In fact, as I have said elsewhere, Emile has all the freedom of a programmed computer. His entire development, his character and his life, have been carefully mapped out for him, controlled at every point, from babyhood on. He cannot even choose his own wife, do his own courting, or make love to her without supervision. The method and the purpose of Rousseau's system of education—and of politics (*both are essentially forms of control*)—are revealed in these words of the tutor:

> You cannot imagine how docile Emile, at the age of twenty, can be. . . . It took me fifteen years of careful work to win that hold on him. I was not bringing him up then, I was preparing him to be brought up. He is now sufficiently brought up to be docile. . . . I leave him, it is true, *the appearance of independence*, but *never has he been more completely subjugated* to me, for he is in my subjection *because he wants to be*. As long as I was not able to *make myself the master of his will*, I remained the master of his person; I never left him. Now I sometimes leave him by himself, because I can still control him.[54]

It is my contention that Rousseau also envisages the prime function of the State and of its "guide," "leader," or "Legislator" as the control of the will, the acts, thoughts, and passions of the citizens, and that the means of controlling all these are essentially the same. And the final aim, let it not be forgotten, is the beneficent one of making men happy—despite themselves, one may say: "Happy is he who is led [to wise living] in spite of himself! What does it matter what guide [means] is used, as long as it leads him to the goal?"[55]

Rousseau, an obsessional personality, had a fixation on certain words, the significance of which for his personality and thought has never been studied. In *Emile* one word that recurs again and again is "docility." Associated with it is Rousseau's fixation on words such as "yoke" and "subjugate" ("put under the yoke"). These words are specifically applied to the "will," or to the self-directed natural ego of the individual. The responsibility for happiness is shifted from the individual (who cannot achieve it, since in our societies he is at war within himself and with other men) to the State and its Wolmarian leaders. They must attain complete control (subjugation, docility), and Rousseau's system is an explication of the means to that control. The most important of these falls under the heading of "education," which he considered to be, as we see in *Emile*, almost all-powerful. Education must be, consequently, an aspect of politics and the most efficacious instrument at the disposal of the State.

To complete the context in which the *Social Contract* should be viewed, we must glance at Rousseau's later political writings, especially those which are a deliberate application of his theory: *Projet de Constitution pour la Corse* (*Project of a Constitution for Corsica*) and *Considérations sur le gouvernement de Pologne* (*Considerations on the Government of Poland*). Working realistically within the context of existing historical circumstances, he modifies his abstract theory, or more exactly, the institutions, in each case; but he never loses sight of his constant ends and means. The kind of society he has in mind is always the same.

In 1765, as a result of the *Social Contract*, Rousseau was invited by the Corsican leaders to write a constitution for their country. The idea appealed to him because Corsica was the kind of relatively "uncorrupted" people, without a formed government, to which his theory could be applied with some modifications. It will require much "art," he warns, to keep the Corsicans in this healthy state, an art that belongs to the guide or Legislator. We are not surprised when the latter tells the people that the laws he is giving them are "the only laws of nature." He leads them where he wants, employing the usual techniques, but convinces them that they are free. In the Corsica Rousseau plans there will be a minimum of private property and strict control of every aspect of economic life, which will be kept on a Spartan level, so that the citizens will not stray from virtue and will be easily controlled. Control is used to maintain simple living at a primitive level, and simple living enables control to be effective. To a large extent Rousseau envisages a form of socialism or State capitalism, and he outlines the idea of what the Chinese communists call communes.[56] Authoritarian, probably draconian, methods will be needed to prevent the natural movement toward cities, luxury, commerce. Complete control, then, is exercised in several directions—over economic life and over the "passions."

The Corsicans must not be able to imagine a better condition. "Not being able to leave this condition, they will want to distinguish themselves in it." [57] This is "virtue," a word that does not refer to moral standards, as such, but to devotion and sacrifice to the collective good. Morals having been absorbed into politics, the one virtue that matters is thinking of oneself only as part of the whole. We must form "the nation for the government," not adapt the government to the nation.

In the Corsica Rousseau envisions, egalitarianism is exalted, as is military service. Arts and letters, it should be especially noted, are prohibited. Instead of taxes—an easy and meaningless sign of devotion and sacrifice—forced labor is to be exacted of all. But the main point remains the psychological captivity of the individual, his subjugation and docility. "The people must be made to practice this system, to love the occupation *we decide to give them,* to find in it their pleasures, their desires, their tastes, their happiness in general, and to limit their ambitions and projects to it." The State or community will "possess men and all their powers." [58]

In the second part of this treatise, Rousseau draws up a truly astounding program of regimentation. Every aspect of life, including sexual life, marriage, and procreation, is controlled. The theory is the one we have already seen: "I will not preach morality to them; I will not order them to have virtues. But I will put them in such a position that they will have those virtues, without knowing the word, and that they will be good and just, without knowing what goodness and justice are." [59] Thought, feeling, and action must be absolutely certain and automatic. A statement like this one, as well as Rousseau's consistent attitude toward the people in his other political writings, refutes the unfounded argument of those who claim that we cannot draw a comparison between *La Nouvelle Héloïse* (where servants and workers are involved), or *Emile* (where his focus is upon a child), and what Rousseau would do to the citizen. For him the people are always to be treated as children—watched over and guided—because they easily go astray and succumb to nature. Never does Rousseau place any confidence in men's rationality or reasonableness, or in their good will. They must, as he declares, be remade, by conditioning and thought control, so that the desired reactions will be reflexive; and even then the apparatus of controls must be maintained. All rests on this certainty: "fear and hope are the two instruments by which men are governed. . . . From which it follows that those who control a people's opinions [i.e., thought, judgments] control its actions." [60] The voting process fits into the pattern, as the following sentences testify: "Corsicans, be silent. I am going to speak in the name of all. Let those who do not agree leave, and let those who do agree raise their hands." [61] And let it be noted that Rousseau calls this system "a system of liberty." [62]

In 1771 Rousseau wrote his *Considerations on the Government of Poland*, in circumstances which need not concern us here.[63] Although the political institutions designed by him correspond to Polish traditions and politics, the underlying concern is a mobilization of all the means at the disposal of the State to "form citizens," as he would say. The essence of his theory is set forth in plain terms in the first chapter. To write better laws, he declares, is easy. But it is impossible to prevent their being eluded by men's passions. "To put the law above man [Rousseau apparently refers both to those who rule and to those who are ruled] is a problem in politics which I compare to that of the squaring of the circle in geometry." Yet Rousseau calls on the Legislator to solve this problem. If he does, there will be no abuses. If he fails, all else will fail.

There will never be a good and solid constitution except one in which the Law rules over the hearts of the citizens. As long as the legislative power does not go that far, laws will always be evaded. But how do you reach hearts? That is a matter about which our *instituteurs* [those who bring up children] scarcely think.

Rousseau goes on to affirm that even justice is inadequate; "enthusiasm" must be aroused.

How then shall we stir hearts, and create love for the fatherland and its laws? Shall I dare to tell you? By children's games; by practices that seem frivolous in the eyes of superficial men, but which form cherished habits and invincible attachments.[64]

Throughout the *Considerations on the Government of Poland* Rousseau will emphasize the means to this end. Condemning the institutions of existing societies, which foster individual "egoism," he once again holds aloft as models the ancient lawgivers Moses, Lycurgus, and Numa Pompilius. Moses made a people; he gave them institutions that have not changed in five thousand years; he created a permanent autarchy. To do this, he weighed his people down with rites, confined them *("le gêna")* in a thousand ways. As for Lycurgus, he imposed on his people

> . . . an iron yoke, such as no other people has ever borne; but he attached them [i.e., emotionally] to this yoke, identifying them with it, so to speak, by keeping it constantly in their minds. He showed them their country unceasingly, in their laws, their games, their homes, their loves, their feasts. He did not allow them a moment to be with themselves alone. And from this continual constraint, ennobled by its object, was born that ardent love of country. . . .[65]

In these words we encounter again an element that was also of major importance in the systems of control and manipulation Rousseau had developed in *La Nouvelle Héloïse* and *Emile:* destruction of privacy, living under constant observation, or under the eyes of others.

All three ancient legislators, he concludes, had these techniques in common: nationalistic religious ceremonies (he condemns other types of ceremonies); games that brought the citizens together in public; athletic exercises and competitions; historical spectacles designed to inflame the people's hearts and to stimulate "a lively emulation"; poetry and literature put to the same use. In the latter two ideas and in his repeated condemnation of unguided freedom of the arts and letters,[66] we see how Rousseau would harness both the competitive spirit (which is so deadly in present societies) and the arts to the ends of the State. He would make them important instruments of the total regimentation he has in view, of the primacy of the collectivity over the self, which is clearly and constantly implied in phrases like "that ardent love of country founded on ineradicable habituation." [67] His public festivals, which promote, and are manifestations of, unity and patriotism, are still another means toward the same end.

The original character of Rousseau's political thought, and his opposition to the liberal Encyclopedists, is again put in evidence by his refusal to accept the mainsprings of their political theory: reliance on the combination of self-interest and enlightenment. The mechanisms on which he relies depend on the conditioning processes that have haunted his mind ever since *La Morale sensitive:*

> You will give their souls . . . a vigor that will replace the delusive game of idle precepts, that will make them do out of inclination and emotion what is never done well enough when it is done only out of duty or self-interest.[68] It is on such souls that a well thought-out legislation will be effective.[69]

In other words (to use Rousseau's vocabulary), it is necessary to "form" men, to "remake" them first. Rousseau denies to laws the power attributed to them by other *philosophes;* as he had said much earlier, laws can at best restrain behavior; they cannot capture hearts, minds, and wills, cannot create "docility," or the *moi commun.*[70]

The detail of other mechanisms is then supplied. Those who have shown outstanding patriotic virtue should be honored in public ceremonies. Every method must be used to keep the idea of "country" constantly in the minds of the people, "constantly under their eyes," and to make it *"leur plus grande affaire."* Hearts must be turned into "an instrument more powerful than gold." The result should be a feeling of dependency that keeps the people, like Emile, in a state of childlike immaturity: "Many public amusements in which *la bonne mère patrie* enjoys seeing its children play. Let her constantly concern herself with them, so they may always be concerned with her." But an end must be put (again!) to all ordinary amusements and spectacles (that is, "ordinary" in the sense of being undirected by the State to its communal ends), to all that distracts people from country and duty, and to all that isolates them as individuals. New kinds of games and celebrations are to be invented, and the admiration of the people is to be directed toward physical prowess and military qualities, while they must constantly be kept from idleness, effeminate pleasures, and "luxury of the mind." From those who excel, the future leaders will be selected and formed.

As a calculated measure of winning loyalty, the people will be allowed, at certain "pleasant occasions," to be with their leaders and share their pleasures with them.[71] Pomp, on public occasions, is also useful:

> It is unbelievable to what extent the hearts of the common people follow their eyes, and how much they are impressed by ceremonial majesty. It gives to authority an appearance of order and regularity that inspires confidence and dissipates ideas of caprice and whim, which are associated with arbitrary power.[72]

Illusion and stage settings remain constants.[73] So does Rousseau's attitude toward the "people"; a sheep-like mass, *des pauvres d'esprit*, they are to be treated like children, to be kept children, and to be led.

Nothing, however, is as essential as the upbringing of children.

> This is the important article. It is for education to give souls the national form, and so direct their opinions and tastes, that they will be patriots out of inclination, out of passion, out of necessity. A child, on opening his eyes, should see *la patrie*, and until he dies see nothing else. . . . This love fills his whole existence; he sees only *la patrie*, lives only for it. As soon as he is alone, he is nothing.[74]

It is not necessary for us to go through all of Rousseau's prescriptions for this type of education. The children will be brought up together. They will have their play "all together and in public, so that there is always a common end to which all aspire and which excites competition and rivalry." This is necessary to accustom them to rules, to equality and fraternity, "to living under the eyes of their fellow-citizens and to desiring public approval." [75] Furthermore, all must participate, as spectators or as competitors.

Rousseau concludes this chapter with a warning. "Direct in this way the education, usages, customs, and mores of the Poles. . . . But, without these precautions, expect nothing from your laws. . . . They will be eluded and vain." [76] To which we must add the warning with which he had closed the preceding chapter, which is a summary of his theory:

> To forbid things that are not to be done is an inept and vain expedient, unless you begin by making them hated and despised; the law's disapproval is never efficacious except when it supports that of judgment. Whoever puts his hand to forming a people must know how to control the opinions [i.e., thought control], and through them to control the passions of men. [77]

For Rousseau, all this is the price of what he calls "liberty." "Proud and holy liberty! If those poor people [78] could know you, . . . if they realized how your laws are more austere than the harshness of the tyrant's yoke, . . . they would fly from you with fright as from a burden that would crush them." [79]

Liberty, in Rousseau's sense, is also associated (as in the *Project of a Constitution for Corsica*) with a primitive level of culture, an agricultural nation, simple manners, a martial spirit, "courageous and disinterested souls." Military service is universal. Luxury, commerce, and industry must be avoided. "Financial systems make venal souls; and as soon as one's main desire is to make money, one can always get more by being crooked than by being honest." Pecuniary rewards for virtue are no good because they are not public enough, do not speak to hearts and eyes, do not excite emulation. [80] All ranks, honors, and occupations should bear visible signs; everything must be in open view. In fact, concludes Rousseau, the most powerful, the most infallible, means for developing "patriotism" (we know by now that the word had a larger and different meaning for him than for us today) is

> . . . to see to it that all the citizens feel themselves constantly under public inspection; . . . that all are so dependent on public

opinion that nothing can be done, nothing acquired, no post obtained, without it. From the effervescence aroused by this universal emulation will be born that patriotic intoxication which, alone, can raise men above themselves [i.e., above the *moi humain*], and without which liberty is only a hollow word and legislation a chimera.[81]

Similarly, he prefers small States, where "all the citizens know each other and watch over each other." [82] We realize that Rousseau has indeed given the word "liberty" a new and different meaning. The way in which Rousseau would use the power of the State is also clear.

I cannot forbear quoting the following sentences, regarding the representatives, as an extraordinary example of Rousseau's mentality:

> If, then, in an almost unanimous resolution, a single member in opposition kept the right to annul it, I should like him to answer for his opposition with his head, not only to his constituents in the [legislative body], but then to the whole nation whose misfortune he is causing. I should like it to be ordered by the Law that, six months after his opposition, he would be solemnly judged by an extraordinary tribunal established for that purpose alone . . . which could not merely release him as acquitted, but would be obliged to condemn him to death, without any possibility of mercy, or else, to bestow a reward and public honors on him for life, without there ever being any middle ground between these two alternatives.
>
> Institutions of this kind, so conducive to the energy of courage and to love of liberty are too removed from the mentality of our times to hope that they will be adopted or liked. But they were not unknown to the Ancients; and it was by them that their founders were able to exalt hearts and inflame them when needed with a truly heroic zeal.[83]

In sum, then, the consistency of Rousseau's ideas in writings that cover the span of his productive years, and particularly in the major works composed within the same period as the *Social Contract*, gives rise to a strong presumption that the latter work embodies the same thinking. Would it not be unreasonable to suppose otherwise? The evidence shows that in his mind all these writings were parts of one whole concept, one vast scheme, which he had originally intended to develop in a work on political institutions. To assume that the *Social Contract* turned out to be a program for liberty as we conceive it, for an open or pluralistic society, would be a very strange assumption indeed, one that would require powerful reasons from outside the text to support it. Such reasons have never been found.

In approaching the *Social Contract* we must bear in mind Rousseau's rather absolute ideals of order and justice, his belief that men in society are inevitably selfish and aggressive and are split hopelessly, both within themselves, because of the conflicting demands of nature and culture, and among one another, according to their personal interests. We must remember his desire to put an end to this state of war, to redirect the aggressive, competitive instincts into a co-operative social harmony in which alienation would be overcome. This end requires that the natural self (the *moi humain* which he execrates) be replaced by the collective self, the individual will by the general will. The accomplishment of a purpose so difficult and far-reaching cannot be entrusted to law itself, to good will, the sense of duty, or enlightened self-interest. Rousseau, in fact, rejects the belief in enlightenment and enlightened self-interest, not only explicitly, but implicitly, in his exclusive reliance on duplicity, manipulation, and reflexive conditioning. We must not forget that his program requires control not only of behavior, but (as he so often says) of wills, thoughts, and emotions—the determinants of behavior. That is why he twice writes that his system requires "the docility of a young nation." That is why, too, he insists constantly upon the fomenting of patriotic zeal and upon the pressure of public opinion. All of the means he proposes lead to that "docility" (one of his word-fixations) which he calls "liberty"—that dependence on impersonal force (the general will) in place of personal power. He has shown how, through controlled child rearing, conditioning, suggestion, and habituation, conduct is shaped, and how men are made even to desire such treatment. Pride and the competitive instincts, which are too profound to be extirpated or bypassed, are cleverly utilized to frustrate the individual's natural purpose of atomistic egoism or self-aggrandizement. "Openness" is artificially cultivated as a means to control egoism, to invade effectively private life. These and other techniques, especially the mobilization by the State of what we now call the resources of propaganda or indoctrination, are developed and brought to bear on the individual with a pressure of overwhelming force.

It is not the purpose of this essay to investigate the psychological motivations that underlay Rousseau's thinking.[84] It is enough to say that, according to contemporary psychological and sociological studies, he was a perfect model of what we now refer to as "the authoritarian personality." The roots of his personality deformation lay in his obsessionality and his paranoid tendencies. An alienated "outsider," tormented by feelings of inferiority, worthlessness, and guilt, he condemned a world that to him seemed unreceptive and hostile. He compensated for his own inadequacies in all kinds of fantasies, especially in fantasies of a harmonious dependency or, contrariwise, of isolated, godlike self-sufficiency (or power). In his intellectual fantasies his own moral and personal weaknesses were redeemed by a need for rigid moral values and puritanical discipline, his own disorder by a vision of rigidly stable order. He achieved the feelings of superiority and moral self-approbation which he needed by projecting himself into such all-powerful figures as Wolmar, Emile's tutor, and the godlike Legislator—each of whom, impassive and olympian, achieves the control over others that he could never achieve over himself.[85]

Notes

[1] *Correspondance générale,* ed. Dufour-Plan (Paris, 1924), I, 367–79.

[2] P. Burgelin considers the dialectic of order and existence to be the axis of Rousseau's philosophy. (See *La Philosophie de l'existence de Jean-Jacques Rousseau* [Paris, 1952], hereinafter referred to as *"La*

Philosophie.") R. A. Leigh writes: "This poet of solitude and indolent reverie, this fierce defender of his independence, this enemy of all obligation nonetheless sketched the outline of a society founded on the idea of obligation in its most rigorous form." (*Correspondance*, I, xiii.)

3 *Discours sur les sciences et les arts*, ed. G. R. Havens (New York, 1946), p. 160.

4 *Réponse à M. Bordes*, in *Oeuvres*, ed. B. Gagnebin and M. Raymond (Paris, 1964), III, 80. This edition of *Oeuvres* hereinafter will be identified as "*Oeuvres*, Pléiade edition."

5 *The Political Writings of Rousseau*, ed. C. E. Vaughan (Cambridge, 1915), I, 453. This work hereinafter will be referred to as "*Political Writings*."

6 It is not surprising that he misinterprets Jesus' purpose as a political one, that of "making his people free and worthy of being so." This statement is followed by one which reveals his unconscious self-identification with Christ: "But his vile and cowardly compatriots, instead of listening to him, developed hatred for him precisely because of his genius and of his virtue, which were reproaches for their unworthiness." ("Lettre à M. de Franquières, 15 January 1769," *Correspondance générale*, XIX, 62.)

7 *Oeuvres*, ed. Ch. Lahure (Paris, 1865), V, 108. This edition will hereinafter be identified as "*Oeuvres*, Hachette edition."

8 *Correspondance*, II, 223 (letter dated June 1753).

9 J. C. Herold, "The Solitary Wanderer," *Horizon*, IV (1964), 99.

10 The formulation comes from the later *Dialogues*, or *Rousseau, juge de Jean-Jacques*, in *Oeuvres*, Hachette edition, IX, 108.

11 I. Fetscher, "Rousseau's Concepts of Freedom in the Light of His Philosophy of History," *Nomos*, IV (1962), 49. (This essay will hereinafter be referred to as "Rousseau's Concepts of Freedom.") Fetscher goes on to say that Rousseau will reduce the material dependency by a Spartan agrarian economy, and the spiritual by the establishment of community.

12 *Discours sur l'inégalité*, in *Political Writings*, I, 203.

13 In *Political Writings*, I, 449.

14 J. N. Shklar, "Rousseau's Images of Authority," *American Political Science Review*, LVIII (1964), 919. There are some coincidences between Dr. Shklar's excellent article and my own thinking, which was, however, first developed in an article written in 1962 and published at about the same time as hers ("Rousseau et la voie du totalitarisme," in *Rousseau et la philosophie politique* [Paris, 1965]). The ground covered is, however, quite different, and the conclusions are often opposed. For Dr. Shklar, Emile is really free, Saint-Preux really cured and liberated, the end of political authority real freedom. It is difficult to understand the contradictions in her treatment of Emile. (pp. 930–31.)

[15] Rousseau may have read in Aristotle's *Nicomachean Ethics* (X, 10) that the State must train men to virtue, as in Sparta, in which alone "the legislator seems to have undertaken to control the nurture and pursuits of the citizens." Rousseau emphasizes the indirect, or hidden, control.

[16] All education, of course, does this to a degree. But there is, we shall see, a vast difference between minimal control and emphasis on individual autonomy, on the one hand, and what Rousseau has in mind. He wants children to be "formed" to orient themselves to the collectivity. As in current Soviet education, the judgment and sanctions of the peer group (properly guided) become a powerful coercive force. Education, in a word, is an extension of politics.

[17] See L. G. Crocker, "Rousseau et 'l'opinion,'" in *Studies on Voltaire and the Eighteenth Century,* LV (1967), 395–415.

[18] G. Besse, "De Rousseau au Communisme," *Europe,* No. 391–92 (1961), p. 169.

[19] P. Burgelin speaks of "the transcendence of the City and its value, source of other values, since it is through the City alone that we rise to the moral." (*La Philosophie,* p. 511.)

[20] See L. G. Crocker, "The Priority of Justice or Law," *Yale French Studies,* No. 28 (1962), pp. 34–42.

[21] P. Burgelin, *La Philosophie,* p. 551.

[22] *Emile,* ed. F. and P. Richards (Paris, 1951), p. 279. According to O. Vossler, Rousseau wishes to suppress the dualism of the individual-society opposition by identifying the State and the individual. By putting the ethical and the general will on the same level, every moral act becomes political—morals and politics are one. It follows that morals become a problem of training the will (the subject of *Emile* and the *Social Contract*). This is the job of the State. Rousseau is "a pedagogue, not a politician." (See W. Hempel's review of O. Vossler, *Rousseaus Freiheitslehre,* in *AJJR,* XXXVI (1963–65), 315–17.)

[23] "He is a member of the group without ceasing to be himself, for his personal interest is identified with that of all." (P. Burgelin, *La Philosophie,* p. 517.)

[24] *Political Writings,* I, 245.

[25] *Ibid.,* I, 246.

[26] Exception must be made for Burgelin, who speaks of the universality, in Rousseau's character and thought, of dissimulation, trickery, lying, duplicity, ruse, illusion. (*La Philosophie,* pp. 298–302, 557.) Burgelin, however, does not draw the ultimate conclusions.

[27] *Political Writings,* I, 248.

[28] *Ibid.,* 255–56.

[29] *Ibid.*

[30] *Ibid.,* 326.

[31] "It must be emphasized," writes I. Fetscher, "that Rousseau was *not*

a liberal and individualistic thinker. . . . Rousseau neither was, nor wished to be, the theorist of the kind of democracy that is possible in a modern bourgeois society." But Fetscher maintains that Rousseau cannot be called totalitarian even though he rejects rights, individual freedom, political self-expression, and free competition, since he was seeking to turn away from the modern world toward "a higher moral and political freedom." ("Rousseau's Concepts of Freedom," p. 56.) I find this reasoning neither clear nor convincing.

[32] *Confessions,* in *Oeuvres,* Pléiade edition, I, 409.

[33] *Julie, ou la Nouvelle Héloïse,* ed. R. Pomeau (Paris, 1960), Part IV, Letter XI. The whole passage must be read, as an essential exposition of his outlook.

[34] *Lettre à M. d'Alembert sur les spectacles,* ed. M. Fuchs (Lille, 1948), p. 169.

[35] Professor Allan Bloom defends Rousseau's call for censorship of the arts exercised in the light of "the good of the whole," overlooking the basic point of prior determination of that good by those who wield authority. It is, he thinks, "a defense of the arts against their degradation," rather than their submission to politics. For Rousseau, however, politics included the particular moral ends of the State, and the control of all the means necessary to its ends. The eighteenth-century theory of necessary restraints (Montesquieu, Rousseau) referred to agrarian, egalitarian societies which had no form of representative government. Bloom properly refers to the model of Geneva, which, however, under a façade of self-government was a tight and repressive oligarchy. (See A. Bloom, Introduction to *Politics and the Arts. Letter to M. d'Alembert on the Theatre.*)

[36] *Lettre à M. d'Alembert sur les spectacles,* pp. 89–90.

[37] "*Julie,* ou la nouvelle duplicité," *AJJR,* XXXVI (1963–65), 105–152.

[38] See *ibid.* Social and psychological pressures cannot change his subjects' true feelings.

[39] By "denaturing" men Rousseau means that they are made to place the *moi commun* above the *moi humain,* or more exactly, to replace the latter with the former, or to consider the latter as only part of the former.

[40] That is, the creation of voluntary action that is self-reinforcing through the reward (pleasure) or punishment (pain, disapproval) that it *automatically* entails.

[41] In the *Social Contract* (II, 7) Rousseau describes his Legislator in these terms: "He would need a superior intelligence that saw all of men's passions, without feeling any of them; which had no relation with our nature, and knew it completely." The description fits Wolmar.

[42] *La Nouvelle Héloïse,* Part IV, Letter X, p. 452.

[43] The servants, at any rate, will not believe that it exists, or that their

masters are usurpers, if anyone tells them so. They must be prevented from reflecting on the equality of men and the inequality of their social condition. Shklar asserts that in Clarens there is "less cause for dissatisfaction and hostility than in other societies." ("Rousseau's Images of Authority," p. 928.) It would perhaps be more accurate to say that such reactions are less possible, because of the constant pressures and controls.

⁴⁴ For instance, see Book II, Chapter 6, where he says that the citizens need "guides," so that they may know their true will.

⁴⁵ *La Nouvelle Héloïse,* Part IV, Letter X, pp. 435–36.

⁴⁶ *Ibid.,* pp. 431–32. (Italics added.)

⁴⁷ Rousseau also denies the servants and workers the right to education or the development of their abilities and talents. I do not impugn his sincerity when he writes, in *La Nouvelle Héloïse,* "It is never permitted to degrade a human soul for the advantage of others." On the next page, however, he justifies the stifling of talents, saying that in order to do otherwise "the number of those possessing [talents] would have to be in exact proportion to society's needs." Apparently Rousseau did not believe that the servants and workers were being degraded when they were made part of a harmonious order. The individual is obviously less important to him than the social group. He does not desire a mobile society in which mobility of social roles is based on ability, because this would involve competition and "warfare"; he prefers, instead, a regulated, stable order with each individual in his place. The collective or "public" happiness is what matters most; indeed, he will assert that the individual should have no other.

⁴⁸ See the concluding note of the third chapter.

⁴⁹ *La Nouvelle Héloïse,* Part V, Letter III, p. 571.

⁵⁰ *Emile,* p. 121.

⁵¹ Again it is a question of Rousseau's vocabulary. The tutor manipulates Emile as he wills (*Ibid.,* p. 80), but Emile is "free." The tutor is "master of the child" (*Ibid.,* p. 85), but the child is "master of his will" (*Ibid.,* p. 121). These apparent contradictions are only applications of the central paradox which is a hinge of Rousseau's thought: the "guides" must make people "free and docile." It is sometimes argued that Emile is free, because he has been liberated from his lower appetites and from the pressures and "opinion" of society. The liberation, however, is accomplished at the price of a total surrender, or rather, seizure of his self.

⁵² *Ibid.,* p. 217.

⁵³ *Ibid.,* p. 416.

⁵⁴ *Ibid.,* p. 414. (Italics added.) The Swiss writer J. H. Meister, in a chapter entitled "Morale des sensations," quotes *La Nouvelle Héloïse,* and declares: "We have a strong disposition to becoming machines, that is, to be the next day what we were the day before . . . without any choice, without any reflection." Since these automatic actions are those we

do best, in the proper conditions "that purely machine-like way of being" is most desirable. (*De la morale naturelle* [London, 1788], pp. 19–21.) Meister apparently had grasped the drift of Rousseau's *"morale sensitive."*

[55] *Emile*, p. 549.

[56] *Projet de constitution pour la Corse*, in *Political Writings*, II, p. 338.

[57] *Ibid.*, p. 332.

[58] *Ibid.*, p. 340.

[59] *Ibid.*, p. 354.

[60] *Ibid.*, p. 344. Rousseau also gives "voluptuousness and vanity" as the motives, and later, power. (pp. 344, 345.)

[61] *Ibid.*, p. 349.

[62] One cannot help thinking of the lines from Peter Weiss' *The Persecution and Assassination of Jean-Paul Marat . . .* (New York, 1965), in which Sade is made to say (p. 49):

> Now I see where
> this revolution is leading
> To the withering of the individual man
> and a slow merging into uniformity
> to the death of choice
> to self-denial
> to deadly weakness
> in a state
> which has no contact with individuals
> but which is impregnable.

(Translated by Geoffrey Skelton and Adrian Mitchell. Copyright © 1965 by John Calder, Ltd. Reprinted by permission of Atheneum Publishers.)

[63] For an account of the composition of both works, see *Oeuvres*, Pléiade edition, III.

[64] *Considérations sur la gouvernement de Pologne*, in *Political Writings*, II, 427.

[65] *Ibid.*, pp. 428–29.

[66] *Ibid.*, p. 430.

[67] *Ibid.*, p. 431.

[68] Vaughan here refers to similar ideas expressed in three other works. See *ibid.*, p. 432, *n.* 6.

[69] *Ibid.*, p. 432.

[70] Rousseau recognizes that "man can be made to act only out of self-interest." (*Ibid.*, p. 477.) That is why his whole, unconcealed intent is to "remake" men, so that by proper conditioning they will think of themselves only as part of a whole, and have no feeling of self-interest contrary to the interest of the collectivity.

[71] The same technique is used by Wolmar—another example of the consistency of Rousseau's thought.

[72] *Ibid.*, p. 435.

[73] Cf. *Emile*, p. 611: "Sweet, charming falsehood, more valuable than truth."

[74] *Political Writings*, II, p. 437. (Rousseau also speaks of "liberty" in this passage; but by that word he here means national independence.) In totalitarian societies, writes a modern psychologist, "one of the postural insignia is the mask of enthusiasm. Because silent obedience is an uncertain quality, the citizen body is denied the right of silence. 'Nobody can hope to be left alone by claiming political ignorance or lack of political interest.'" (See M. R. Stein, *et al.*, *Identity and Anxiety: Survival of the Person in a Mass Society* [Glencoe, 1960], p. 303.)

[75] We must emphasize here the double antithesis: his condemnation of competitiveness and of living according to the "opinion" of others, both of which referred to existing societies of anarchic individualism. (See my article, "Rousseau et 'l'opinion.'")

[76] *Political Writings*, II, 441.

[77] *Ibid.*, p. 437.

[78] He refers to "abased peoples" who are the playthings of factions.

[79] *Political Writings*, II, 445.

[80] *Ibid.*, p. 479.

[81] *Ibid.*, pp. 491–92.

[82] *Ibid.*, p. 442.

[83] *Ibid.*, pp. 469–70. For "zeal," we may read "fanaticism." This quotation is deliberately taken out of its context, which relates to the liberum veto; we are not interested here in its substance, but in the spirit that animates it.

[84] See Preface, note 5.

[85] One has only to read pp. 404–6 of *Emile* to be struck by the abnormal, obsessional character of Rousseau's fantasies of power. He apparently tried to play a role of this kind with Mme. d'Houdetot, after his rejection by her. It should be added that his relation to his imaginary power-figures was in all likelihood a dual one: he probably also experienced satisfactions of submissiveness and dependency, as when he projected himself into the role of Saint-Preux. His constant ambivalence toward authority and "opinion" expresses a fundamental character trait, whose immediate cause was his sado-masochism and inferiority feelings, and which is ultimately related to his obsessionality (the characteristic of which is, precisely, ambivalence). Fantasies of independence and power or of submissive docility thus yielded satisfactions which, more than alternatives, were contrary needs.

2. The Social Contract

WE are now in a position to interpret the institutions Rousseau devises in the *Social Contract* and the underlying theories which he expounds in this treatise. There are several reasons for the conflicting interpretations they have occasioned. For one, his vocabulary, and sometimes his ideas, are ambiguous; and he sometimes gives his words special meanings of his own. The result is that each reader is apt to peruse Rousseau in such a way that he finds what he seeks, rather than what the author intended him to find. This is much more possible in Rousseau's writings than in those of most authors. A second reason is that his institutions have sometimes been analyzed without adequate reference to their spirit, as if they were ends in themselves, instead of means to the significant ends they serve; that is, the kind of society they were meant to create. To be sure, the relation is reciprocal, and the institutions must be understood if we are to understand the society. With Rousseau, however, the reverse is more important.[1]

The *Social Contract,* we must above all remember, is part of the same philosophy and the same program that Rousseau developed in *La Nouvelle Héloïse* and *Emile,* as well as in various other writings. Its function in the whole, as he conceived it, is to treat one aspect of a vaster program for a reconstructed (perhaps we should say a *constructed*) society—a *real* society. That aspect is political *institutions* and processes. I underscore "institutions," because all of these works are *political*, in the broad sense of that word. All deal, in one way or another, with the problem of how to govern individuals who must live in a community—the problem of the individual and society.

Rousseau's political philosophy has been described many times as totalitarian in character, or at least as authoritarian and despotic. The basis of this charge has usually been the political organization and functioning of his State, or the political relation of the individual to the State. I have little argument with this conclusion, except that the method does not go far enough, and so has not been strong enough to convince those whose love and admiration for Rousseau have taken the misguided form of an apologetics that would make him a liberal and the father of our democratic societies.[2] Because of the democratic character (a cultivated illusion far more than a reality) of certain of his political institutions, Rousseau has often been called a supporter of freedom by writers who neglect what he contemplates doing to the individual.[3] Not enough has been made of the interrelationships between his strictly political ideas and the ideas concerning the management of individuals, which we discussed in the first chapter. Too often, those who speculate on his political philosophy have approached him from the "outside," with a set of concepts already in their minds and with too narrow an understanding of the term "political." It is necessary to approach Rousseau from the "inside"—that is, bearing in mind his life, personality, and experience in the world, his dreams, and his shape of mind. Only in this way, I think, can we determine what he meant and wanted, and the importance to him of key elements such as duplicity, docility and dependence, unity and order. It is when we understand what kind of society he dreamed of (and, preferably, why) and how he would treat the individual in that society that we can interpret with greater certainty the institutions and processes of the *Social Contract*. Only then can we grasp the place of the latter work in the grand scheme, and how it serves that scheme. Only then can we come to realize that the chief danger in Rousseau's system, and also his most original and remarkable creation, is what I have called his "program of

behavioral engineering." As we discuss the institutions and processes, we shall see that he has not lost sight of this, the core of his
system.[4]

As we look back on Rousseau's earlier writings, we see that
they are based on a radical critique of society, which is condemned for what it has done to man's life and character. He
would like to restore some of the qualities he attributes to "original man"—such as sincerity ("transparency"), closeness to nature, and independence of others (or of "opinion"). But social
structure is inevitable (if not "natural"), and Rousseau always
said that man is potentially far better off in society than in the
state of nature. Only in society does he become a moral being,
"transformed from a stupid and ignorant animal into an intelligent being and a man." At the same time, man may be said to be
naturally wicked in society, because of the effects of *amour-
propre*.[5] Furthermore, social structure creates what may be called
"social facts," which change everything. Given the existence of a
social structure, it is no longer possible for man to make a simple
regress to an earlier state and its qualities. Time's arrow flies in
one direction only. We cannot, then, escape the necessity of
working within the social fact. For Rousseau this means making
man into a being of virtue (rather than of goodness), a social
being rather than an ego-centered will or the divided, unhappy
being that he now is.[6] Civilized right—the analogue of primitive
pity and empathy but superior to it—can triumph only through
a will to right which is strong enough to combat natural impulses
and self-interested will, which does not will a common self.

If the first estate of man was independence, the second is
competition and dependence on others; and the third will be
co-operation or equal dependence on the whole of society. Rousseau's view of the world had been made explicit in the second
Discourse, and again in *Emile*, when he said that each man
(being free and so not submitted to nature's harmony) regards
himself as the center of the universe and orders all others in
relation to himself—a principle of disorder on which Sade was to
capitalize. Just as cosmic chaos is harmonized in God's order, so
on earth the collective State, God's substitute, is the common

center that harmonizes the disorder of individual wills. Since conscience is weak, virtue must be founded, remarks Burgelin, "not on the natural aspiration to happiness, but on consideration of social order." [7] This process of secularization makes man the originator of his own values and of his own salvation; but it can be accomplished only with the inspired guidance of a semi-divine legislator-preceptor. Sincerity or transparency among the citizens requires, paradoxically, the use of duplicity or "illusion" by those who govern and lead. Closeness to nature can be achieved (as in Julie's garden) only by artifice and planned control.

According to the distinguished Italian political philosopher Sergio Cotta, the essential element in Rousseau's thought is the reduction of ethics to politics, a view that negates both the Christian and the Natural Law traditions.[8] It rests ultimately on his rejection of the Fall (evil is attributed to social developments) and of the Christian postponement of the realm of justice until the next life. Rousseau was the first to adopt this position, which is close to the Marxist theory that historical societies have alienated and corrupted man and given to human relations the character of war. Both Rousseau and Marx saw the remedy in a new and perfect society. The corrupted individual cannot regenerate himself. Virtue must replace the lost innocence. But whereas the Christian looks to grace for redemption, Rousseau relies on political action. "In his system, the City finally takes God's place, becomes divine and thereby becomes essentially totalitarian." The renewal of the inner man is Rousseau's primary concern; but this can only be accomplished by the State, and excludes autonomy.

Society must pursue principles diametrically opposed to nature. Rousseau says that natural inclinations are usually harmful in society. In place of individuality and independence, we must establish complete submission to the totally integrated community, a single will allowing no diversity of viewpoints or opinions. This Rousseau again makes clear in a personal document, the *Letters to Sophie*. There he writes that he has decided to give up the innocence or simple goodness he would have had in solitude.

Recognizing his dependence on other men, he states, "It is manifest that I must no longer consider myself as an individual, isolated being, but as part of a great Whole, as a member of a greater body, on the conservation of which my own depends absolutely, and which could not be badly ordered without my feeling that disorder." [9] It follows that virtue will have to be social; internal moral independence would only reinforce individualism. The "great Whole," substituted for natural independence, must dominate the individual without the possibility of contest. "Democratic totalitarianism," observes Cotta, "is thus founded and justified in its principle. . . . And if democratic totalitarianism does not succeed in making men virtuous, we shall have to go to despotic totalitarianism." This Rousseau says quite firmly in a letter to the Marquis de Mirabeau to which we shall later refer (see pp. 178–79). Proceeding with rigorous logic from the original innocence of man to the concept of the ethical State, Rousseau's thought is "necessarily totalitarian in its essence." We owe to him, concludes Cotta, the myth that politics can solve man's problems.[10]

Rousseau was, then, the great defender of culture against "nature"—the latter word being taken in the sense of the aggressive, egoistic vitalities that are our biological inheritance. But the "culture" he defended was of a different kind from any which existed in his time, and it departed radically from the theories of the *philosophes.* They defended the social passions born of *amour-propre*—pride and power—as being productive of knowledge, art, industry, and commerce; he condemned both the passions and their products. He charged, moreover, that the nature doctrine of the *philosophes* contained anarchistic or nihilistic potentialities (which were being overtly developed in his time); and Rousseau was, above all else, a lover of *order.* He wanted a truly human community, one which no longer depended on the motives of power, greed, and vanity (though these were to be utilized for purposes of directing and controlling individuals), and was based instead on a law recognized as inwardly binding and necessary.

Although Rousseau drew much from his own inventiveness,

he had models in mind.[11] One was Geneva—partly the Geneva
that Rousseau knew, but far more, the Geneva of Calvin, which
he idealized. He carried with him an image of its institutions and
traditions, and especially the spirit of Calvin, from whom he
learned that men, being evil, must be distrusted. They need
leaders and authoritarian control, even in their private lives.
Puritanism and the unity of the City were Calvinistic ideas. It is
noteworthy that Rousseau considered Geneva the home of liberty.[12] Yet in Geneva there was little if any legal protection for
rights or personal freedom. People were subjected to a broad
censorship and to surveillance, and there was a fairly rigid control of behavior.

The other influence was the ancient *polis,* or city-state, of
which Rousseau also formed an ideal image, which he related to
Geneva. He knew, of course, that in the city-state there were
classes and slaves, and that a minority were citizens. There was
no idea of representative government. The citizen was by definition one for whom participation in public affairs was the principal concern, not something to be taken up and laid aside at will.
He was one who identified himself with the community, and
was tied to it by a spiritual bond. Legislation was intended to
regulate private as well as public life. This was held to be no
sacrifice, for the individual, it was believed, realized himself in
the whole.[13]

Nevertheless, while there is no doubt that Rousseau had a
model of the *polis* in mind, he went further along his own path.
First of all, we must remember that there was a marked difference among ancient city-states, and especially between Athens
(which Rousseau derided) and Sparta (which he admired).
Despite Aristotle's statement, the Athenians placed great value
on individual judgment and critical thought, on individual rights
and self-realization. Athens, the home of freedom of the mind,
cherished its full exercise in speculation. It was by no means,
then, a monistic, unanimous State. "The freedom we enjoy in
our government," writes Thucydides, "extends also to our ordinary life. There, far from exercising a jealous surveillance over
each other, we do not feel called upon to be angry with our
neighbor for doing what he likes. . . ."[14] In Thucydides' mind

the contrast with Sparta was pointed. The Spartan ideals, as we know, were adopted by Rousseau, and he frequently holds them up as a model. Surely this is significant. In Sparta control of individuals and living for the State were well-nigh absolute. In government Sparta's popular assembly, unlike that of Athens (but like Rousseau's in the *Social Contract*), never had a chance to debate the proposals placed before it by a council of elders. As in Rousseau's *Project of a Constitution for Corsica*, it signified its assent or dissent by shouting. Real power lay in the hands of the five ephors, who enforced the laws and controlled morals and education with the help of the secret police. In a word, what Rousseau admired in Sparta was the *disciplined State* that was able to overcome the anti-social elements in the human personality and "make men one."

Plato's State, in the *Republic*, was inspired not by Athens, but by Sparta. The Spartan idea has supported every self-denying society since ancient times. Its aim was to create the ideal citizen, who would be selflessly devoted to the common good. Rousseau's model of the city-state is, then, that of Sparta, though he also approved some aspects of the early Roman republic that were of a like nature.[15] In his ideal city, as in its ancient ideal model, regulation of private life actually means complete control toward the end of zealous patriotism and absorption into the organic society of the *moi commun*. He goes beyond identification to the creation of a "superior person" who controls the parts of its body toward the single end sought by the Whole. It has already been made clear, but it will be clearer still, that, as the individual's mind and self are submitted to the mobilized forces of the State, in which all right and power inhere and which is determined to remake the "divided" individual into a true social unit, there is in the personality no sanctuary that is inviolable. This is the purpose of Rousseau's institutions. The State, in the person of its legislators, guides, and censors, takes over the function of Wolmar and of the tutor—and does the same things to its charges.

Some of Rousseau's basic considerations are developed in the important pages which he excluded from the final version of the

Social Contract, and which we fortunately have recovered in the discarded manuscript of the original draft (the Geneva manuscript) that was first published toward the end of the nineteenth century. The most important excluded chapter is at the beginning of the first book (Chapter II, "On the General Society of Mankind"). It is obviously written as a reply to Diderot's article "Droit naturel" ("Natural Right") in the *Encyclopédie,* and we can therefore date it from the end of 1755 or not long after. It is closely related to Rousseau's article "Political Economy," as is evidenced by the repetition of a passage on the family and the State. In later years, at least from the time of his letter of February 26, 1770, to Saint-Germain, Rousseau became convinced that he was the target of Diderot's fierce argument against the anarchist or nihilist in "Natural Right." In an addition to the *Confessions* he intimated that Diderot, and not he, was the enemy of society who ought to be choked to death. But at that time Rousseau was in a psychotic or semi-psychotic state, and there is no reason to think that he had already conceived such a suspicion in 1755, before their quarrel. In any event, the suspicion was entirely baseless, and a projection of his own hostilities. Diderot was interested in an abstract question of morality and politics, and his target was the rebellious immoralist, who was later to become the *Lui* of *Rameau's Nephew,* Father Hudson of *Jacques the Fatalist,* or Nero of the *Essay on the Reigns of Claudius and Nero.*

In this chapter Rousseau is interested, as he was in the second *Discourse,* in the origins of society and of government; and he begins along the lines he had developed in that earlier work. Primitive men, he argues, were made wicked and enslaved by new needs which required them to depend on each other. Thus weakness was the origin of a loose, ungoverned "general society"; and our weakness, he adds, with his usual arbitrary distortion of vocabulary, "comes less from our nature than from our cupidity." This was the state, lying between the natural and the civil, which he had described in the second *Discourse* as a golden age, and which he now turns into one of great unhappiness because of its constant instability and lack of order. In such a (Hobbes-

ian) state there is no discernible good or evil, and no protection
or shelter for the weak man, who is bound to perish "a victim of
this deceitful union"—"deceitful" because each sees only his
own self-interest and seeks to satiate his own passions. Consequently (and this is the significant point), there is no "object of
common felicity" and "one man's happiness makes the unhappiness of another." The essential result, which underlies Rousseau's thinking about society, is this: "the sweet voice of nature
is no longer an infallible guide for us, nor is independence . . . a
desirable state." He goes even further. Now he says that independence is never good, because it prevents the formation of a
whole. "Each would remain isolated among so many others, each
would think only of himself." No moral life, no intellectual
faculties would develop.[16]

All this theorizing is preliminary to an assault on Diderot, who
had tried to demolish the nihilist's arguments against social control by postulating a general will prior to civil society, based on
the identity of human nature (a "general society of mankind").
This was really equivalent to a secular Natural Law—the "general will" of the human race.

It is against this idea that Rousseau has been arguing. The
history of all societies proves that the results we should expect
from such a condition as Diderot describes have never come
about—that is, a condition which would make of mankind "a
moral person," with a universal motivation causing "each part to
act toward a common end, relative to the whole." Now this is
precisely what Rousseau is aiming at. Natural Law (which he
properly calls "rational law") is insufficient, for it develops only
when passions, which nullify its precepts, have also developed.
Civil society, it also follows, is an act of will, not a fact of nature.
It establishes what Diderot's supposititious "general society"
would possess if it existed: "qualities of its own, distinct from
those of the individuals who compose it"—what I have called
"social facts." Under it, the public welfare is not merely the sum
of the well-being of its individuals; greater than such a sum, it
lies in "the links that unite them," and is the source of individual
welfare. Such a definition actually tends to set up an abstract

general welfare over and above the concrete welfare of the individual.[17]

Diderot's nihilist was right, then. Nature tells us to place ourselves first and to seek our happiness at the expense of others. What Rousseau intends is to reverse this, by the force of the social regime. Enlightened self-interest, preached by Diderot and his group, is a farce, because no one can depend on others to place the general interest first, and so cannot be certain he will not become a dupe if he does so himself. In other words, Diderot has not found the way to overcome the natural "order" (that is, not the *original* natural order, but the one that obtains when men associate in societies) by seeking the remedy in another "natural order" that does not exist. Rousseau further infers that no society (doubtless with the exception of Sparta) has overcome this natural order, or, more exactly, disorder. Even God is not a help with the common masses, who follow gods "as irrational as they are"—gods that enable them to satiate their thirst for blood. Neither God nor Natural Law, he now declares, is an innate idea.

Relentlessly, Rousseau continues his smashing of Diderot's construction. Suppose the nihilist consults the general will, or consensus of mankind, and suppose it tells him what he ought to do. This still does not answer the main question. Why should he subject himself to that rule? Why is it his self-interest to be just? (It may well be that one reason why Rousseau avoids defining the general interest as that of the majority is that such a definition would make it impossible to answer the nihilist's question.) Rousseau admits Diderot's definition of the general will as "a pure act of the understanding [in individuals] which reasons in the silence of the passions on what each man may require of his fellow man, and on what his fellow has the right to require of him." [18] But what man can do this? What man "can separate himself from himself"? The common man could never reach such a level, and even well-intentioned persons would err, mistaking their own inclinations for the law. (Rousseau will again evoke this idea in proposing the need for a guide.) To do what Diderot supposes would be against nature, Rousseau argues.

Thereby he deprives conscience of any efficacy, and reduces behavior to naturalistic terms of self-interest. The laws of conscience, like the written laws, come from the social order that is already in existence. "We begin really to become men only after we have become citizens."

The implication is clear: a way must be found to make men rise above nature and individualistic motivation. Diderot's appeal against injustice was to the abstract sense of justice in men. For him the question was a moral one, and so he reacts against Rousseau's exclusion of traditional Natural Law in the second *Discourse.* Rousseau, who will absorb morals into politics, adds a new political dimension. There is no purely moral answer to the nihilist; there can be only a political answer. Rousseau drives toward new ground—the general will and the "collective self" of his authentic society. The traditional Natural Law becomes irrelevant, as well as inefficacious. In the Preface to the second *Discourse* he had written that reason finds itself forced to reestablish Natural Law "on new foundations, when, by its [i.e., reason's] successive developments, it has finally stifled nature"— that is, as he explains in a passage omitted from the final version of the *Social Contract,* when self-interest has stifled humanity in our hearts and passions have rendered its precepts powerless. Then reason, the corrupter, becomes the remedy.

In his conclusion Rousseau asks us to face the fact that men "who are living simultaneously in the freedom of the natural state and the subjection of the social state" can care nothing about justice and equality (for "living in the freedom of the natural state" means that to a certain extent they can do as they wish, regardless of the effect on others or on the community).

> Let us strive to draw from the ill itself the remedy that is to cure it. By new forms of association, let us correct, if we can, the faults of the general association. . . . Let us show him [the nihilist] in art perfected, the remedy for the ills that art, once begun, wreaked on nature. . . . Let him see in a better organization the reward for good actions, the punishment for bad ones, and *the lovable harmony of justice and happiness.*[19] Let us illuminate his reason with new lights, let us warm his heart with new feelings, and let

him learn to multiply his being and his felicity by sharing them with his fellow-men. (II, 2.)

For Rousseau, then, no refutation of egoistic nihilism is to be found either in nature or in present societies. His own position is that the source of meaningful moral values is in civil society itself; that is, law is prior to justice, as he often says. By true collectivization of man we can overcome the contradictions in him and remedy what nature failed to supply. In utopian fashion Rousseau declares that the first law of the new society will be that each prefer in all things the good of all to his own good. Nature will thereby be reversed.

> Protected by that society, . . . the natural repugnance to do harm no longer being balanced in us by the fear of being harmed, we are led by nature, by habit, by reason, to treat other men as we treat our fellow citizens; and from this disposition, reduced to acts, are born the rules of reasoned Natural Law, which is different from Natural Law properly speaking, which is founded only on a feeling, true but very vague and often stifled by self-love.[20]
>
> Thus the first distinct notions of the just and unjust are formed in us. For Law is prior to justice, and not justice to Law. And if the Law cannot be unjust, it is not because it is based on justice, which may not always be so, but because it is against nature to want to harm oneself, and to this there is no exception. (II, 4.)

Thus at one blow Rousseau reduces justice to utility and sets up the law as the sole criterion of right and wrong. Justice is identified with the Law, which creates it, and from that Law there is no moral appeal, for the Law is morality.[21] The entire chain of arguments leads to one objective, the making of the citizen—a man who sacrifices personal interest to the general, or, more exactly, as we saw in *La Nouvelle Héloïse,* one who is induced by various means of indoctrination to believe that the general interest *is* his personal interest. We must remake men so that there *are* no nihilists, rather than try to argue with nihilists and persuade them to accept our views. We must remake society so that no one has an interest in being an anarchistic, atomistic individual. The *Social Contract,* it now becomes evident, is the logical complement of the second *Discourse.*

One cannot help asking why Rousseau suppressed this important chapter. The answer suggested by Vaughan is the most reasonable supposition. The chapter "was fatally relevant; because he became aware that in refuting this idea of Natural Law, he had unwittingly made a deadly breach in the binding force of the Contract," and he had no other principle to put in its place as the foundation of civil society.[22]

The contract contains two essential elements for Rousseau: freedom (in its acceptance), and the element of collective compulsion, which only the freedom of its acceptance justifies. This theory Vaughan deems preposterous, since a contract can be effectuated only in civil society; to use it as an explanation of society "is to bring forward the effect as an explanation of its own cause": that is, there is no sanction to establish the validity of the original contract—except Natural Law, which Chapter II of the first version effectively denies. No wonder Rousseau was tempted to establish society on the notion of general utility instead, for that he realized the flaw in his theory is clear when he states: "How can we count on promises, which nothing can force the contracting parties to make good, and which, when the interest that makes them acceptable changes, they will inevitably desire to break?"[23]

The whole weight of the coercive forces which Rousseau wants society to use against the refractory individual is destined precisely to forestall that desire.

At the very outset of the *Social Contract* Rousseau declares that his purpose is to find a way of governing men that is "legitimate and sure, taking men as they are"—that is, as self-centered, aggressive beings. His first chapter begins with a ringing phrase: "Man was born free, and everywhere he is in chains." This statement has often been misinterpreted as a cry of revolt, but it is nothing of the sort. Rousseau means only that in the state of nature men were independent, while now their wills are subjected to social and governmental restrictions. His intention is made plain immediately, when he asks, and promises to

answer, the question "What can legitimize this change?" Albert
Schinz once wrote that, far from denying the necessity of
"chains," Rousseau "was only proposing the substitution of another kind." [24]

"The social order is a sacred right which is the basis of all
other rights." That is, all rights are founded on conventions. For
Rousseau, it is fair to say, so-called rights in the state of nature
are not rights, but powers. A right is a moral and legal entity,
and these categories come into existence with civil society.

But civil society is itself the result of a convention. To prove
this fundamental point, Rousseau in the following chapters eliminates other alternatives. The family is not the origin of civil
society, although it is the only natural society, because its links
are dissolved with maturity.[25] In a magnificent argument he
demonstrates that the law of the stronger can never be a right,
and so can never be a legitimate power that creates the obligation
of obedience. Then the justifications of slavery are refuted one
by one, with eloquence and logic, in an effort to show that
slavery is not a foundation of civil authority. Force and slavery,
on the one hand, right, on the other, are contradictory and
exclusive terms.

The social order can only have been founded on mutual
consent—the social compact. Although Rousseau, as in the second *Discourse*, writes as if he is recounting history, he undoubtedly believes that the social contract, in its true and proper form,
is an ideal that has never yet been adopted, or put into effect, in
any society. His originality is to insist on the act that creates civil
society as prior to and distinct from any other contract, such as
the supposed contract between ruler and people creating government. Without such a prior agreement, there would be no obligation for the minority to submit to the majority. Majority rule
"presupposes that there has been unanimity at least once." (I,
5.) This limiting of the notion of government was a novelty that
others found hard to understand; in the traditional view, government was an exercise of sovereignty.

What, exactly, is the nature and meaning of the fundamental
pact? Men, it is to be supposed, have reached a point in cultural

evolution at which they need each other. The problem then becomes this: "to find a form of association that will defend and protect with the entire collective force the person and the property of each individual; and by which each individual, uniting himself to all, will yet obey only himself and remain as free as before." (I, 6.) It is obviously the second part of the proposition that contains the essence of the solution created by Rousseau's intellectual ingenuity. The attentive reader will at once be reminded of his "solution" of the dichotomy of discipline and freedom in both *La Nouvelle Héloïse* and *Emile*. We shall find that Rousseau has not changed his thinking or his special use of vocabulary.

"To unite with all" means simply but absolutely this: "the total alienation of each associate with all his rights to the collectivity." [26] All the clauses of the social contract reduce themselves to this. Contrary to Locke and Spinoza, Rousseau eliminates any residual natural rights at the start. "For, if any individual rights remained, there being no common superior to decide between individuals and the generality, each person being at some point his own judge would soon claim to be it in all points." The authority of the community, embodied in the political State, must be absolute. Once again, it is obvious that Rousseau intends to eliminate any theoretical or institutional limit to law (the will of the community). For Locke and Spinoza, as for the writers of the American Declaration of Independence, society's function is to protect certain rights which men do not surrender.[27] The people in what we call a free society do not give themselves absolutely to anyone, not even to an association of equals or a mythical "collective self." The State's function is to take the necessary measures—including educational and disciplinary—to protect and enhance the individual's own life, rather than to control and re-direct the private sanctum of his inner being for its own purposes, however well intended they may be. Rousseau's view of the relation between the individual and the State is exactly the reverse—a reversal, as Vaughan says, that is "nothing less than a revolution in political speculation." [28] Locke further assumes that no powers belong to the community except such as have been expressly entrusted to it; its sovereignty is therefore limited. Thus the *traditional* social contract theory implies a limitation of governmental or communitary authority by Natural Law and natural rights.

For Rousseau total alienation, or total authority, is the necessary condition for equality under law; and only equality under law can prevent the strong from reducing the weak to dependency, and so from exploiting them. "Each, giving himself to all, does not give himself to anyone." Since there is a perfect mutuality of surrender and of claims, no one, Rousseau maintains, loses anything. He was convinced, according to Vaughan, "that such a community as is presented in Locke's *Treatise* was incapable of the keen public spirit, the strong communal life, which was to him the supreme good attainable in the State. Rome and Sparta, with their constant sacrifice of private to public interests, always hovered before his imagination." He had "a deep conviction that no theory which does not rest itself upon the passions of man, as well as their calculating [i.e., aggressive, evil] instincts, can hold water for a moment." [29]

The concept of equality under law is in itself a liberal one. However, leaving aside for the moment the fact that Rousseau is not entirely faithful to it, let us note only that in his mind it exists in close partnership with an aversion to dependency on others that has quite different implications. Rousseau says over and over again that a man who is dependent on other men cannot be free. What is needed is mutual interdependence, achieved through a complete dependence of each on the whole. Each being equal in dependency, he will not be subject to the will or compulsion of other individuals or groups. "Each giving himself to all gives himself to no one." [30] This is the concept of the "body." The price of being independent of other individuals is total dependence on the collective whole, on the organic society Rousseau wishes to create. "The alienation being without reservations, the union is as perfect [i.e., complete] as possible." That is why the compact excludes the retention of any rights vested in the individual. And later (Chapter 7), "That each citizen is given to the Fatherland is the condition that guarantees [the individual] from all personal dependency." Rousseau recognizes (Chapter 7) that each man, "as a man," has a will that may be different from the general will which is his as a citizen; that his interest may be quite opposed to the general interest. His own existence is "naturally independent" and it alone is of real importance to him. He may desire to enjoy his rights as a citizen and evade the duties of a citizen. All these facts are used by Rousseau to justify repression ("he will be forced to be free"). Only by "giving each citizen to the nation" can he be "guaranteed from dependency on persons." This is the condition "which alone makes civil engagements legitimate"—the question Rousseau set out to answer at the beginning of his book. In a later work, *Lettres écrites de la Montagne*, Rousseau phrased his precept in unmistakable terms:

> The essence of sovereign power is to be unlimited: it can do everything, or it is nothing. . . . It can recognize no rights except its own and those it grants. Otherwise the possessors of those rights would not be a part of the political Body. They would be strangers to it because of those rights, which would not be in it; and the moral person, *lacking unity*, would vanish.[31]

Typical of Rousseau's dogmatic shape of mind, there is only one "right" contract. He allows no choice as to terms, declaring that the slightest modification makes it null and void.

It is clear, then, how "each is united to all." But how does each remain "as free as before," and "obey himself alone"? This puzzler becomes clear only by reference to the writings we have previously discussed. His words make sense, but only because what is actually implied is a complete change in the nature of the self, and in the meaning of "freedom." Rousseau does not make this entirely apparent. This is what he says:

> Each of us puts his person and all his power in common under the supreme control of the general will; and we receive each member into a body as an indivisible part of the whole. At that instant, instead of the private person of each contracting party, the act of association creates a moral, collective body composed of as many members as there are voters assembled, which receives from the

same act its unity, its collective self ["*moi commun*"], its life and its will. (I, 6.)

Thus a "public person" is created—"a moral and collective body" (*Emile*). The unitary self no longer exists, at least from the viewpoint of the "public person." It is alienated, absorbed, transmuted into the "collective self," whose will and imperatives —possibly quite distinct from those of the former private or "human" selves—are morally superior and commanding.[32] "What is a public person?" Rousseau had asked in the first version. And he had answered: "It is that moral being called 'sovereign,' which the social pact has brought into existence, and all of whose acts of will bear the name of laws." In other words, it is the only will that creates obligation, thus answering the opening question in the first chapter.[33]

Rousseau's social contract is not really a contract at all, but a covenant, in the Old Testament sense. This is so not merely because there is no prior law to assure respect of the contract, but for other and more interesting reasons. A contract is between people who do not trust each other and its purpose is limited; Rousseau's covenant is among people who trust each other, and it is completely open-ended. It involves not only a specific act, but a commitment to future decisions as yet unknown. Rousseau denies any contract with the ruler; but his covenant, which he claims to be one among all the people (I, 3), is in reality between the people and the *moi commun*, or the general will. The surrender of the individual is as complete and absolute as in Hobbes. Rousseau simply skirts this by identifying the general will with the individual—with each individual and all, regardless of their differences—by stipulating that it is their true will and true self. Thus metaphysics is brought into politics.

Since the nature of the self is transformed, that of liberty is transformed accordingly. If to be free is to obey oneself alone, then for the socialized man, with his new collective self, the only true freedom is to obey the collective or general will, and not his private will, which should no longer exist as such. In a sense, this "political liberty" is essentially the same as natural liberty. We do not obey other *men*; we obey only our own will.[34] Only the notion of will has been radically changed, alienated to an abstract entity.

It is scarcely necessary to say that freedom is swallowed up by this collective monolith, this all-devouring general will. And this is as Rousseau wished. In *Emile* (Book II) he declares that in the state of nature, when men were self-sufficient, individual liberty was fine. "Before prejudices and human institutions had altered their natural inclinations, the happiness of children as well as of men consisted in the use of their freedom." But individual liberty can only be harmful in society, since "it is proved that no private will can be integrated into the social system."

Rousseau undoubtedly knew that there was a measure of illusion and duplicity in his argument. There is a total surrender; but, he argues, it is really to oneself, not to another person. That is, the surrender is not literally to oneself—or at least not to the same self—but to a new self, which he supposes and claims to exist in a relationship of complete identity with the individuals who compose it, for it now becomes the true self, the superior self. It follows that no matter what constraints the individual suffers, no matter how much his personality is violated, he is still obeying his will and is free. "We are free, although subjected to laws; not when we obey a man, because in the latter case I am obeying another's will; but in obeying the law, I am obeying only the public will, which is as much mine as anyone's." [35] Rousseau knew, however, that power and will were really alienated either to the majority or ultimately, as we shall see, to a "guide." I think he also knew that the identification of the general will with each individual's own true will rests on the dubious validity of an argument which commits in advance the whole of the future, and cannot be called into question on each new occasion, regardless of what a law requires us to do. In a disguised way, then, he reaches the same end as Hobbes—unlimited power of the Sovereign. [36] But the Sovereign no longer is a despotic monarch; it is an all-powerful general will. In fact, the potential tyranny is much greater in Rousseau, because the *moi commun* is to have, as he puts it, the impersonal necessity of things; or as he writes in

Emile, if laws had "an inflexibility which no human force could overcome, the dependency of men would again become a dependency on things. . . . We would join to the liberty which keeps man free of vices the morality which raises him to virtue." [37] The yoke of necessity, he tells us in *La Nouvelle Héloïse,* is "impersonal, inflexible, hidden." Furthermore, Rousseau in this section gives the delusive impression that he will be satisfied with voluntary compliance with the general will, its acceptance as one's own. The truth is that he will have no reliance on good will or reasonableness. The "ought" that replaces impulse or instinct (Chapter 8) will become a crushing force.

We readily see the difference between such a concept and the notion of an agreement to submit to majority rule in the limited sense of conforming our actions to it. The individual may be deprived not only of his "rights," but of his personality and conscience by such a force. Yet, if we follow Rousseau's definitions, oppression by the State becomes, by definition, impossible; since we have agreed to it, since it has become our will, it cannot be oppression. It is not surprising that he prefers not to talk of rights and avoids defining them.

In the liberal view, as Diderot expressed it in the *Encyclopédie* ("Political Authority"), "true and legitimate power is necessarily limited," regardless of the person or organ of society that wields the power. This is precisely what Rousseau proceeds to deny even more emphatically in his next chapter. From the individual's dual position as a member of the Sovereign and as subject of the Sovereign, Rousseau concludes that the Sovereign's laws bind the subjects (because there are in effect two contracting parties—the Sovereign making the law and the subject whom it controls), but cannot bind the Sovereign itself (since the Sovereign or Law-maker cannot contract with itself or make itself the object of its own laws, else it would become subject, not Sovereign). The power of the Sovereign, he states categorically, "has no limits other than the public utility properly understood." This means that the Sovereign cannot "impose on itself any law that it cannot break," and that "there is and can be no kind of obligatory fundamental law [i.e., fixed constitution or Bill of Rights] for the body of the people." [38] In other words, sovereignty, or the collective will, cannot be limited by obligations it has undertaken by previous acts or weakened by constitutional safeguards.[39] Rousseau refuses to conserve any distinction between an order of fundamental laws (natural or constitutional) and an order of positive laws. To put it even more clearly: "the sovereign power has no need to give guarantees to the subjects, because it is impossible for the body to want to harm its members. . . . The Sovereign, by the very fact that it is, is always all that it should be." [40] The whole notion of natural, prior, or supervening rights of the individual is out of the question. What are called "rights" on the theory of *droit naturel* are really passions, expressions of *amour-propre*, anarchic demands of the individual. "The individual could only have rights," writes Alfred Cobban, "so long as he continued to be conceived as a distinct moral entity, separate from the State." [41] Let us note here the persistent Aristotelian imagery of a body and its members ("limbs" is an alternate meaning in French), and the similarity to Hegel's idea that the State is the highest form of moral existence.[42]

In Rousseau's theory the idea that a body cannot *wish* to harm its members is intended as a protection against the abuse of power by the State or the general will. Obviously, this theoretical protection is quite without substance; not only because of the reality of where power lies in his system (the guides, leaders, or at best the majority), but because, as his own writings prove, what the Sovereign does in the best interests of its members, and without *wishing* to harm them, may be to take away their freedom and to control their lives.[43] Rousseau, I am convinced, was aware of all this. How skillfully he has slipped from a theoretical level to a pragmatic one! The reasoning is analogical. The collective will, embodied in the State, cannot *want* to harm its members, even as the body will not harm the limbs. Previously (Chapter 6) Rousseau had also argued, in like fashion, that since the total alienation is equal for all, "no one has any interest in making it onerous to others." Here it is the individual who will not want to authorize any too very rigorous action by the collectivity. These arguments make implicit and not necessarily valid psychological assumptions. But Rousseau has known all along that to maintain equality (which is essential to his special idea of liberty), the State will have to use the maximum possible power; and he will provide for this in his own planning. Furthermore, the protection derived from the axiom that no one wants to hurt himself rests on the instinct of self-love or self-interest. But this self-interest, it has been pointed out, is the self-interest each individual has *qua* citizen, not *qua* individual, the latter being (in Rousseau's words) always opposed to the general interest. We are therefore brought back to the problem of "making citizens," that is, of "denaturing man." [44]

In fact, Rousseau quickly goes on to emphasize strongly that the proposition about guarantees is not reversible. The Sovereign must require guarantees of the subject, since an individual's will as a man may clash with his will as a citizen (the "general will") and speak for his self-interest. This is precisely what Rousseau wishes to eliminate. In such a case the individual's natural independence rebels against his new dependence, and the ruin of the political body ensues. The Sovereign must therefore be able to compel the subjects' obedience. In Paul Léon's words, " 'communitary autonomy drains away individual autonomy.' " [45] Such compulsion of the private will (which may involve control of his personality, and of his person) does not deprive the individual of his liberty, in Rousseau's terminology, as it would in the anarchic state of nature. To force him to obey the general will "means only that he will be forced to be free." As one political philosopher has put it, man is free " 'only if he passively obeys the State [or, as Rousseau would say, if he exhibits "docility"—a passive readiness to be led or taught]. . . . The more omnipotent the State is, the freer man is.' " [46] There is no other way to "guarantee him from all personal dependence"—and for Rousseau, as we have made clear, liberty is clearly freedom from personal subjection, at the price of a complete but equal subjection to a collectivity whose will *is* his own, inasmuch as he is part

of the Sovereign to which he has alienated his *moi humain*.
Since dependence on the whole is by its necessity, impersonality,
and equality analogous to dependence on nature, Rousseau considers his society, however artificially brought about and maintained, to be a more "natural" one.

To be free, declares Rousseau, is to obey only the law. Now in
all civil societies the fictitious social contract implies the State's
power to compel obedience to law; but there is the important
matter of a limit to law itself and of the individual's residual
rights *vis à vis* the law. "To obey only the law" is a necessary, but
not a sufficient, condition of liberty. Even if Rousseau intended
—which we shall see he did not—that citizens should "prescribe
the law to themselves" and that they should obey only the law,
his doctrine tells us nothing about how the laws are drawn up or
what they prescribe. For Rousseau, the principle of government
is the power of the Whole over each of its parts.[47]

Rousseau, to be sure, does not intend to rely on open, external
constraint. Coercion is sometimes necessary, because refractory
individuals do not accept laws that are not ego-aspirations but
ego-controls or frustrations. We must not forget all that he has
said, time and again, about capturing wills. A captured or controlled will autonomously, freely wills what it is supposed to.
Since being a citizen more than a man is contrary to nature, a
whole system of thought control and character formation (as
illustrated in the other writings) is required. Citizenship
("virtue") must replace natural instincts that have become degenerate and corrupted in society.

It follows that the individual has no firm protection against
this Whole, which will turn out to be, in theory, the majority,
and in practice, its "guides." Early in the nineteenth century
Benjamin Constant pointed out why the liberal cannot accept
Rousseau's political system. " 'It is false,' " he noted, " 'that society as a whole possesses an unlimited sovereignty over its
members. . . . There is a part of human existence which necessarily remains individual and independent, and which is by right
outside of the competence of society.' " [48] This is precisely what

Rousseau's political theory, and his plan to remake men into social beings who think of themselves only as part of the whole, denies.

But Rousseau is consistent. If to disagree with the general will means to disagree with yourself, obviously you cannot be allowed to do that. If the Sovereign can have no self-interest against that of its individual citizens, then the general will cannot err—and who has the right to err or to oppose his own true interest? J. I. McAdam has shown how incorrect is Derathé's claim that in Rousseau's theory all natural rights are returned to the individual reinforced by the authority of the State. Rousseau does not accept the traditional theory that natural rights are rights possessed independently of the State or Sovereign and which can, if necessary, be claimed against them. According to Rousseau's theory of surrender, the State becomes the subject or possessor of these rights. The individual has rights only as a member of the collective association. This is clear in Rousseau's contrast between the state of nature and the civil state, the latter being one of complete mutual dependence in which the citizen "can be nothing by himself." [49]

A pluralistic society is impossible under this regime. While Locke's society was a bargain among individuals intent on preserving their rights, while Montesquieu sought a balance among social groups and forces, Rousseau emphasizes the welfare of the whole community, which can be achieved only by total commitment to it and by diminishing the individual and all lesser groups. In Rousseau's State there is no right to be wrong, no toleration for "error" or heresy. Liberals have never ceased criticizing Rousseau for allowing no real, or practical, limit to the State's power, on the theory that its only effect is to force men to be free, by making them do what they really want (or ought to want) to do. [50]

Let us summarize the consequences attained thus far. In the State that the implementation of the contract effectuates, moral duty succeeds instinct and appetite, and natural freedom gives way to civil liberty—that is, a freedom determined and limited by the general will and protected by the social force against the play of individual aggressions. Dependency on nature is replaced by an equally absolute dependency on the collectivity, whose laws must be made to have the necessity of natural laws. This is what Durkheim called "a mechanically solidary society," in which people are homogeneous in beliefs and conduct, directed by a "collective conscience" that imposes a totality of sentiments. The members of a mechanically solidary society cannot morally refute its collective conscience, and any offense against it becomes a moral offense.[61]

The difference between the natural and the social orders is sharply defined in the matter of property. On entering the social order, the individual surrenders all his possessions along with his person and his independence. Since individual rights are derived from the prior right of the State, the right of the first occupant, traditional in Natural Law and recognized by Locke, no longer obtains as such. It now takes a positive act by the State to reestablish it and to make him a proprietor. But what he has now is a true *right* of ownership, protected by the community, instead of usurpation or mere physical possession. Individuals are protected against aggressions; at the same time, by putting them into dependency, we engage their fidelity to the State. In this way, too, the collectivity can prevent the rise of that disastrous "artificial inequality" Rousseau had condemned in the second *Discourse,* and even attenuate the effects of natural inequality. Unlike eighteenth-century communists, Rousseau does not dream of abolishing the property he had condemned in the earlier work, because in society new and legitimate rights and duties are created. This shortcoming and the failure to theorize the class struggle (which he was one of the first to comprehend, in the second *Discourse*) have provided the chief grounds for the reproaches levelled against Rousseau by modern Marxists, who have otherwise found valuable elements in his writings. Rousseau in this regard seems close in his thinking to Aristotle, who denied that evils in society stem from property: "They proceed from the wickedness of human nature . . . . It is not so much the *property* as the *desires* of men that need equalizing"; and that cannot be done unless the people are trained "not to desire more." [52] It was not *socialism* that Rousseau proposed, but *socialization* of the individual, and Marxist theory requires both. But Communists do recognize, as one of them has put it, that "Rousseau created the theoretical basis for distributive action by the State." [53]

In the first book Rousseau has outlined the theory of a rational collectivity, or a just and truly social State founded on the contract. Following Hobbes and Pufendorf, but transforming their ideas, he has made the State into an artificial moral and juristic person, investing in it unlimited sovereignty and all rights. In the second book he will describe the operations of such a State.

His first consideration—one which is directly related to the total character of the desired socialization and the collectivity's resultant power over the individual—is that sovereignty is inalienable and belongs exclusively to the collectivity. That sovereignty inheres in the "people" is a democratic notion; it may even be considered as liberal when considered relative to the institutions of monarchy and feudal aristocracy, to which Rousseau was firmly opposed. There is no doubt that the historical influence of his doctrine worked in this direction, as liberal thinkers throughout the Western world seized upon it without understanding its function in Rousseau's grand scheme. It is also true that one of his motives was to prevent arbitrary power, or power *not* used for the general welfare. And he doubtless had Geneva in mind, where the executive had destroyed the legislative. But his chief purpose was an end beyond this. It was to insure the *total participation* of the citizen in the collective acts, and so their total control over him. Hence he argues that the general will can alone direct the State to the general welfare, and then that the "collective being cannot be represented except by itself." (II, 1.) Its power may be delegated (to the officers of government), but not its will, or law-making function. Were that done, an individual would consent in advance to *another's* will, or would be engaging himself simply to obey, and would thus lose the character of Sovereign to become only subject.

Behind this rationalistic insistence lie two essential notions.

The first is that an organic collectivity cannot exist as a mere confluence of individuals or groups united for common purposes, because the unity is constantly ruptured by competition and "war." Parliamentary government is the playground of special interests, and the whole point is to overcome separate wills. "Only the ensemble of citizens, obeying a single feeling, a single will," writes one commentator, "is inspired by the common interest." [54] Rousseau's concept of the general will implies that the State is, "in the fullest sense, a corporate body, with a life of its own quite apart from that of the individual members of which it is built up." [55]

The second notion, that of total participation, we shall also bear in mind later in discussing the voting process. But it is obvious at this point that when Bauclair, a contemporary opponent of Rousseau's, defended the representative system, his argument brought out precisely the thing Rousseau was fighting against. According to Bauclair, deputies can represent the general will *if* the people consent to it and they are chosen for that purpose; it follows, however, that "my will is not enclosed in theirs." [56] Parliamentary democracy would nullify the total alienation and participation that Rousseau must have.

Sovereignty is not only inalienable, but indivisible. It may not be separated (as Montesquieu proposed) into the legislative, executive, and judicial, although government must have such divisions. It remains total, like that of a body, and is not "a fantastic being or a collection of pieces, as if they made a man out of several bodies, one of which would have eyes, another arms, the third feet, and nothing else."

Rousseau heads the third chapter "Whether the General Will Can Err." The question is tautological, since by prior definition the general will is that which tends to the general good, that which creates right and justice. But now Rousseau's purpose is not so much to underscore this definition as to draw certain important consequences from it. He has now gone from the theoretical to the political or pragmatic level; we must be aware of this. His first point cracks his whole rational structure wide open, for purposes that immediately become evident. It does not follow, he says, that the deliberations of the people are always right (i.e., that they express or discover the general will). The general will and the action of the collective Sovereign may be different things, and the people cannot after all be trusted. "We always want what is good for us, but we do not always see it." If we read carefully, we can grasp the significance of these statements. The general will is an abstract entity, *pre-existing* the collective vote. The "will of all" is only a sum of private wills, and thus is concerned only with private interests. Discovery of the general will, Rousseau tells us, results from a cancellation process in which contrary opinions annul each other, leaving a remainder that is the true general will. It is not clear just what this means, since such is the process of any vote, and the same error may come out of the collective judgment. A distinguished scholar in political science calls Rousseau's cancellation method nonsense.[57] Certainly, the whole process contains difficulties. The general will can be confirmed (or discovered) only if each citizen votes according to his own private opinion; but the worth of any private opinion remains to be determined by the general will. Moreover, since the people may be mistaken, the vote reveals only the will of all, which is not necessarily the general will.[58] Rousseau is aware of the difficulties, and what really is significant is the way he takes to get out of them. At this point, he gives us only a glimmer of what will turn out to be a process of indoctrination or control.

> If, when the people, *sufficiently informed, deliberates,* the citizens have had no communication amongst themselves, from the great number of small differences the general will will always result, and the deliberation will always be right. But when there are *factions,* partial associations at the expense of the great association, the will of each association becomes general in relation to each of its members, and private in relation to the State. . . . The differences then become less numerous and give a less general result. (II, 3.)

I have italicized the essential words. The phrase "sufficiently informed" conceals the indoctrinating process, to which Rousseau will later return. Unless they are "informed," they are "a blind mob." (II, 6.) The word "deliberates," as the context makes clear, means only "reflects"—even as Wolmar had said, "For whom do I deliberate?"[59] In his isolation the individual cannot become subjected, in his thoughts or his loyalties, to any group interest. He remains uniquely and totally committed to the collectivity, and his only relationship is with it.[60] That is why no factions (analogous to political parties) can be tolerated; in each "interest group" there is a lesser general will, which serves its own interest. The consequence would be a government by compromise and counterpoise among the several wills and group interests—one such as exists in all liberal societies. A true collectivity can tolerate only one will, to which, once it is formulated, there can be no opposition.[61] To oppose the general will is to be an enemy of the people, a criminal, and such a person must be forced to be free—or expunged.

Rousseau could conceive of the clash between factions only as one of group or class interests. He could not conceive of it as a method of enquiry. He would be close to the current Soviet view that free debate merely allows the dissemination of error. In the world of the totalitarian mind there can be no solutions by conciliation and consent. The conflict must always end in unconditional surrender. There is no such thing as the harmonizing of interests. The writers of the Federalist Papers, on the other hand, thought that "factions" (group or class interests) were useful in preventing what they most feared, the tyranny of the majority. They held that without the right of association "the individual is left helpless in the presence of the State. He can neither secure the redress of his own grievances, nor influence public opinion for the benefit of the whole mass."[62] They sought compromise and consensus, not unanimity, which, given the self-interest motivation, they held to be impossible unless property were abolished. For Rousseau, on the other hand, the idea of the general interest emerging from a counterpoise of conflicting interests, the idea of the lions and tigers lying down together in peace, was a hopeless illusion. The whole point is, rather, to eliminate the conflict, and so to eliminate all the lesser "particular wills." Only individual wills, kept carefully in isolation, will remain. These it will be easier to "form," to direct or "guide" into an organic, co-operative society. Factions, like parliaments, would be buffers between the "collective self" and the "human self," and would prevent the direct relationship on which depends the complete absorption of the latter into the former. Doubtless he might also have argued that in his ideal democracy there is no need for parties; the identification of private and general interest having been achieved, all individuals are in the same situation and have exactly the same interests.[63]

The aim, then, is unanimity, and not the free play of interests and wills, which would only perpetuate the state of war and disharmony. Rousseau frequently uses phrases such as "collective body," "moral and collective body," "political body," "public person," "community," "collective self," "the Sovereign considered collectively." Only by considering the State as a person or a body can we speak of "public good" and of a general will. What makes a "person" is spiritual unity.[64]

According to Charles Eisenmann, a major flaw in Rousseau's theory of liberty ("I am free because I have consented to the laws that bind me") is not the obvious objection that the general will is not my real or present will, but the retreat from unanimity to majority rule. (IV, 2.) This concession, though practically necessary, "ruins the thesis of the total liberty of each individual in a government of direct democracy." Rousseau's evident uneasiness about the whole matter leads him to "contrived and generally absurd ratiocinations about the meaning of the citizen's legislative vote and of the defeat of the minority," according to which his consent to majority rule means that he really wants any law the majority enacts, which plainly is not so. The citizen, moreover, is not called on to vote for or against a law, but to vote on what is the general will relative to the proposal. The vote, then, turns out in the last analysis to be only the expression of his opinion of what the result of the vote will be! There is still another consequence: since he agreed to submit to the general will as his own, he really did want the law to pass even though he voted negatively. Such is the result of Rousseau's insistence that the citizen will be as free, and as obedient to his own will, as the individual living outside of society.[65]

Rousseau does not want a tyranny of the majority (Derathé is quite correct in asserting this), for it could not produce the unity and harmony to which he aspired.[66] In other words, he does not intend that majority rule should take the place of the general will. To avoid these dangers, he has another card to play. The majority rule must be made to coincide with the general will.

The character of this whole process becomes even clearer when Rousseau talks about the law. "The People, who are subjected to the laws, should be their author." (II, 6.) But there is no way, he continues, for the people to propose laws, to draw them up, or to know what they should be. "Does the political body have an organ to express its will?" Obviously it does not, since no elective body can represent it. This denial is a crucial one, and it completely upsets Halbwachs, who had been trying to interpret Rousseau's theories apologetically. "At the moment when we are about to reach port, we are thrown back on to the high seas. The sovereign has been constituted, its members assembled, and it needs 'an organ to express' the general will." [67]

The stage is set. This is the moment for Rousseau to bring the Legislator on the scene.[68] He does so partly to solve a dilemma which he faces: the collectivist State must be the creation of the moral will; but the moral will can be transferred from the conceptual to the existential realm only in the conditions created by such a State. The concept of the Legislator enables him to escape from this vicious circle; but it does so at the cost of contradicting the principle of the collective origin of the general will. It leads directly to the principle of a "guide" or superior individual. The fact is that Rousseau has no intention of allowing the people to govern themselves. The people, he says again, are too stupid to see beyond the immediate or beyond their self-interest.[69] Rousseau's concept of freedom here is in no way different from what it is in *La Nouvelle Héloïse* and *Emile*. He has no confidence in the individual, and even less in the "people." Nature must be constantly controlled and remade.

How could a blind mob ["multitude"], which often doesn't know what it wants, because it rarely knows what is good for it, execute by itself so great and difficult an enterprise as a system of legislation? By themselves the people always want what is good, but by themselves they do not always see it. The general will is always right, but the judgment that guides it is not always enlightened. They must be *made to see* things as they are, sometimes as they should *appear* to them. It is necessary to *show them* the road they are looking for, *protect* [*"garantir"*] them from the seduction of private wills. . . . Individuals see the good but reject it; the public wants the good but does not see it. *All have the same need for guides.* It is necessary to *compel* the first to make their wills conform to their reason; it is necessary to *teach* the second to know what it *really wants.* (II, 6; italics added.)

One function of the guide, or Legislator, is, then, to tell the people what they ought to think and what they want. It is he who makes the people "sufficiently informed." The "educational" role of the State begins with the Legislator, and the purpose of "education" is to prepare consent ("docility") and "liberty" by changing wills. That the people should will consent ("of their own desire") is necessary; therefore the "docility" which Saint-Preux and Emile exemplify is essential. Since the voting process is a defective mechanism, Rousseau knows that without the guide his "general will" may be only the oppressive will of the majority. The role of the guide is to see to it that the citizens make their own decisions as they should; that while they do as they wish, they wish what they *should* wish. For it is the general will that is always right, and that of the people, affirms Rousseau, is not always so. There is really nothing left for them to decide. But their confirmation is necessary; the people must be the final judge. (In a moment we shall see why.) Rousseau is the inventor of what is now euphemistically called "guided democracy." The tenor of his political philosophy is akin to Jacobinism and to all totalitarian regimes, in that the inspired, charismatic leaders are held to be more representative of the deepest will of the nation than an elected body could be—more even, than the people themselves.[70]

"Legislator" is a word that Rousseau uses without great preciseness. In the chapter bearing that title (I, 7), as in much of the *Social Contract*, he is thinking of the Lawgiver as one who forms a nation, rather than as a person who formulates laws in later times. But in the preceding chapter the term seems to have a more general import, with apparently no distinction being drawn between the Legislator and the guide. Rousseau is interested not only in a single act, but also in setting up continuing institutions. He establishes no mechanism for the drawing up of laws and makes it clear that the people will still need to be guided in voting. Regardless of the title by which the persons who fill the leadership roles are known, the roles continue to exist. In a later chapter of the *Social Contract* (II, 12, fourth paragraph), it is quite clear that Rousseau specifies a continuing Legislator, who is also the "guide." In "Political Economy," it is the *"homme d'Etat"* who, avoiding overt show of power, captures control of the citizens' wills. The "leaders" who know the general will are specifically the heads of government. In the *Considerations on the Government of Poland*, Rousseau proposes holding the government in check by having its officers or magistrates act "only under the eyes of the Legislator." He adds: "It must be he who guides them. That is the true secret of preventing their usurpation of his authority." [71] In the same work he speaks of "leaders" and "guides" in a way that suggests they are not necessarily wielders of overt power. They are not Hitlers.[72] In general, the initial, semi-divine Legislator sets up a pattern, a tone, a methodology. These must be maintained; and they require the guide, or wielders of authority and power that are everywhere in evidence. The character of the society and the basic mechanisms for preserving its integrity are not going to change. A semi-divine Lawgiver is needed only at the start. But Wolmar must be replaced by another Wolmar, if Clarens is to continue; each generation of Emiles needs a new tutor; each generation of citizens needs new leaders and guides—to form them, "give them *moeurs*," and inspire them with patriotic zeal; to "denature" them and to guard against the ever-present menace of the *moi humain* which would fragmentize the artificially created unity of the political body. Rousseau makes it fully clear that the pressures must be maintained. It seems to me that in his mind the three words, Legislator, guide, and leader, are associated, and this association may be seen in the historical paragons he idolizes, in the heroes he creates in his fictions, and in the charismatic shadow-figures of his political writings.

The original Legislator (or Lawgiver) who shapes a people and gives them their laws is a rare, almost superhuman individual "who sees all the passions of men and is affected by none of them." He knows the general will in advance. He is Wolmar, Moses, Lycurgus, Rousseau's imaginary or legendary "guide." He must be wise and disinterested. In Rousseau's mind the Lawgiver is always an individual, a leader whose superior force of mind and character, combined with a magnetic personality and rhetoric, make him a Pied Piper to the common herd. Never does it occur to Rousseau that a group of men can sit down, deliberate, and write a constitution to "form a people." Something beyond the rational is necessary.

Where can such a man be found? "It would take gods to give men laws." Such a superior being cannot be chosen by the people; he wins his place by inherent merit. Wolmar was a man-god. Why is this so? Rousseau's reply sums up his political philosophy:

> He who dares to undertake the formation of a people [i.e., of a collective society] must feel himself able to change, so to speak, human nature; to transform each individual, who by himself is a perfect and isolated whole, into a part of a greater whole from which that individual will receive in some way his life and his being; to alter the human constitution in order to reinforce it; to substitute a partial and moral existence for the physical, independent existence that we have all received from nature. It is necessary, in a word, to deprive man of his own forces to give him others that are foreign to him and which he cannot use without the help of others. The more these natural forces are dead and annihilated, the greater and more enduring the acquired forces, the more solid and perfect will be the institution. So that if each citizen is nothing, and can do nothing, except through all the others, and if the force acquired by the Whole is equal or superior

to the natural forces of all the individuals, one may say that the legislation is at its highest possible point of perfection. (II, 7.)

Once more, then, he restates his major thesis: independence is to be transformed into total dependence and the atomistic individual submerged into the collective self as a co-operating unit in an organic body. It is no different from what he says in "Political Economy," *La Nouvelle Héloïse,* and *Emile.* The passage we have quoted is the rationale for a process of conditioning and indoctrination, the implementation of which will be drawn up in Rousseau's later writings. As Rousseau clearly said in the other three works, and repeated time and again, the essential task is to control wills and minds, in order to make of people what the guides, or the government, want them to be. The control must be absolute and certain, and have, "like [the laws] of nature, an inflexibility that no human force could overcome." To accomplish this, men must, he said again and again, be "denatured." It is obvious that this goal requires a process of complete conditioning and indoctrination. *La Nouvelle Héloïse* and *Emile* are experiments in such a process.

Rousseau has made it clear that the people are not qualified to formulate laws, not even to approve of them unless they are properly "informed." [73] In "Political Economy" he had asked: "How can the leaders know the general will in those cases in which it has not declared itself?" Very easily, he replies; and, if the nation is not assembled, "all the more so, because it is not certain that its decision would be the expression of the general will." [74] Consultation is not necessary—not for *this* purpose— "because the leaders know that the general will is always the decision that is most favorable to the public interest, that is, the most equitable." In other words, some know the general will in advance and speak for it, in the name of all. These are the ones who formulate the propositions and who have the task of guidance. In fact, then, the people are expected to approve (though they theoretically may also disapprove) what is proposed. It is evident that Rousseau's vote has the character of a plebiscite (a term he uses in the second *Discourse*), in which the people are called on to say "yes." There is no way for them to debate or to amend the proposition, which neither they nor their elected representatives have formulated.[75]

This analysis enables us to understand the purpose of the vote. Why does Rousseau insist on popular ratification, in spite of the fact that the general will not only exists before the vote, but is actually known to the "guides" or leaders? The vote is necessary because the leaders know, but the *citizens* do not know. They have to discover it for themselves (or, with proper guidance, be made to discover it). But why does Rousseau think it so essential that they do this? Here lies the whole point. If they were only *told* by the leaders that a proposal represents the general will (i.e., *their* will), such a procedure would not be effective. If we think of laws as imposed by ourselves (and unless we have had a part in making them they will seem imposed by others), we may think of ourselves as free. The people, following Wolmar's words, must "want all they are obliged to do." The general will is only an abstraction; it must be made existential. By the vote, the citizens are engaged in a total commitment. Rousseau's goal is the creation of a unity, a "body." The vote, in a word, is the means by which the *moi commun* is created. That is why the act of voting takes on the character of a solemn ceremony or ritual.[76]

It is obvious that there is a bit of duplicity in all this. Rousseau intended it to be so, as we shall now see. The only way to control people, he has told us, is never to let them realize that they are being controlled, and to let them think they are doing freely what you want them to do, and willing freely what you want them to will.[77] He again states this clearly in the *Social Contract*, in a remarkable and often unnoticed reference (Durkheim deliberately passes it by) [78] to what is unmistakable thought control. The most important kind of laws, he has said, are those to which a people give their emotional loyalty. "I am speaking of mores, of customs, and *above all of opinions*; a sphere unknown to our political writers, but on which the success of all the others depends; a sphere which the great Legislator looks after in secret ["the hidden hand"], while he seems to limit himself to particular rules." (II, 12.) [79]

Rousseau gives the game away. He has assured the reader that his citizens are free because they obey only the laws (which they supposedly make). But he also says, and says again, that the law is not enough, because, in controlling only actions and not wills, it cannot create docility. And this, he now insists, the Legislator must do—and do secretly. Obviously, then, his citizens will be obeying *something other than the law*: they will be obeying the whole hidden process. Duplicity conceals the real control. Rousseau, a realist, knew that his "impersonal yoke" had to be controlled by persons, and he wanted it so to be.[80]

The technique of balloting, as we have seen it, confirms this. One thing that is generally overlooked is that Rousseau does not intend that the vote be taken by secret ballot. This fact is not clear in the *Social Contract*. In the *Project of a Constitution for Corsica*, however, it is made clear in the following lines: "Corsicans, be silent. I am going to speak in the name of all. Let those who do not agree leave, and let those who agree raise their hands."[81]

Freedom, we have been told, lies in consenting willingly to what is necessary ("the yoke of necessity"). We shall need, then, a certain dose of what Rousseau calls "illusion" in order to make the general will seem "necessary," even as there is calculated illusion in making Emile see certain things as necessary which the tutor wants him to see as such. In each case there is someone who decides what it is that is beneficial and must be made to seem necessary and so become "the yoke."

The duplicity may also be viewed from a theoretical level. Rousseau's condition that the people be the sole judge of whether the will of the Legislator or guide is the general will simply cannot be fulfilled. This, too, he knew. As one scholar has astutely formulated it, "It is precisely because the people does not in fact judge according to the general good that the Legislator is necessary in the first place; how then can it judge whether or not the Legislator's will is really the general will?"[82] Since the general will is not the sum of individual wills, but what they would will in the silence of the passions, only the judgments of those who will morally really count. In fact, there is no empirical way of determining the identity of the Legislator's will and the general will. We could only measure his will and that of his opponents—if any were allowed. If the general will is nothing until it becomes actual in individual wills, there are no grounds on which to decide in which individual wills the general will has become actual. Rousseau's arithmetical hocus-pocus is no solution at all.

Indeed, Rousseau is not really satisfied that he has supplied all the mechanisms needed for control. Toward the end of the chapter on the Legislator, he emphasizes the difficulty of the beginnings, of starting a people out on the right path. We are startled to encounter this sentence: "Thus the Legislator, being unable to use either force or reasoning [the people (who are to vote to determine the general will!) being too stupid, Rousseau says], it is necessary for him to have recourse to an authority of another order, which can win them over without violence and persuade them without convincing them." Duplicity, again, to the rescue. This is necessary, Rousseau continues, "in order that peoples, submitted to the laws of the State *as to those of nature,* . . . should *obey with freedom* and bear *with docility the yoke* of public happiness." (II, 7.) [83] This last passage is an epitome of some of Rousseau's essential ideas: the transposition of natural necessity into political life, reflexive submission, the equivalence of docility and liberty, "beneficent illusion," and the conception of liberty as a "yoke."

One minor point should be added. It is a mistake to think that Rousseau's universal suffrage meant exactly that. With the government of Geneva in mind, he meant that only citizens could vote. In Geneva, at least, only a very small minority were citizens. In the eighth of the *Lettres écrites de la Montagne* he distinguishes between "the most vile populace" and "men really worthy of liberty," who are the true members of the Sovereign. In the *Project of a Constitution for Corsica* he distinguishes citizens, patriots, and aspirants. To a certain extent the *Social Contract* is an idealization of the constitution of Geneva, with the absorption of various ideas from the partisan tracts of 1718–38 (as well as from other political writers).[84] His mind was always shifting between anger toward Geneva as it was and love of his ideal Geneva.

In sum, then, total participation is one of the principal techniques, within the larger process we have been examining, toward the end of forging and maintaining the collectivity and the collective self, and of overcoming the "human self." [85] In order to approach the desired mechanical necessity in the citizen's obedience to laws, two conditions are postulated as necessary: they must apply equally to all, and the citizens must ratify them. Rousseau, in contriving the satisfaction of the second condition in the way he has done, has aimed at a psychological conquest. The general will taking on the shape of the citizen's own "true" will, as well as having (so he has been "informed") an axiomatic value of right, the citizen can no longer advance opinions he deems true, try to modify the law, or try to change a minority to a majority: there is no other right way. Thus by total participation he becomes totally committed, and unanimity is achieved. We cannot, then, separate the two phases, the goal of capturing the will of the citizen for the community (or the *moi commun*) and the voting procedure. We cannot, as is customarily done, take the second while ignoring the first. For Rousseau they are two parts of one process. For Rousseau the very meaning of freedom in a true or organic society is to act in accordance with the will of the *moi commun*, rather than in the service of the *moi humain*, and freely to will such action. The individual will, then, must be captured by the collective organism. In an open society, on the other hand, an individual's participation in the State is always partial. He helps to choose his representatives, but is not completely bound either by their acts, or by the vote of all, or even by his own vote. He remains *himself*; his possibilities of opposition and resistance, of judgment and will, have not been alienated by his action or any other action.

As for the first of Rousseau's two conditions, that the law must apply equally to all, it, too, contains a grave flaw, which Eisenmann has emphasized, one that may well involve another conscious duplicity, inasmuch as Rousseau was clearly aware of it. This idea of equality under law is, by his own statements, an essential ingredient of his concept of liberty, as well as a necessary condition of reflexive obedience.

> There is no one who does not apply to himself that word *each,* and who does not think of himself while voting for all. . . . The general will, to be really such, must be general in its object as well as in its essence; it must come from all to apply to all; and it loses its natural rectitude where it tends to some individual and specific object. . . . Thus, by the nature of the pact, any act of sovereignty, that is to say, any authentic act of the general will, obligates or favors all citizens equally, so that the Sovereign knows only the body of the nation, and distinguishes none of those who compose it. (II, 4.)

Scarcely has Rousseau established this vital principle when, not without some embarrassment, he retreats from it—just as he had retreated from unanimity to majority rule. It is enough, he affirms, that a law regulate the juridical status of an abstractly defined category of individuals, provided they are not specifically designated individuals.

> When I say that the object of the laws is always general, I mean that the law considers subjects in bodies and actions as abstract, never a man as an individual nor a particular act. Thus the law may well decree privileges, but cannot give any to a definite individual; the law may establish several classes of citizens, . . . but it cannot name such and such persons as admitted to them. (II, 6.)

Here Eisenmann exclaims:

> What a fall! What a retreat! The whole argument founded on the natural rectitude of the general will collapses in this sense, that it is no longer valid when applied to the adoption of laws which are merely general, that is, which apply only to a part of the citizenry— and why not a very small part? [86]

If the laws can be merely "general and abstract," or impersonal, the door is open to laws "contrary to the interests of certain citizens," either by imposing special obligations or burdens, or by exclusion from an advantage. Once again, Rousseau has been trapped by upholding an excessive thesis. He really admits it in several pessimistic statements.

The aspiration to liberty under the safeguard of laws is vain. Laws? Where are there laws? . . . Everywhere you have seen only the private interest and the passions of men rule under that name. . . . The universal spirit of all countries is always to favor the strong against the weak, and the one who has against the one who has nothing; this fault is inevitable; there is no exception to it.[87]

And again in the *Considerations on the Government of Poland*: "To put the law above man is a problem in politics that can be compared to the squaring of the circle. . . . But until then you may be sure that wherever you think you are making laws rule, it will be men who rule." [88] Such statements give further confirmation to my contention that the vote is designed as a tool to create the *moi commun*, and not really as a method of legislation. It is those who control opinion who govern, in the most inclusive sense of that word.[89]

The rejection of representative government, based on a theory of inalienable sovereignty,[90] contributes to the same ends of unity and control. Rousseau's political organization prepares the way for a government in which the basic relationship is between the leader and the people, with no effective intervening body. As Montesquieu had written, "The great advantage of representatives is that they are capable of discussing problems. The people is not able to do this." Rousseau knew this, too, having read his *De l'Esprit des lois* very carefully, but it was precisely what he wanted to avoid. Representative government, with its partial participation, its shield of a legislature between the people and the power of the general will (or the State), before which the individual otherwise stands naked, as before a crushing force, makes impossible the *kind* of general will he envisions. No doubt Rousseau was concerned about a representative body's assuming the sovereignty and becoming a place where conflicting pressure groups could fight a war in which the victor would be unlikely to be the general welfare and the general will. These are the conditions that cause a society to degenerate, he says: "When private interests raise their heads and small groups influence the great society, the common interest is altered and encounters opposition; unanimity no longer reigns in the vote, the general will is no longer the will of all, contradictions and debates arise, and the best opinion is not accepted without dispute." (IV, 1.) And again: "The more opinions approach unanimity, the more the general will is dominant; but long debates, dissension, tumult, signal the ascendancy of private interests and the decline of the State." (IV, 2.) [91]

Everything points to a monistic or closed society. The general will, by definition, cannot oppress anybody, and a tyranny of the general will is a contradiction in terms. One cannot quarrel with oneself, as one may with one's representatives. In a liberal society, on the other hand, minority rights are carefully recognized and protected because it is never supposed that any will is always or axiomatically right.[92] Consensus, not a unanimous will, is the objective. The vote is, therefore, the expression of wills, the forging of a will that is not pre-existent. Individuals and minorities are deemed to require protection against the State, the government, and the majority. It is held that through disagreement and conflict change is fostered, and that the possibility of change is the condition of a relative stability. But in Rousseau's State, his ideal of absolute order and stability rests on antithetical assumptions, for the continuing disagreement and conflict of pluralism seemed to him an intolerable disharmony. In the open society one is not a "member" of the State in Rousseau's sense:

> If the State or the City is only a moral person whose life consists in the union of its members, and if the most vital of its functions is self-preservation, it must have a universal and compulsive force to move and control each part in the way most suitable to the Whole. As nature gives each man absolute power over his limbs [in French, "members"], the social compact gives the political body absolute power over all its members, and this power, directed by the general will, bears, as I have said, the name of sovereignty. (II, 4.)

What Rousseau has created is a *Volksgemeinschaft*, from which there is no appeal to any higher instance. To oppose it is to be a dangerous egotist and to exclude oneself from the community of the people.[93]

I have asserted that in Rousseau's scheme an individual's continued opposition to the general will makes him a criminal, or an enemy of the people. This idea, which is implicit in his theorizing, seems to become explicit when he generalizes from the right to put murderers to death.

> Besides, any evildoer who attacks the social law becomes by his crimes a rebel and a traitor to the fatherland, and even wages war on it. Then the self-preservation of the State becomes incompatible with his; one of the two must perish, and when the guilty person is put to death, it is less as a citizen than as an enemy. The trial and judgment are the proofs that he has broken the social compact, and consequently, *he is no longer a member of the State.* (II, 5.)

The consequences of the unlimited sovereignty of the general will are portentous. Living according to one's own conscience (at least in matters of public concern) is atomism; the moral will of the "collective self," free from false judgment and egoistic natural will, is what the individual conscience should be. "Right" is conventionalized will: "the general will being in the State the rule of right and wrong. . . ." [94] In "Political Economy" theft is declared to be just when ordained by law—for the general will is *ipso facto* just. In view of this attitude and of the possibility of legislating for groups of citizens, it is not difficult to see how a minority—a whole group of people—might be excluded (or even destroyed—though such an idea would have been repugnant to Rousseau). It is often claimed that Rousseau does propose a safeguard for individuals and minorities in stating that every law must apply to all citizens equally. But, again, we have seen that he does not really mean this after all. The sovereign power, he has also declared, has no limit—other than the general welfare. And, "There is no right to put anyone to death, even for the sake of an example, except him who cannot be kept without danger." (II, 5.) But, as P. Grosclaude has asked, "Where does danger to the social body begin?" [95] Far from being a safeguard, such a doctrine opens the doors to arbitrary acts.

The general will has the power, then, to determine who belongs to the State and who is excluded from it. Another instance of this principle will occur in the matter of the civil religion. In the *Project of a Constitution for Corsica* exclusion from the community is specifically involved as a punishment for those who refuse to marry, and in the same work its use among the Romans is applauded. It would be possible, then, for a group to be declared enemies of the State and excluded from the protection of law. If the law, Rousseau has said, cannot ever be unjust, "it is not because it is based on justice, which might not always be true, but because it is against nature to want to hurt oneself." Yet, despite such reasonings we know that "a wrong cannot *become* a right because the majority wills it—perhaps it becomes a greater wrong." [96]

Still another safeguard for the individual is offered by Rousseau. After saying that the State has a universal and compulsive force over all its members, an absolute and therefore an unlimited power, he goes on to propose a limit. We must distinguish, he declares, the rights of citizens, as men, from the rights of the Sovereign over them as citizens. What the basis of such "rights" is after the total alienation of the social contract is not clear, and we are given only a weak, general statement. ". . . all that is alienated, by the social compact, of [the citizen's] power and his freedom, is only the part of all that whose use is of importance to the community; but it must also be agreed that the Sovereign is sole judge of that import." (II, 4.) This statement, or the first part of it, contradicts the preceding statement which opens the chapter. Moreover, the concluding part of the "safeguard" again opens all the doors. If the State *can* do anything it decides is useful, there is really no protection at all. After all, there is no fundamental law that is not revocable by a single vote of the citizenry. Rousseau's own proposed constitution for Corsica will make a mockery out of the "safeguard." What, in his mind, is not "of importance to the community"? [97]

Both totalitarianism and democracy imply a concept of man. In the totalitarian view (as in Rousseau's in the second *Discourse*), man is not defined by thought or reason; it is assumed that most men are determined not by those faculties, but by instincts and passion. This, too, Rousseau has said many times, from the "Epître à M. Parisot," where he spoke of "the imbecilic people" to *La Nouvelle Héloïse,* where he had written, "I soon realized that it was impossible to make the multitude listen to reason." Men, unless they are remade and under continuous control, cannot be trusted to distinguish between good and evil, or not to prefer the personally useful to the socially harmful. Judgment and decision therefore belong to an elite of leaders. The people, unable to think or will correctly, are called on to obey and to believe. Because Rousseau has no confidence either in their reason or in their impulses, his whole thinking points to a system of hidden control by a few Wolmarian leaders under the guise of self-government and liberty.[98] Docility remains the necessary condition of what he calls liberty. Though more masked than overt in the *Social Contract,* the idea is constantly implied and appears overtly from time to time. It is necessary, we are told, to "catch" a nation before customs and prejudices are established. "Most peoples, like men, are docile only in their youth." (II, 8.) And again, the kind of people that can be legislated for is, "in a word, one that joins the consistency of an old people with the docility of a new one." (II, 10.) Rousseau had explained the need for the Legislator to make laws seem divine in these words: "so that the peoples, submitted to the laws of the State as to those of nature, and recognizing the same power in the formation of physical bodies and the moral body [the same idea we have noted in *Emile*], will obey with freedom and bear with docility the yoke of public happiness." (II, 7.)

Equality before the law (even granting the point), together with nominal popular sovereignty, does not constitute liberty in a controlled, collectivist State. On the contrary, human nature being what it is, equality, conceived of as independence from oppressive groups of individuals achieved through equal dependence of all on the collectivity, is incompatible with liberty as we understand that word. Of this Rousseau was fully aware. Equality means that "no one has the right to require another to do what he does not do himself . . . so that each citizen may be completely independent [*"dans une parfaite indépendance"*] of all the others, and completely dependent [*"dans une excessive dépendance"*] on the City. . . . It is only the force of the State that can make the liberty of its members." (II, 12.) [99] Later, speaking of liberty and equality as the ends of legislation, he implicitly tells us his concept of the former word when he writes, "Any dependence on individuals is that much power taken from the body of the State."

Nor should "equality" be interpreted as implying a classless, economically levelled society.

> That word should not be taken to mean that the degrees of power and wealth are absolutely the same, but rather that power is below the level of constraint and is exercised only by virtue of rank and the laws; and as for wealth, that no citizen is opulent enough to buy another, and none so poor that he is obliged to sell himself. (II, 11.)

This, too, is the object of legislation. Furthermore, equality is not really conceived of as individual right, but rather as an essential of the social contract or a *sine qua non* of *community*.[100]

At this point some additional observations on the idea of the general will, which has tormented Rousseau's explicators more than any other of his notions, may be useful. They have sought in vain some clear, decisive definition. It is not surprising that they have not found it, or that Rousseau himself was never able to, either. As his friend Count d'Escherny later reported, Rousseau wrote to Mirabeau that the problem of finding the general will resembled that of squaring the circle; as to what it is, d'Escherny adds: "As a theoretical principle it presents only a vicious circle and contradictions; as a practical principle, it means only a tendency toward well-being." This statement comes close to the heart of the problem. Rousseau's general will exists on two levels, and he could not find a way of going from one to the other. It is first of all a metaphysical entity, existing independently of any actual wills; but it must also be realized existentially in actual wills. The voting process, including "informing" and the majority that remains after cancellation of contrary views, is the method of actualization he proposes (except on rare occasions when the leaders make the decision by themselves). But there is no guarantee that even this process will be free from corruption and error. However, "Does it then follow that the general will is annihilated or corrupted? No, it is always constant, unalterable and pure." That is why it exists prior to the vote and can be known in advance to the wise Legislator who guides and "informs" the people. It is precisely the fact that Rousseau (contrary to Locke) usually distinguishes between the general will and the majority will, that makes his concept an illiberal one. Being distinct from what is actually willed, being absolute and unique, it cannot brook dissidence. The problem then becomes one of making this abstract entity existential; which, in practice, can only mean bringing existential wills into agreement with it. The techniques for doing this are both psychological and institutional (the voting process).

This "split level" is a trap from which Rousseau cannot escape. "The majority will," comments Halbwachs, "is both a diminution and a change in the nature of the general will. But the latter cannot be actualized in any other way." [101] In other words, the vote is the attempt at a positivistic determination of something that has no similar (phenomenological) existence. On the other hand, the abstract level enables Rousseau to justify both the guide and the subjection of dissidents. When a law is proposed, the people are not called on

> . . . to approve or to reject the proposition, but to say whether or not it conforms to the general will which is theirs. . . . When, therefore, the opinion contrary to mine wins, it only proves that I was wrong, and that what I thought to be the general will was not. If my own view had won, I should have done something else than what I wanted, and it is then that I would not have been free. (IV, 2.)

Rousseau is compelled to suppose—though he tries to cover this —that the majority vote confirms or discovers the general will, for in his theory to obey the general will is to obey oneself (even though it be an ideal self which is both subject and Sovereign) and not the will of others, whether they be minority or majority.

Were this not so, Diderot's nihilist in "Natural Right" would have the right to revolt. In the words of one critique, Rousseau "was asking, what form of society will do away with the right to revolt by restraining men with perfect justice?" [102] Obviously he would not be able to argue that to obey the majority (*qua* majority) is also to obey oneself if one is not part of the majority. Rousseau does say that the original contract provides for obedience to majority rule, and in a special and extended sense this could be taken to prove the contrary. There is another bit of jugglery in this. The contract does not establish an identity between the general will and the majority will. Cobban is apparently aware of the difficulty, because he comments that majority rule is identical with the general will only when it satisfies the conditions of the general will. But who is to determine whether or not it does? It can only be either (1) the majority itself, which sets up a vicious circle, or (2) the "guides" or Legislators who prepare laws, inform the people, and direct the elections.

When Rousseau, whose statements about the general will are often apparently contradictory, declares that it is present in all citizens, he obviously does not mean that it is the actual will of those whom he has described as stupid or selfish. Only in a metaphysical sense is it present in them, as the will of the "collective self," not of the "human self." Only in this light can we understand why Rousseau says that virtue is the conformity of our personal will with the general will; and why he also declares that the personal will is always opposed to the general interest (or that the interests we have in common are far fewer than those that oppose us to each other). In this way he sets up a level of "authentic interests" or "true will."

This dichotomy makes it possible to say that one who follows his private will is guilty toward himself. The collective self is the only self to be considered in matters of public importance, so that a person's true will is what some think he ought to will. A person's will may be not what it is, but rather what it ought to be. The question of freedom remains, even if we accept this definition. Who determines the "ought"? In all totalitarian systems there is only one central source of the "true" and the "ought"—an all-inclusive system, allowing no alternatives. It also follows that the citizens must be "conditioned" to vote and to think in the way Rousseau describes; for to do so is not "natural." Men become capable of this function, comments Vaughan, "only when they have lost their personal identity in the corporate unity of the State." [103]

This set of concepts is in opposition to what in the eighteenth century would have been called the laws of nature and also to the traditional Natural Law. Rousseau has little use for the latter, although he occasionally makes a nod in its direction. As for nature, it is separated from culture and relegated to the state of nature. The general will is not a natural phenomenon. A moral order of the State is opposed to the natural order of the species or the universe. The civil order, Rousseau tells us at the beginning of *Emile,* must put an end to the primacy of natural feelings. How different from the effort of Rousseau's contemporaries to unite the moral and natural orders in the ethics of enlightened self-interest! Rousseau derided their idealism, because he was so sure that men are not virtuous or wise enough to choose the general good without coercion (preferably concealed). He also made the law an expression of human (collective) will rather than, as it was for Montesquieu, a relationship deriving from "the nature of things." The collective State is not natural, and it is a superior moral person.

Rousseau's views were strange to his former friends, who had little sense of the collective as such and never thought of the general will in the way he did. Yet in a sense its moral character is, in his mind, founded on a purely natural principle: no person, single or collective, can want to hurt himself. That is why the general will is essentially *will.* Had he not shown in his devastating critique of Diderot's "Natural Right" how useless are purely rational solutions? The general will seeks the useful without necessary reference to prior moral value, and it establishes moral value. It is, remarks Burgelin, an "egocentric and self-preservative force." [104] It makes no claim to other than national applicability or validity. Rousseau's contemporary critic Pierre Naville warned: "This is to open the door to injustices, as soon as they are useful to the State, a very dangerous principle." [105]

Neither nature nor rationality, Rousseau thought, will ever create or permit the identity of self-interest and the general interest. In another sense, to be sure, the general will depends on the rationality and love of virtue of each individual, reasoning in the silence of the passions. [106] But this the individual will not do in the purely natural course of events. Thought, for Rousseau, is not a value in itself, but a weapon to transform "that which is" into "that which ought to be." Myth and illusion are preferable to knowledge, and rhetoric (a lost art, he says, referring to what we would call demagoguery) is better than demonstration in leading peoples.

Rousseau's general will, according to Paul Léon, is opposed both to the arbitrary will of isolated, unsocial individuals, and to the juridical will of a society based on force. [107] For these he substitutes the juridical monism of the nation-State. Rousseau believes it will be effective because it absorbs all partial wills and sublimates them into a new, unanimous will, changing the individual's independence into complete dependency—like that of a limb of a body—and transforming his natural self into a social self with a different will, so that it can truly be said that he is forced to be free and that what he wants as a concrete (or individual) self is not what he wants as an abstract (or social) self. Both "selves" are, of course, in all men, but Rousseau's point is that they cannot coexist without warring with each other, and to this inner division an end must be put, by absorption of the ego into the social unit. [108] In this fashion the Legislator will accomplish his end of a harmonious, co-operative society by replacing the inexorable necessities of nature with the equally impersonal force of laws conceived in the spirit of an ideal general will. [109]

The character of Rousseau's general will stands out clearly in a comparison with Diderot's general will (in "Natural Right"). Both men intended that their general wills should will the right. But for Diderot the right is rationally available in a way that is independent of the fact of will. Rousseau tells us that whatever the general will wills is *ipso facto* right, by virtue of its generality (i.e., its divorce from individual self-interest, or its expression of the *general* interest) and because no body can want to hurt itself. There seems, then, to be no check on this will, either by individual consciences (each of which is submitted by the contract to the "superior moral person"), or by the decent opinions of mankind (there being no general society of mankind). There is an implicit assumption of the identity of will and right, based on a definition of right as the good which one wills to oneself. In other words, Rousseau replaces the natural order of laws, for which other *philosophes* were looking, with voluntarism. We were correct in affirming that ethics is absorbed into politics. There is no effective right in a Platonic sense, or in the Humean sense of the impartial, disinterested observer.[110] Further comparison reveals that Diderot's theory does not imply a total commitment to, or participation in, whatever is proclaimed by the body politic as the general will. The individual conscience remains inviolate and uncoerced, even though conformity to law is maintained. Rousseau's theory of the general will, on the other hand, like most of his doctrines, is ultimately directed toward his main purpose of "capturing wills." His general will is not a harmony of particular wills, but their transmutation. In the first version of the *Social Contract* (I, 7) he had written that we must "subject men to make them free";[111] and that we must "chain their wills of their own desire." With opposition between the individual and communal wills thus eliminated, harmony, unanimity, and community may be attained.

Rousseau, of course, did not conceive of the general will as a form of oppression, but as one of liberation or liberty. Yet, one would think he had some notion of this potentiality, for he occasionally stipulates limits to the general will: the concept of public utility, its expression in law which must be ratified by the people, and the prescription that the Sovereign must return to individuals the "rights" which it does not need for the general welfare (a need which the Sovereign itself defines). We know from Rousseau's own writings how ineffective and meaningless these vague protections are. The unchecked public power gradually absorbs everything. In his framework of remaking men into social beings who have no existence except in and for the community (as he says), there is no alternative.[112]

Many critics have held that there is no relation between the general will and the social contract. This view, in my opinion, is incorrect. In Rousseau's mind the contract establishes the authentic civil community by an act of association and surrender. Thus is created the "public person" or "collective self" whose will (the general will) exists as soon as it comes into being, and cannot exist before. From this will, justice and obligation ensue. That is why there can be no right to oppose that which, by definition, *is* right. Rousseau completely disallows the possibility that a situation of "right" can ever grow out of a historically established situation, one of "might." In Burke's words, he is always " 'at war with governments not on a question of abuse, but a question of competency and a question of title.' " [113]

The theory of the general will added a mystical element to political thought. A corporate body, as such, cannot express its will or execute it. Thus the general will created, speculatively, a power vacuum that would enable a leader, or guide, to proclaim, "It is I who know it, speak it, am it." The more the community is exalted, writes Sabine, "the more authority its spokesmen have, whether they are called representatives or not."[114] Whether or not Rousseau was conscious of this direction—and I believe he was—these factors were capitalized on by Robespierre and by many tyrants after him.

ˋThe third book of the *Social Contract* analyzes the forms and character of the various kinds of government. Aside from passages we have already borrowed from this section, there is little of prime interest, as the analysis proceeds along classical lines (but with Rousseau's general views always in mind). The chief novelty is his insistence that the establishment of any government lies outside the contractual relationship. The officers of government are servants of the citizenry, who alone have sovereignty, and who may replace the magistrates any time they choose to do so. (This idea was embodied in the Constitution of 1791, which declared the king to be a servant of the people.) He prefers, moreover, that the magistrates be chosen by lot, and not by elections.

In the fourth book Rousseau returns to his main preoccupation, the socialization of self-centered, atomistic individuals. All the forces of the State must be massed and brought to bear on each individual, to "re-form" him. Two of these mechanisms are not described in the *Social Contract*, but we have observed them in the other writings: "education," as we have described it, without which laws are ineffectual; and the institution of communal activities, popular festivals, or manifestations which create patriotism, pride of citizenship, emotional involvement, and a feeling of belonging to one unanimous body. There is little doubt that the vote, too, is a kind of solemn *fête*, fostering the feeling of a unanimous act. All systems of this kind demand universal participation and the whipping up of zeal (Rousseau's word) because of the threat of apathy as a corrosive factor.

Two other mechanisms are carefully described in the *Social Contract*. One is censorship, which is Rousseau's word for thought control and surveillance of behavior—morals, speech, and actions—even as it was in Geneva. "Just as the general will is declared by the law, so the public judgment is declared by censorship; public opinion is the kind of law of which the Censor is the minister." (IV, 7.) Rousseau has said that "opinion" includes preferences, desires, ways of striving for happiness —in a word, the motives of behavior. He has also said, we remember, that it is "opinion" which the Legislator (or guide) must above all control, and control secretively. The same deception, the same illusion of freedom, obtain here as with the vote and the general will. We see it in a statement such as this: "Far from the censorial tribunal being the arbiter of the people's opinions, it only expresses them, and as soon as it departs from them, its decisions are null and void." But how do the censors discover the people's opinion? How are their erroneous decisions made null and void? There is no word on these crucial matters.

Is there any doubt that once again the guides, or moral guardians, will speak in the name of the people? And once they have spoken, no dissent is tolerable; their judgments are not subject to revision. This is "legitimate," we may suppose, because, as with the imperium of the general will, it has been consented to in advance. Rousseau had said that rights are created by the Sovereign. But it is clear that there is no right to escape or to oppose the censorship or the dictates of the general will. Again we see how idle it is to talk of a "residue of rights." The extent of what Rousseau means by "opinion" and the importance he attaches to its control are brought out in the following lines:

> It is useless to distinguish the morals of a nation from what it esteems. . . . Among all the peoples of the world, it is not nature but opinion that determines the choice of their pleasures. Reform the opinions of men and their mores will purify themselves. They always love what is fine and what is esteemed as such, but it is in their judgment that they err: it is therefore that judgment which is to be controlled ("*réglé*"). . . . Censorship maintains morals by preventing the corruption of opinions, by conserving the rectitude of opinions by wise applications, sometimes even by forming them when they are still uncertain. (IV, 7.)

It is not unjust to Rousseau's views and attitude to infer that from this would flow the State control of the publication and the dissemination of books, the regimentation of art and the theater (already urged in the *Letter to d'Alembert*) and eventually, could he have conceived of their existence, of the media of mass communication. There can be little doubt that "private" or personal deviations from the ideals and the theory of his State—not to mention outright opposition—would not be tolerated. From what he has said here and elsewhere and from what we are about to read concerning the civil religion, it follows that everyone is open to surveillance at all times, and there are no secrets from the government. When privacy is gone, when everyone fears that his thought and words may be used against him, liberty, too, is gone. It matters little. Nothing must be allowed to rupture the unity of the collectivity or to impede the State in its work of socializing refractory individuals. Opposition and dissent must be wholly destroyed. ("I speak of mores, of customs, and above all of opinion, a sphere that is unknown to our statesmen, but on which success of all the others depends.") Rousseau, like Helvétius (and unlike Montesquieu or Aristotle), specifically declares that morals and politics are inseparable. In his mind and work, as I have noted, both become politics, and every phenomenon has a political significance. Nothing is neutral or indifferent. Virtue, the identification of private and public interest, becomes a national concern. All forces must be harnessed by the State for the accomplishment of its task. In the organic society of the *moi commun*, the luxury of having an individual ego and an individual "opinion" (in Rousseau's broad sense of the word) is intolerable. The ultimate significance of the individual as the bearer of values is annihilated.

Another of the forces that must be made part of the total effort is religion. It, too, is one of the mechanisms of the State, and Rousseau has already explained why the Legislator needs its help. But Rousseau is not referring to the institutional Christian religion; here, as in the *Profession de foi du vicaire savoyard* (*Profession of Faith of a Savoyard Vicar*), he considers Christianity a force of dissension and resistance to social control. A religion that adds not its force to that of laws is harmful. "Whatever ruptures the social unit is worthless. All institutions that put man in contradiction with himself are worthless." (IV, 8.) The religion of the Gospels and national religions are also dangerous. The former detaches men from the State and weakens the "social spirit" (a criticism taken from Machiavelli's *Discourses*). It is typical of the authoritarian mind to despise Christianity for Rousseau's reasons: "Christianity, in addition, preaches only servitude and dependence. . . . True Christians are made to be slaves." National religions have the great merit of "making the fatherland the object of worship" and of teaching the citizens that "to serve the State is to serve its tutelary God." Rousseau does wish to have the religious feeling transferred in great measure to the State, because he knows its depth and power; but national religions are false and tyrannical. His solution, then, is "civil religion." [115] This is "a purely civil profession of faith whose articles it is the Sovereign's task to determine, not exactly as religious dogma, but as feelings of sociability without which it is impossible to be a good citizen or a faithful subject." Among these dogmas (he does use that word, after all) are belief in a providential and all-powerful God, immortality, the reward of the good and the punishment of the wicked (in the *Profession of Faith* he accepted the former but not the latter), the sanctity of the social contract and of the laws, and the abjuring of religious intolerance. Rousseau, despite his dislike for other religions, demands their toleration, except when they violate the civil religion, or except when they are, like the Roman Catholic Church, exclusive and intolerant; to do otherwise would promote the dissensions and disharmonies he is most eager to suppress. It is not a question of truth, in any of this; it is a question of political expediency. What matters to him is not the truth of religion, but its persuasive and disciplinary power.

The citizen can no more escape this religion than he can the censorship. In *Emile* Rousseau had said that anyone who disputes the dogma of the civil religion must be punished, for "he is the disturber of order and the enemy of society." In the *Social Contract* he is more specific. Anyone who does not believe and profess his belief, whether skeptic or atheist, is to be banished from the State, not for impiety, but for being unsociable. If he violates his allegiance, he is to die—for treason to the State, obviously, rather than to religion.

But how does one determine violation? A passage in the "Lettre à M. de Beaumont" (1762), concerning the civil religion, is particularly illuminating.

> Why does a man have the right of inspection over another's beliefs? And why does the State have the right of inspection over those of its citizens? It is because we suppose that men's beliefs determine their morals. . . . In society, each of us has the right to inform himself whether another person believes himself to be obliged to be just, and the sovereign has the right to examine the reasons on which each person bases that obligation.[116]

Could it be plainer that for Rousseau thought control involves constant spying and surveillance, with the inseparable implication of denunciation? Denunciation, which Rousseau had defended and used in the *Letter to d'Alembert* and *La Nouvelle Héloïse* is, as we have come to know, a strangulating, terror-inspiring system to which it is difficult to set a limit.

But even worse is to come. "If anyone," he continues in this chapter of the *Social Contract*, "after having publicly accepted these dogmas, acts *as if* he did not believe them, let him be punished by death." In other words, the State has a right to conclude from a person's action—or, implicitly, from his non-action—what his *real* beliefs or opinions are, to accuse him of perjury, and to put him to death. What is this, if not the doctrine of arrest on suspicion of wrong thinking? We need take only one further step to punish people for lack of enthusiasm. The effect of such a state of affairs on people's conduct can easily be imagined from similar situations in later history.

If Rousseau shifts here from the inspection of consciences to that of conduct, we may assume that it was because he realizes the former to be difficult or impossible. What he writes about censorship and the capturing of wills must be considered conclusive in this regard.

Although Rousseau insists that tolerance extend beyond the limits of the civil religion, Robert Derathé has convincingly shown that the civil religion cannot but lead to intolerance:

> The liberal State which prescribes what may be the most unpleasant obligations denies itself the right of penetrating within consciences and is not concerned with beliefs or opinions. Now, according to Rousseau, the State has the right and the duty to penetrate consciences, to proceed to an *inspection* which, as I see it, bears a frightening resemblance to an inquisition.[117]

At what age, asks Derathé, is the citizen to take his oath? And what happens if his beliefs change? According to M. Dehaussy, who comments on Derathé's article, it is not only this thought control that is totalitarian; the implied utilitarianism—which makes of religion, as of education, only a means to "manufacture good citizens"—is totalitarian, too.[118] H. J. Tozer had reached a similar conclusion many years before:

There is something almost ludicrous in this solemn renunciation of intolerance after Rousseau's declaration that a citizen may be put to death for a constructive act of disbelief in a set of speculative dogmas. It matters little whether a man be treated as a rebel or an apostate [as unsociable or impious], and whether the judge be a civil magistrate or an inquisitor; the intolerance is equal in either case. . . . Thus once again we find that the doctrines of Rousseau are fatal to individual liberty. The State would become a persecutor.[119]

C. E. Vaughan was particularly critical of this aspect of Rousseau's system. Rousseau, he charges, opens the door to persecution by imposing a religious test on all members of the State. He should have known that tests are "a premium on hypocrisy. . . . It is obvious that the man who has no sense of duty will not scruple to commit perjury." Such a test "may admit those who are morally worthless, and exclude those who are morally beyond reproach." Rousseau imposes penalties not for acts, concludes Vaughan, but for opinions. On no theory of justice can beliefs be a proper matter for punishment.[120] However, as we have just seen, Rousseau's demand that we infer beliefs from behavior holds even more dangerous potentialities than Derathé or Vaughan have pointed out.

One purpose of the civil religion, as well as of the public demonstrations and *fêtes* Rousseau recommends, is to make the citizen love his duties and to make the "engagement," or the renunciation expressed in the contract, a sacred act. The duties of the man and the citizen must be joined. "The divine and human laws being always united in the same subject," wrote Rousseau in the first version, "the most pious theists will be the most zealous citizens, and the defense of the sacred laws will be the glory of the God of men." (IV, 8.) Religious and political authority, religion and civism, must, as in Geneva, be united. There cannot be two allegiances. Not only must institutions not put man in contradiction with himself; they must work together to the same end of unanimity. According to Talmon, there is no essential contradiction between the subjective religion of the *Profession of Faith* and the civil religion; they supplement each other. The State or society exists under the providence of God and embodies right and justice. The "religious sense of awe and patriotic piety not only need not clash, but are likely to become fused into the Robespierre type of mysticism. There are no priests other than the magistrates; religious and patriotic ceremonial are the same; and to serve your country is to serve God." [121] As Jean Starobinski has astutely commented, Rousseau both secularizes Christ and sacralizes the Legislator. But his doctrine, according to Starobinski, is fundamentally secular, since he channels the psychic energies of religion into the political domain; politics does not depend on religion, and the accent is on men's will.[122]

The liberal view in the eighteenth century was expressed by Voltaire, among many others. Men, he said,

> . . . do not realize that every kind of religion must be separated from every kind of government; that religion should be no more a matter of State than ways of cooking; . . . and that as long as laws are obeyed, the stomach and the conscience should be completely free. That will come some day, but I shall die with the sorrow of not having seen that happy time.[123]

The more militant *philosophes,* like d'Holbach, demanded that every cult contrary to reason be banished—a no less tyrannical solution.[124] Rousseau's civic religion is not a matter of reason, but is based rather on the assumption that man is not sufficiently reasonable.

On this note the *Social Contract* ends. From the foregoing pages we can judge the fallaciousness of the charge that Rousseau's whole system is an inverted Hobbism, with the many-headed multitude supplanting the despotic monarch. This is only the appearance. In the organic society of the *moi commun* there is no dictatorship of the proletariat, or even of the citizenry. In fact, the individual and the mass are controlled, by a small, élite leadership, in one way or another, in the very depths of their being. Rousseau demands that this be done; and he applies theory to practice. To deny it is to contradict Rousseau himself, in order to make him into a more pleasing image.

Notes

¹ "The essence of Rousseau's republic can be better understood if one starts from its *function,* its *purpose,* rather than from its formal structure as depicted in the *Contrat social." (*I. Fetscher, "Rousseau's Concepts of Freedom," p. 44.) Professor L. Thielemann writes, in an unpublished note, "The abstract political principles of the *Contrat social* can be evaluated only in the context of the educational and legal institutions they imply. This approach constitutes a useful corrective to the abstract apologies which are so often made for Rousseau's political principles on the assumption that Rousseau's rhetoric of resounding words always has the accepted semantic values."

² One of the latest examples is in M. A. Cattaneo's *Le Dottrine politiche di Montesquieu e di Rousseau* (Milan, 1964). The alienation of rights stipulated by the contract, according to Cattaneo, is really fictitious. Why? Because the contractants receive a new liberty in return. To this reasoning I make the following objections: (1) it assumes what is to be proved; (2) the "old" liberty is still given up—in other words, a return in a different coin does not annul the payment; (3) the "new" liberty depends on the alienation's being real and *not* fictitious—that is, the alienation is the very condition for its coming into being; (4) Rousseau would have no reason to insist on it so strongly as he does throughout the *Social Contract,* if it were fictitious.

³ Miss Ann Callahan, in her unpublished thesis on the Legislator, points out the impact of the idea of popular sovereignty in an age of divine right. According to Miss Callahan, to most it seemed to incarnate the democratic idea and resistance to tyranny. Rousseau, however, looked far beyond this.

⁴ Rousseau owed a debt, to be sure, to Helvétius, who develops, but only in a general way, the idea of controlling men by conditioning. Jacques Ehrard has pointed out that before Helvétius, La Mettrie expressed the idea that a philosopher prince should teach men "the art of making men docile and of putting a brake on them, when they cannot be led by the natural lights of reason." (*Discours préliminaire,* in *Oeuvres* [Berlin, 1796], I, 38.) We note the word "docile." This education, continues Ehrard, will be "scarcely respectful of each individual's personality," and will aim at "creating mental automatisms," according to "a science of psychological conditioning." No longer is it a matter of demonstrating that virtue has utility (as with other *philosophes*), only of habituating men to think that it has. (*L'Idée de nature en France pendant la première moitié du XVIII° siècle* [Paris, 1963], I, 393–94.) The possi-

bility of an influence of La Mettrie on Rousseau is not to be excluded. Neither Helvétius nor La Mettrie developed his ideas into programs.
[5] "Men become wicked and unhappy when they become social beings." (Fragment 12.) Again, in *Emile* Rousseau says that in society men are irremediably evil and devour each other. (pp. 99, 579.)
[6] "It will always be great and difficult to submit the dearest natural feelings to country and to virtue." (*Ibid.*)
[7] P. Burgelin, *La Philosophie,* p. 344. "Love of order," Rousseau wrote to M. de Beaumont, "is the good which is proper to the soul." (*Oeuvres,* Hachette edition, III, 64.) I. Fetscher concludes that the function of the conscience is to lead each individual to "integrate himself into the order of the whole instead of placing himself at the center of his world." ("Rousseau's Concepts of Freedom," p. 43.) But for Rousseau this is quite abstract and theoretical, and having no confidence in the unreconstructed individual, he gives the job to the State.
[8] S. Cotta, "La Position du problème de la politique chez Rousseau," in *Etudes sur le "Contrat social" de Jean-Jacques Rousseau* (Paris, 1964), pp. 183–90. (*Etudes sur le "Contrat social" de Jean-Jacques Rousseau* will hereinafter be referred to as "*Etudes sur le 'Contrat social.'* ")
[9] *Ibid.,* p. 188.
[10] R. Mauzi has remarked that virtue, order, and will, imposed as a law from outside the conscience, are the principle of all tyrannies. (*L' Idée du bonheur au XVIIIᵉ siècle* [Paris, 1960], p. 634.) Rousseau, of course, prefers to mold consciences so that the individual may, by virtue of his docility, feel free.
[11] Rousseau was also influenced by Plato, Aristotle, Hobbes, Spinoza, the Natural Law theorists, and others; but this essay is not concerned with his sources.
[12] *La Nouvelle Héloïse,* Part VI, Letter V, p. 644.
[13] I am indebted to Miss Ann Callahan for this formulation. M. Bourguin once summarized Rousseau's political theory in these words: "What we have here is the ancient ideal of the all-powerful State, absolute master of persons and property, supreme regulator not only of external conduct, but also of domestic relations and of individual conscience." ("Les Deux tendances de Rousseau," *Revue de métaphysique et de morale,* XX [1962], 366.)
[14] *History of the Peloponnesian War,* trans. R. Crawley (New York, 1950), p. 123.
[15] ". . . the same pride, the same mores, the same maxims, above all, the same enthusiasm for the fatherland. . . . Both established many spectacles, assemblies and ceremonies, many colleges and private societies to arouse and foment among the citizens those sweet habits and that innocent and disinterested intercourse which form and nourish love of country." (Fragment, *Oeuvres,* Pléiade edition, III, 538–43.)

[16] Rousseau will become more and more convinced that in society individual freedom or independence is really slavery. "The more I examine the work of men in their institutions, the more I see that by dint of wanting to be independent, they make slaves of themselves, and that they wear out their very freedom in vain efforts to insure it. . . . It is you, oh my master, who have made me free by teaching me to yield to necessity." (*Émile*, p. 603.) We must remember that in Rousseau's societies, the moral law is to acquire the quality of necessity characteristic of physical laws—this being the work of the conditioning processes.

[17] As we have already seen, Rousseau thinks of the State as a superior moral person. The idea of person includes will, judgment, and even happiness. He separates public from private happiness, and implicitly gives precedence to the former. The weakness of individual happiness is its complete subjectivity, the impossibility of establishing fixed rules and verifiable criteria for its existence. "But that is not the case with political societies; their welfare and their ills are all open and visible; their internal feeling is a public feeling. The common people may be taken in, of course; but what does not fool them? For any knowing eye, they are what they seem to be, and one can judge their moral being without rashness." (Fragment, in *Political Writings*, I, 325–26.)

[18] The *Social Contract* (I, 2), in *Political Writings*, I, 452. Hereinafter references to the *Social Contract* will be made in parentheses, by book and chapter, following the quotation in the text.

[19] (Italics added.) This is Rousseau's ideal goal.

[20] It is then only, Rousseau adds in Chapter 8, when "the voice of duty replaces physical impulse and right replaces appetite, that man, who until then had considered himself only, is forced to act on different principles, and to consult his reason before listening to his inclinations."

[21] For a fuller discussion of the implications of Rousseau's view on justice and law, and of Diderot's contrary (liberal) view, see the Index to L. G. Crocker, *Nature and Culture. Ethical Thought in the French Enlightenment* (Baltimore, 1963).

[22] C. E. Vaughan, ed., *Political Writings*, I, 441.

[23] Fragment relating to the *Social Contract*, in *Political Writings*, I, 322.

[24] A. Schinz, *Etat présent des travaux sur Jean-Jacques Rousseau* (New York, 1941), p. 398.

[25] In "Political Economy" and in the fifth chapter of the first version of the *Social Contract* Rousseau had insisted more emphatically on a number of differences between these two kinds of "societies."

[26] One source of Rousseau's ideas may have been Spinoza, in the *Tractatus theologico-politicus;* see also *Ethic*, Book IV, 37, Schol. 2.

[27] Compare Wollaston: "A man may part with some of his natural rights, and put himself under the government of laws . . . in order to

gain the protection of them. . . ." (*The Religion of Nature Delineated*
[London, 1726], p. 150.) It is true that Locke occasionally spoke of a
complete surrender, and is not consistent. Rousseau may have found a
suggestion in Aristotle: "It is indeed quite false to imagine that any
citizen belongs to himself. The Spartans deserve our admiration." (*Aristotle's Politics and the Athenian Constitution*, ed. and transl. by J.
Warrington [London, 1959], pp. 83, 221.)

[28] C. E. Vaughan, ed., *Political Writings*, I, 40–41; 48–49.

[29] *Ibid.*, 49.

[30] It is obvious that Rousseau's argument that one gains the same rights
over others that he yields over himself has nothing to do with liberty and
involves only equality.

[31] *Political Writings*, II, 219. (Italics added.) The importance of
"unity" in Rousseau's thinking—indeed, in his whole mentality and outlook—can scarcely be overemphasized. It runs throughout his political
writings. Even in the *Dialogues* (*Rousseau juge de Jean-Jacques*) we
come upon the statement that our laws are bad because they produce "multitudes of new and often opposing relationships, which pull in contrary
directions." (*Oeuvres*, Hachette edition, IX, 209–10.) The longing for
unity is related to one for simplicity.

[32] We have covered this basic idea in Rousseau's other writings. We
must recall what he wrote at the beginning of *Emile:* "He who wants to
keep the primacy of natural feelings in the civil order does not know what
he wants. Always in contradiction with himself, he will never be a man or
a citizen. . . . Good social institutions are those which best denature
man, deprive him of his absolute existence, and transport his self into the
community." (pp. 588–89.) In *Emile* Rousseau also included a summary
of the *Social Contract*.

[33] G. H. Sabine comments: "The general will, therefore, represented a
unique fact about a community, namely, that it has a collective good
which is not the same thing as the private interests of its members. In
some sense it lives its own life, fulfills its own destiny, and suffers its own
fate. In accordance with the analogy of an organism . . . it may be said to
have a will of its own. . . . (*A History of Political Theory*, rev. ed. [New
York, 1950], pp. 588–89.)

[34] Rousseau's theory had been summarily stated by E. de Vattel in *Le
Droit des gens* (Washington, D. C., 1916), I, 101.

[35] *Du Contrat social*, ed. M. Halbwachs (Paris, 1962), p. 97 (first
version). Also in *Lettres écrites de la Montagne* (Lettre VIII).

[36] In a nineteenth-century edition of the *Social Contract*, H. J. Tozer
pointed out that Rousseau kept Hobbes' conception of sovereignty as a
supreme coercive power, "although he strove to dissemble its despotism.
. . ." (H. J. Tozer, trans., *The Social Contract* [London, 1895], p. 63.)

[37] *Emile*, pp. 70–71. Implicit, here again, is Rousseau's concept of

freedom as docility in view of what is an impersonal necessity, and independence of other individual wills.

[38] There is "no fundamental law that cannot be revoked." (III, 8.)

[39] See J. I. McAdam, "Rousseau and the Friends of Despotism," *Ethics*, LXXIV (1963), 34ff.

[40] It is impossible because (according to T. H. Green) "all merely private interests are lost in it." The law cannot be unjust, because the whole people cannot be unjust to the whole people. "The practical result," Green continues, "is a vague exaltation of the prerogatives of the sovereign people, without any corresponding limitation of the conditions under which an act is to be deemed that of the sovereign people." The people's will, rather than the "true general will," constitutes justifiability. (T. H. Green, *Works* [London, 1893], II, 387–90.)

[41] A. Cobban, *In Search of Humanity* (New York, 1960), p. 97.

[42] For the idea of the State as a "moral person," and the subjection of the individual, see E. de Vattel, *Le droit des gens*, I, 85, 101.

[43] We cannot say, as Derathé seems to imply, that a law, just because it is a law (i.e., it expresses, in theory, the general will), promotes and protects liberty. (*Rousseau et la science politique de son temps* [Paris, 1950], p. 357.) According to Tozer, the assumption that no one wishes to injure himself leads Rousseau to the fallacious deduction that the general will is always just and equivalent to the common good (H. J. Tozer, trans., *The Social Contract*, p. 64). Rousseau's argument is perhaps the reverse: what is good for the social unit *is* the general will; that is why the wise leader knows it in advance of the vote and can be a guide.

[44] R. de Lacharrière, *Etudes sur la théorie démocratique: Spinoza, Rousseau, Hegel, Marx*, reviewed by R. Derathé, in *AJJR*, XXXVI (1963–65), 358.

[45] P. Léon, *L'idée de volonté générale chez J. J. Rousseau et ses antécédents historiques*, reviewed by B. Constant, *AJJR*, XXV (1936), 289.

[46] M. Davy, quoted in *Du Contrat social*, ed. M. Halbwachs, p. 112.

[47] According to Burgelin, the law "conciliates the liberty of each man, who bows only to reason," with the authority of the State, and enables him "to give up being a monad in order to be a moral being." (*La Philosophie*, p. 530.) This is an idealistic interpretation. Rousseau's theory of law is indeed abstract and idealistic. But he operates on two levels. On the realistic level of function and power (and he was, fundamentally, very much the realist), he knows that law is not pure reason, but also will; and that his citizens, in the mass incapable of pure reason, must be formed and led. Moreover, the reflexive type of reaction he emphatically prefers is not really *moral*; nor is the binding to the yoke of what they are made to believe is "necessity."

[48] B. Constant, *Principes de politique* (1815), quoted in *Du Contrat social*, ed. M. Halbwachs, p. 112. While Rousseau does at one point (I,

4) make a distinction between individuals as "private persons" and as "subjects," we recall that he gives the State complete power to set the limits of the private sphere, and that he practically annihilates it in his own writings. We have seen, and shall again observe in the *Social Contract*, that the citizen's private life is far from invulnerable. While some "private affairs" doubtless remain, the only limit in Rousseau's mind seems to be what can be realized in restricting them; indeed, he writes that the fewer they are, the better the State. (III, 15.)

[49] See J. I. McAdam, "Rousseau and the Friends of Despotism." Nor is restitution after alienation, as Derathé thinks, the same as reservation of rights and a partial alienation. I fail to see a basis for his further assertion that the real purpose of the alienation is not the formation of a collective whole, "but to assure individuals the exercise of their essential rights." (*Rousseau et la science politique de son temps*; p. 344n.) We have already explained what Rousseau means when he says there is no real renunciation. As Tozer puts it, there can be no genuine conception of the rights of individuals, while the power of universal compulsion "is regarded as the characteristic thing in a State." (H. J. Tozer, trans., *The Social Contract*, p. 67.)

[50] I am at a loss to follow Derathé's reading, when he refers to the beautiful pages "of individualistic inspiration" in the second part of "Political Economy," in which Rousseau speaks of the "protection the State owes its members," and concludes that the authority of the State never intrudes on their liberty. (See *Oeuvres*, Pléiade edition, III, lxxviii.) The beautiful pages he refers to say nothing of the kind and deal not with individual liberty, but with the idea of community, the idea that all are parts of the same body and under the protection of the "common mother of the citizens" (note here again the idea of citizens as children). Now Rousseau does say that "the laws should be *in their eyes* only the guarantee of their common liberty." (Italics added.) Immediately after (p. 255), we see what he means by "liberty," when in his earliest passage setting forth the idea of behavioral engineering he demands that citizens be conditioned from childhood never to think of themselves except in relation to "the Body of the State" and "to perceive their own existence only as a part of its existence"; and when he talks of changing "our natural inclinations" and destroying the "human self." All this will produce "virtue," without which "liberty" cannot exist.

[51] Summarized in F. Tönnies, *Community and Society* (East Lansing, 1957), p. 13.

[52] *Aristotle's Politics and the Athenian Constitution*, pp. 44–45.

[53] In *Emile* Rousseau says that the Sovereign may not touch an individual's property, but that "it may legitimately seize the property of all."

[54] M. Halbwachs (ed.), *Du Contrat social*, p. 137.

[55] *Political Writings*, I, 61.

[56] P. L. de Bauclair, *Anti-Contrat Social* (La Haye, 1765), p. 191.

[57] J. Plamenatz, *Man and Society, Political and Social Theory* (New York, 1963), I, 393.

[58] H. Barth, "Volonté générale, volonté particulière," in *Rousseau et la philosophie politique* (Paris, 1965), p. 48.

[59] *La Nouvelle Héloïse,* Part VI, Letter XI, p. 695. That the word was taken in this sense is evidenced by P. L. de Bauclair's *Anti-Contrat Social:* "It means nothing to suppose the people sufficiently informed, and the citizens without communication with each other; public deliberation is always subject to error. Man does not need to talk to others to be seduced; his own heart and his passions, always at war with reason, succeed in corrupting him in solitude as in society. . . ." (p. 54.)

[60] Burgelin asserts that in isolation the individual can follow his reason, protected from "all falsifying influences." (*La Philosophie,* p. 549.) Like Rousseau, then, Burgelin assumes that the guide's voice is not falsifying and that all other voices are. We know, too, that Rousseau has no confidence in this reason, limited and corrupted as it is.

[61] Compare Diderot: "Nevertheless, this right of opposition even when the sovereign orders the good is sacred; without it, subjects resemble a herd whose demands are scorned on the pretext that they are being led into fat pastures." Despotism, he adds, is characterized by the extent and not by the use of authority. (*Réfutation d'Helvétius,* in *Oeuvres,* ed. Assézat and Tourneux [Paris, 1875], II, 620.) A strong reply to Rousseau was made by L. S. Mercier in *L'An deux mille quatre cent quarante* (see, in particular, Chapters 57 and 72). S. Cotta contrasts Rousseau's idea of a "unitary whole," exclusive of factions, which "originate in the grip of passions that blind the light of reason," with Montesquieu's idea of union as a *concordia discors.* For Montesquieu the common good is not a univocal reality, but the outcome of the struggles between different ways of thinking. "The common good is freedom, freedom to express and realize one's own conception of social life, freedom of political confrontation, on the condition of recognizing the same right of others." Rousseau's ideology is antithetical to this whole outlook. ("L'Idée de parti dans la philosophie de Montesquieu," *Actes du Congrès Montesquieu* [Bordeaux, 1956], pp. 260–61.)

[62] *Political Writings,* I, 60. In the tenth Federalist Paper, Madison wrote: "There are two methods of removing the causes of faction; the one, by destroying the liberty which is essential to its existence, the other, by giving to every citizen the same opinions, the same passions, and the same interests." He rejects both.

[63] J. Dehaussy, "La Dialectique de la souveraine liberté dans le *Contrat social,*" in *Etudes sur le "Contrat social,*" p. 137. The reasoning is the same in contemporary Communist states.

[64] M. Francis, "Les Réminiscenses spinozistes dans le *Contrat social* de Jean-Jacques Rousseau," *Revue philosophique*, 141 (1951), 68–69.

[65] C. Eisenmann, "La Cité de Jean-Jacques Rousseau," in *Etudes sur le "Contrat social,"* pp. 197–98.

[66] R. Derathé, *Rousseau et la science politique de son temps*, pp. 362–64.

[67] M. Halbwachs, ed., *Du Contrat social*, p. 172n.

[68] Or Lawgiver. We shall use the usual translation.

[69] We recall Rousseau's statement in "Political Economy" (p. 243) that "unfortunately personal interest is always in inverse ratio to duty," and his insistence in *La Nouvelle Héloïse* on not giving the common people an education which would allow them to develop their talents. The opinion of Diderot, a liberal, was that the humble are as entitled to education as anyone else; only ability matters; and talents, genius, and virtue will come, he predicts, from a hut more often than from a palace. (*Plan d'une université* in *Oeuvres*, III, 433–34.)

[70] According to J. N. Shklar, the law in Rousseau's view inevitably declines without an inspirational leader, for it cannot long withstand the assaults of the *moi humain*. ("Rousseau's Images of Authority," p. 922.) T. H. Green pointed out that in order for the general will to be represented by power (*Social Contract*, II, 1) "there must be a permanent accord between it and the individual will or wills of the person or persons representing it. But such a permanent accord is impossible." (*Works*, II, 389.)

[71] *Political Writings*, II, 449. Rousseau's singular does not refer to the entire Senate, which, moreover, is not in continuous session.

[72] One would guess from Rousseau's description that certain figures in the Senate might exercise that role, and also the king. (See *Political Writings*, II, 465.) However, the institutions proposed for Poland are not his ideal institutions, but compromises.

[73] Compare Aristotle in *Politics*: "The virtue peculiar to the subject is definitely not prudence in this sense of directive wisdom, but only right opinion." (*Aristotle's Politics and the Athenian Constitution*, p. 75.)

[74] *Political Writings*, I, 247. This was no casual statement. Rousseau repeats it a few paragraphs later.

[75] "It is for the government alone to propose laws," writes Derathé, and it alone has the right to discuss them. ("Les Rapports de l'exécutif et du législatif chez Jean-Jacques Rousseau," in *Rousseau et la philosophie politique* [Paris, 1965], pp. 164–65, and *Social Contract*, IV, 1.) Much earlier, in the Dedication of the second *Discourse*, Rousseau had urged that only magistrates should have the right to propose laws; the people are asked only to give their consent, "deciding in a body on the report of their leaders." (*Political Writings*, I, 128.)

[76] It also explains why the vote is conceived of as a discovery or a

confirmation, and not, as in open societies, as a construction. Ratification of laws by the citizenry is also a part of Rousseau's theory of sovereignty, the essence of which lies in the legislative function. As we have seen, this theory of sovereignty is designed to prevent exploitation by the few and to make unanimity possible.

[77] "There is no subjection so complete as that which keeps the appearance of freedom; that is the way to capture the will itself." (*Emile*, p. 121.)

[78] E. Durkheim, *Montesquieu and Rousseau: Forerunners of Sociology* (Ann Arbor, 1960), p. 122.

[79] (Italics added.) We are reminded of Mussolini's statement, one which succinctly summarizes Rousseau's thought: "Everything turns on one's ability to control the masses like an artist." (Emil Ludwig, *Conversations with Mussolini* [Boston, 1933], p. 127.)

[80] Cf. B. Constant: " 'In vain do you pretend to submit the rulers to the general will. It will always be they who dictate that will and all the safeguards become illusory.' " (Quoted in *Du Contrat social*, ed. M. Halbwachs, p. 112.) For Constant, representative government was the only way in which power could be controlled.

[81] *Political Writings*, II, 349. Public voting was in the tradition of popular democracies; Montesquieu calls it "a fundamental law of democracy," adding that "the common people must be *enlightened* by the leaders, and contained by the gravity of certain personages." (*De l'Esprit des lois*, ed. J. Brethe de la Gressaye [Paris, 1950–61], Book II, Chapter 2. Italics added.)

[82] L. Gossman, "Rousseau's Idealism," *Romanic Review*, LVII (1961), 176.

[83] Italics added.

[84] See J. S. Spink, *Jean-Jacques Rousseau et Genève* (Paris, 1934), pp. 13–29.

[85] Conditioning ("education"), indoctrination ("informing," control of "opinion"), and the judicious use of duplicity or "illusion" are the others.

[86] C. Eisenmann, "La Cité de Jean-Jacques Rousseau," pp. 200–201. ("General" is used in the sense of applicability to *more than one* individual, but not to the entire citizenry.) Eisenmann's criticism is also advanced, in essence, by R. de Lacharrière: " 'The generality of the law which is part of equality does not subsist in legislative practice and can therefore no longer be, for the citizens, a guarantee against oppression.' " (Quoted in R. Derathé's review of *Etudes sur la théorie démocratique, Spinoza, Rousseau, Hegel, Marx*, in *AJJR*, XXXVI, 357.)

[87] *Emile*, p. 280.

[88] *Political Writings*, II, 426–27. For other important criticisms, see R. de Lacharrière, "Rousseau et le socialisme," *Etudes sur le "Contrat social*," pp. 520–21, 535.

[89] As Shklar puts it, "Perpetual denaturalization cannot be maintained

except by perpetual tutorial vigilance." ("Rousseau's Images of Authority," p. 923.)

⁹⁰ See above, and *Social Contract* (II, 7; III, 15).

⁹¹ In the *Considerations on the Government of Poland* Rousseau is
obliged to accept representation, though he does not approve of it. But
there, too, there is no right of protest against laws: "The Diet . . . can do
anything." (See *Political Writings*, II, 450–52.) He refers back to the
Social Contract (III, 15–18).

⁹² W. E. Hocking criticizes Rousseau and his idealistic successors for
making the general will a real entity with a distinct center of consciousness and an unreal perfection. This, he says, is an unjustified idealization,
for no will is good merely by self-definition. (*Man and the State* [New
Haven, 1926], p. 406.)

⁹³ E. Ritter, "Direct Democracy and Totalitarianism," *Diogenes*, No. 7
(1954), pp. 64–65.

⁹⁴ Fragment, in *Oeuvres*, Pléiade edition, III, 484.

⁹⁵ P. Grosclaude, Commentary in *Jean-Jacques Rousseau et son oeuvre*,
Actes et Colloques (Paris, 1963), p. 263.

⁹⁶ F. Neumann, *The Democratic and the Authoritarian State*
(Glencoe, 1957), p. 156.

⁹⁷ "His sovereign power, which imposes no useless burdens, injures
none of its subjects, and always aims impartially at the common good
without prejudice to individual interests, is an ideal." (H. J. Tozer,
trans., in the preface to *The Social Contract*, p. 65.)

⁹⁸ The weight of evidence seems to make this Rousseau's real and
enduring opinion, even though he declares at one point in the *Social
Contract* that "straight-forward, simple men are difficult to deceive and
that the Swiss peasants are able to conduct the affairs of State under an
oak tree."

⁹⁹ R. Derathé sees in the power of the State a protection against the
power of groups. (*Rousseau et la science politique de son temps*, pp.
363–64.) And so there is; but it is obvious that there is no protection
against an all-powerful monolith, and that absolute sovereignty is an
invitation to the use of force. Moreover, that which acts can only be a
person. The one or the ones who control decision become the "moral
person" speaking in the name of the general will. That the leader
inevitably assumes he speaks in the name of all, or of the general will, has
been shown in the passage quoted from the *Project of a Constitution for
Corsica*. (See p. 29.) The same objection refutes Cassirer's claim that
present societies are compulsory and obedience to Rousseau's general will
is freedom. (*The Question of Jean-Jacques Rousseau* [New York, 1954],
pp. 55, 97, *et passim*.) The fact that one may consent to the total power
to condition and to coerce him (even if the consent is not engineered,
even if it is real and binding—which it is not in the case of a vague,
general contract) does not mean that he is free. Cassirer's reasoning leads

him to conclude (p. 97) that voluntary obedience must be unqualified and unlimited: in other words, one *must* freely obey!

[100] R. Polin has analyzed Rousseau's dialectic of equality and inequality in an important article, "Le sens de l'égalité et de l'inégalité chez Jean-Jacques Rousseau" (in *Etudes sur le "Contrat social,"* pp. 143–64). He points out that Rousseau expresses, in *Lettres écrites de la Montagne,* a preference for aristocratic government along with popular sovereignty, and that the model society of *La Nouvelle Héloïse* is based on the idea that each must be in his proper place. But the *feeling* of equality is essential, as is equality before the law.

[101] M. Halbwachs, ed., *Du Contrat social,* p. 355*n.*

[102] J. Bronowski and B. Mazlish, *The Western Intellectual Tradition* (New York, 1960), p. 299.

[103] C. E. Vaughan, ed., *Political Writings,* I, 426. E. H. Wright defined Rousseau's idea of freedom as enabling man to act as he ought. But this depends on whether the "ought" is freely determined and freely embraced. (Otherwise the act, we may add, has no moral quality.) Wright, sensing the trap, says: "When our will becomes *autonomously* one with principle, we shall know the ultimate freedom." (*The Meaning of Rousseau* [London, 1929], p. 29.) This evasion sets up two kinds of freedom, one that we do freely, and one that we don't, but which is freedom because it is in accord with "principle." In this latter sense freedom is defined by a so-called general will, or by those who define and announce the general will. Wright does not ask what will make our will *freely* (autonomously) desire a principle. But we have seen how Rousseau takes care of this.

[104] P. Burgelin, *La Philosophie,* p. 541.

[105] P. Naville, *Examen du Contrat Social de Jean-Jacques Rousseau* . . . , *AJJR,* XXII (1933), 72.

[106] See *Julie, ou la Nouvelle Héloïse,* (Part II, Letter XI), ed. D. Mornet (Paris, 1925), II, 295–96, and Book I, Chapter 2 of the first version of the *Social Contract* (*Political Writings,* I, 452). The final version drops the idea of "the silence of the passions," which is on the abstract or idealistic level. Now the general will comes out of the vote, Rousseau proposes, because "there is no *one* who does not appropriate for himself that word, *each,* and think of himself in voting for all." (II, 4.) This is a more realistic approach, but a *non sequitur* none the less.

[107] See review of *L'idée de volonté générale chez J. J. Rousseau et ses antécédents historiques,* in *AJJR,* XXV, 289.

[108] See quotation in Note 32, above.

[109] The latter phrase is that of Paul Meyer, "The Individual and Society in Rousseau's *Emile,*" *MLQ,* XIX (1958), 100. It is interesting to compare Rousseau's ideas with Spinoza's in the *Tractatus theologico-politicus,* Chapter XIX, and the *Tractatus politicus,* Chapter 3, Section 6.

[110] In the *Social Contract* (II, 6), Rousseau concedes the existence of

abstract justice, but affirms that it is meaningless ("*vaine*") among men, because, lacking sanctions, it is not reciprocal. Diderot realizes the lack of sanctions, but attempts to rescue its meaningfulness. Echoing the second *Discourse*, Rousseau adds that such "laws" only "make the wicked prosper and the just suffer."

[111] "Subject," "subjection," "subjugate," and "yoke" are all among his word-fixations.

[112] It is interesting to recall that the Jacobins, who attempted to realize in some fashion Rousseau's general will, found themselves using it as a justification of social oppression. The alienation of individual rights was justified by the need of the community. "Civic virtue" was a mask for terror. Rousseau would not have approved of their application of his theory, but it was none the less open and conducive to such a direction.

[113] Quoted by Vaughan in *Political Writings*, I, 42–46.

[114] *A History of Political Theory*, p. 593.

[115] The theory and justification of Rousseau's civil religion had already been defined by Spinoza, in Chapter 19 of the *Tractatus theologico-politicus*.

[116] In *Du Contrat social*, ed. M. Halbwachs, p. 476. It is important to understand the context of these remarks. Rousseau is protesting against the hypocrisy to which the Catholic religion leads and against the separation between belief and conduct which it causes. He makes this point, which is closely related to his usual criticism of existing societies, in the sentences I have omitted. ("When that is not so, what does it matter what they believe or pretend to believe? The show of being religious only serves to dispense them from having a religion.") Just as men are now in the chains of social subjection, whereas the true society of the social contract would *justify* the loss of independence (*Social Contract*, I, 1), so, in similar fashion, the right to the kinds of inspection Rousseau clearly and unequivocally affirms in the sentences that follow is justified and useful only when a religion based on reason prevails. Only then is the supposition that the beliefs of men determine their moral code and that "their conduct in this life is determined by the ideas they have of the life to come" valid. Rousseau also makes the point that when it comes to opinions that have no influence on morals or actions, such as those concerning the dogma of the hypostasis, or the Trinity, no one has a right to prescribe for anyone else. This, however, only reaffirms what he has said in the *Social Contract*—i.e., that there must be toleration for personal *religious* opinions beyond the dogma of the civil religion. His toleration here does not go beyond religious opinions, and he gives us no reason to doubt that the State will, as usual, determine which opinions influence morals and actions. It is clear, then, that surveillance, useless in existing societies, is a justified and necessary part of Rousseau's society.

[117] R. Derathé, "La Religion civile selon Rousseau," *AJJR*, XXXV

(1959–62), 167–69. In his Letter to Voltaire of 1756 Rousseau denounces the idea that the State has any right over consciences; but he is referring to religious beliefs (as in the *Social Contract*) that are outside the civil religion. Again, Rousseau's toleration is for religions, not for ideas unacceptable to the State.

[118] *Ibid.*, p. 172.

[119] H. J. Tozer, trans., *The Social Contract*, pp. 77–78.

[120] C. E. Vaughan, ed., *Political Writings*, I, 85–93.

[121] J. L. Talmon, *The Rise of Totalitarian Democracy* (Boston, 1952), p. 24.

[122] Cited in M. Launay's account of the discussion on Rousseau at the Collège de France. ("Rousseau au Collège de France," *Europe*, No. 405–6 [1963], pp. 344–45.) See also H. Gouhier, "La Religion du Vicaire Savoyard dans la cité du *Contrat social*," in *Etudes sur le "Contrat social*," pp. 263–75; and especially the luminous article of S. Cotta, "Théorie religieuse et théorie politique chez Rousseau," in *Rousseau et la philosophie politique* (Paris, 1965), pp. 171–94. Cotta properly emphasizes the basic link between the *Profession of Faith* and the civil religion revolving around the idea of order. The general will reestablishes the natural (or divine) order. To Cotta this is a "theological imposture," putting the State *in loco Dei* (cf. Hobbes' "mortal god"), whereas the general will, a human concept, is subject to evil and error. It also follows that, since freedom introduces evil and disorder, total submission to law (the order established by the majority) is necessary. Cotta insists on Rousseau's "deification of the State," the general will taking God's place in "the most intimate recesses of the heart." Rousseau reaches this end because his governing principle is that man's moral and spiritual salvation depends entirely on society, "not on [his] personal initiative." Like morals, religion has been dissolved into politics. J. H. Broome properly compares the surrender to the general will to the surrender to the will of God in the *Profession of Faith*, and adds that "the revealed truths of Christianity have at best a pragmatic value." (*Rousseau. A Study of His Thought* [New York, 1963], pp. 122–23.) I think it somewhat less certain that Rousseau conceived of the law as a "meeting place between man and God, or that his society is "the kingdom of God on earth." Still more dubious is Paolo Casini's opinion, in an otherwise excellent article, that Rousseau's political system is really a theodicy and his "City is a Christian parish"—a view that is reminiscent of Masson. ("Rousseau e Diderot," *Rivista Critica di Storia della Filosofia* [Florence, 1964], p. 266.)

[123] Letter to Bertrand, 19 March 1765, in *Voltaire's Correspondence*, ed. T. Besterman (Geneva, 1953–65), Vol. 57, pp. 213–14.

[124] *La Morale universelle* (Paris, 1820), II, 249.

3. Influences and Analogues

WHILE a complete study of the influence of Rousseau's political thought would require a large volume, or several volumes, it will be useful even to mark some of the highlights. In regard to a man who left so deep an imprint on intellectual and cultural history, it is unpersuasive and arbitrary to suggest that the fortunes of his ideas—what those who came after him did with them—are irrelevant. To explore the radiations and consequences of a set of ideas we may, it seems to me, seek to determine where they have taken root (influences) and to what the ideas may conceivably lead (analogues). Undoubtedly it is dangerous and unfair to judge Rousseau not by what he wrote, but by the light of history's nightmares. My intention, however, is not to judge Rousseau, but only to point to the implications and potentialities of what he wrote; any comparisons are based on the meaning of what he wrote. Critics also assert that it is wrong to judge Rousseau in the light of the misinterpretations of later statesmen. Certainly, he is not responsible for their misinterpretations, nor for their acts. Yet the fact that they turned to him is not devoid of significance, and that significance cannot be dismissed with a pat phrase. He is responsible for what he wrote. Some of what he wrote is unclear and ambiguous. Consequently, Rousseau's influence has been equally strong in opposite directions, and he has been interpreted (or misinterpreted) to support liberal democratic systems and institutions as well as their contraries. Obviously, he cannot be given the credit for one and be protected by his apologists from receiving the debit for the other. I do not think that anyone could have read Locke, Jefferson, or Diderot and been inspired to construct a totalitarian system or State from their ideas. In much of what follows we shall be speaking of relationships, then, rather than ascertainable influences. In some cases ideas may have come directly from him; in others they come from the mainstream of which his ideas were a part. We shall go beyond historical influences into the realm of constructive imagination—the realm in which Rousseau dwelt. By a study of certain interesting analogues, our final conclusions will be deepened and strengthened.

The *Social Contract* was little read during Rousseau's lifetime. In contrast with his other writings, it was arid and impersonal, and despite its temporary notoriety was too easily confused with the mass of speculative treatises. There was, to be sure, the first splash, augmented by the fuss over *Emile*. In 1762–63 no less than thirteen French editions were put out, as well as three English, one in German, and one in Russian. But interest in the work quickly faded. Not until the 1780's did the French public begin to read it more widely. In fact, there was only one new edition between 1763 and 1790. The Rousseau cult was literary and personal, and the times were not ready for his political thought. In 1790, however, four editions were published, and his cult fast became a political one. Three more editions appeared in 1791, and a total of twenty between 1789 and 1796.[1]

It has long been argued whether Rousseau was an optimist or a pessimist. In an absolute sense, he was neither. If he had been a complete pessimist, he would not have outlined a utopian social system in several works, or attempted to show the "right road" to Corsica and Poland. Yet he had little or no hope for the advanced (i.e., "corrupt") societies of his day. In a century prompted by the nascent power of science to look forward to a better future for mankind, he looked backward to early Rome and Sparta, and to a rural, patriarchal mode of life. One scholar writes: "Paradoxically, this rebel, whose message will help to give birth to revolutions, is a reactionary out of spite." [2] There is no paradox in this, for a reactionary may certainly be a revolutionary. But Rousseau was, even more, a conservative, fearful of any changes that might upset the prevailing order. Although he predicted revolution in both the *Social Contract* and *Emile,* he dreaded the horrors of such a cataclysm.

> Just consider the danger of exciting the enormous masses that compose the French monarchy. Who will be able to halt their movement once it is started or anticipate its ultimate effects? Even if all the advantages of the new plan were indisputable, what sensible men would dare undertake to abolish old customs . . . and to give another form to the State. . . ? [3]

But if Rousseau was not himself a revolutionary, he was in revolt; and his work was revolutionary in character. True revolution lies not in violence of action or language, but in the will that rejects the traditional order. When Rousseau censured Montesquieu for concerning himself with what is, instead of with what ought to be, he was being revolutionary, thinking of abolishing the past, which Voltaire had termed a record of crimes and follies; in his mind he was setting up something based on abstract and absolute values—something that had never existed before. He was revolutionary when he wrote in *Emile* that reform of abuses is useless, and that "everything must be remedied at one blow." In the Preface he declared his refusal to write about "possible things," about "some good which can ally itself to the existing evil." He felt strongly that acceptance of reform only makes us a part of what we today call the "Establishment." This attitude was one important reason for Burke's bitter opposition.

There is no doubt that in some important respects Rousseau's thought was opposed to the trend of the Revolution.[4] That matters little, historically; our task is only to examine the various understandings of what his thought was.

During the French Revolution Rousseau was called upon by partisans of both sides, or, more exactly, all sides. Usually they distorted his ideas to favor their own viewpoints. During the first years of the Revolution, the question of his relation to it was

actually the subject of a continuing debate.⁵ A few examples
from the voluminous literature are worthy of mention. One
pamphleteer used the *Social Contract* to attack the National
Assembly.⁶ Rousseau, he reminds his readers, said that the legislature is not sovereign, nor should it concern itself with "particular objects." In 1789 Isnard, the future Girondist, rejected Rousseau's theory that law is only the expression of the general will.
Natural Law, he maintained, exists apart from the will of the
people.

But Aubert de Vitry, in *Jean-Jacques Rousseau à l'Assemblée
Nationale*, pretending that Rousseau was an elected deputy, has
him defend the representative assembly as the voice of popular
sovereignty. The people are "too unenlightened." They must be
"enlightened." "The unfortunate people, who are so easily misled, must be protected against the seduction of our enemies."
The decrees of the Assembly are irreversible, he declares, and
not subject to revision. "No one has the right to oppose them."
Anyone who challenges this is "guilty of *lèse-nation* . . . [and is]
a puppet of the aristocracy who is trying to weaken the public
power by eternal contradictions and the veto of private
interests. . . ." ⁷ There is no such thing as defending the rights
of the people against those who speak for the people. The
example of the American republic, he insists, significantly, is
deadly.

Charles-Francois Lenormant, author of *Jean-Jacques Rousseau, aristocrate*, approves of Rousseau's bust being placed on the
right of the Assembly. In his judgment, it is unworthy of stand-
ing on the left, alongside those of Washington and Franklin, the
defenders of liberty. The *Social Contract* shows that is where he
belongs. "Far from being the author of the revolution of 1789, he
would have been its adversary and scourge." ⁸ Many quotations
from Rousseau's political writings are offered to substantiate this
view. The writer emphasizes the fact that the Assembly has
assumed the popular sovereignty and has not submitted the
constitution or the laws for the people's ratification. Again and
again, he quotes Rousseau about the "stupid, brutish people" and
their need for masters to contain them. Had not Rousseau

warned that one can give new laws only to people who do not yet have any, that it is dangerous to disturb existing institutions or to agitate the masses? Had he not warned, in his plan for the Polish government, of "democratic tumult"?

A certain Father Gudin criticized Rousseau's *Social Contract* in 1791. He accused Rousseau of making liberty an impossible, disheartening goal, quoting his lines:

> "Proud and holy liberty, if those poor people . . . knew how your laws are more austere than the harsh yoke of tyrants, their weak souls, the slaves of the passions they would have to stifle, would fear your liberty a hundred times more than servitude; they would fly from you with fear as a burden ready to crush them." [9]

He blames Rousseau for praising Moses, who oppressed his people, for lauding Lycurgus because he imposed on the Spartans "an iron yoke such as no people has ever borne," for promoting nationalism with all its hatreds, and for exaggerating the worth of governments of times long past.[10] He himself defends the alienation of sovereignty to an elected assembly, and demands the rights of petition, protest, and freedom of the press, which he finds to be excluded from Rousseau's system.

By the end of 1791 the conservatives had lost the argument, and Rousseau became a myth-figure, the idol of the masses. Many even thought that the articles of the Declaration of the Rights of Man were taken from the *Social Contract*!

His general will became a myth, "the will of the people." His bust had been placed in the Assembly in 1790. Borne on a tide of mass emotion, his body was interred in the newly established Pantheon in 1794. The masses, writes Albert Soboul, were impregnated with a vague Rousseauism in their social aspirations and political tendencies. They did not read him, but his ideas were diffused in the penny press, in popular "literature," and by oral means.[11] His influence was deepest on the radical extremists, including the *sans-culottes* masses, who condemned luxury, demanded approximate equality of fortunes, and claimed a popular sovereignty that could not be delegated. Laws, they declared, must be sanctioned by the people, and representatives must be subject to recall. They also demanded censorship, and longed for a unanimous nation.[12] Marat, Billaud-Varenne, Saint-Just, and Robespierre—authoritarian fanatics devoted to an absolute— were steeped in his thought, and there are frequent reminiscences of it in their speeches.[13]

The relation between Rousseau and the Jacobins, as Albert Soboul has shown in an important article, was close but intricate and varying.[14] Rousseau furnished a large part of their ideology, but he was "politically ineffective" in their time of triumph. The Jacobin rule was in many ways an attempt to realize the total, collectivist State of the *Social Contract*, in which "virtue-patriotism" would rule. It made clear the dangers of the absolute, including absolute sovereignty, and the fallacy of the general-will concept of liberty: an individual or a group always arrogates for itself the sole right to speak in the name of the general will, or of the people, and all dissidents become, by definition, enemies of the people, or of the State. Robespierre was to develop the collective idea "in terms of the State as a collective moral and political body, with absolute power over the individual." [15] He condemned the separation of powers. In his theory of public safety and the repression and terror it involved, he based himself less, according to Soboul, on Rousseau's chapter on dictatorship than on the chapter "On the Right of Life and Death." The individual alienates his rights, the community keeps those it needs. "The social treaty's purpose is the preservation of the contractants," wrote Rousseau. "He who wants the ends, wants the means." Like Rousseau in "Political Economy" and in the two constitutional projects, Robespierre planned to shape a new kind of citizen "by exposing him from childhood to inspirational messages and behavioral models," utilizing every artistic and communication medium, as well as schools, sports, and public festivals.[16] Both Rousseau and Robespierre blamed social inequality on property, and neither sought a logical remedy for it. Reasoning juridically, both were guided by purely political concepts, when an economic and social analysis was needed. Both turned their backs on the nascent capitalistic evolution. They had the same intellectual pride, the same rigid attachment to principles, the same certainty that they alone were right. The Jacobin spirit, like Rousseau's, was puritanical in both the superficial and the more profound senses of that word, and it was the puritanical spirit of the "sea-green Incorruptible" that directed the worst excesses of the French Revolution. Robespierre agreed with Rousseau's statement in "Political Economy" that "to be just, it is necessary to be severe"; and he agreed that from the political viewpoint pity is fatal to the establishment of the "reign of virtue" that both called for.

> To prevent pity from degenerating into weakness, it is necessary to generalize and extend it over the whole human kind [abstract love of man]. Then you give way to it only when it is in accord with justice, because, of all virtues, justice is the one that tends to the common good of men. We must, out of reason and self-love, have pity for our kind [i.e., man], even more than for our neighbor. And pity for the wicked is a very great cruelty toward men.[17]

But even love of mankind, while it produces virtues like charity and indulgence, does not, according to Rousseau, inspire courage, or "that energy which [men] receive from love of country and which inspires them to heroism." (Ms. de Neuchâtel.) In both men, we recognize the archetype of the authoritarian mind.

Robespierre, according to one scholar, "was certainly a faithful disciple of Rousseau."[18] He did not misinterpret his master's ideas, but made the error of applying them "to conditions they did not fit." Nevertheless, Rousseau's thought was subjected to many deviations as each party adapted it to its own purposes and deformed it in the act of applying general theories to real situations. This is an inevitable process of which Marx was to be another example. The question, as one historian, C. Mazauric, has put it, "is to know how, in a concrete historical situation, Rousseauism was able to redispose itself in a much vaster ideological field, and become the spring from which most political and social reform movements of the late eighteenth century and doubtless later times have drunk."[19] Nowhere is this more striking than in the case of the communist conspirator Babeuf, who was executed in 1797 after a famous trial.

Like Robespierre, Babeuf started from a utopian Rousseauism

and ended by a commitment to "the tyranny of liberty"—an excellent phrase to describe the commitment of all three men. But whereas Robespierre, a lawyer, had studied Rousseau closely, the peasant Babeuf had, until the Revolution and perhaps after, only vague and secondhand ideas about the man he idealized. Babeuf came to believe that if one has a part in the making of laws he is free. He thought, however, that Rousseau, like himself, wanted an egalitarian, communistic society. He too was convinced that the good society would not be brought about by enlightenment, and for a while he believed that Rousseau's Legislator was the answer—a new Lycurgus. In his mind, the Legislator was also a dictator. The course of events and disillusionment with Danton and Robespierre led him to replace this idea with those of popular insurrection and "the direct democracy preached by Rousseau." [20] The voice of the people would be heard in the committees and sections—the popular assemblies Rousseau had planned, in a revised format. This "direct democracy" really amounted to a popular dictatorship—the means of realizing the general will. Babeuf at first followed the common utopian misinterpretation of Rousseau, according to which equal political rights and control of wealth would by themselves insure that the general will is that of the majority—an interpretation that ignored the real reliance on indoctrination and subtle coercion. But after Robespierre's overthrow on the 9th of Thermidor, Babeuf abandoned this idea, too, and decided that only a select group could be the voice of the people and the general will and that it would have to conspire to seize dictatorial power (the Conspiracy of the Equals). While going beyond Rousseau's system, the conspirators thought they were remaining faithful to his message. In doing this, they also became the precursors of "contemporary socialist [i.e., communist] parties"; for such a dictatorial party would become "the expression and guarantee of the *popular will,* that notion which was elaborated between 1789 and 1795 and which is in sum only the last incarnation of Rousseau's idea of the *general will.*" [21] No longer is unanimity held to be possible; history has shown (writes Mazauric) that the dictatorship of a class and party is the way to realize the spirit of Rousseau.

While it is true that Rousseau was in a sense utopian, he was not utopian in the sense of the usual Marxist criticism of some eighteenth-century fabricators of ideal societies. He did not believe that people would willingly change, or that enlightenment (objective truth, or to use an anachronism, "bourgeois objectivism") was a useful method of reaching the desired end. For him, to "inform" the people involved indoctrination and the "illusion" which he favored—the methods so amply illustrated in *La Nouvelle Héloïse* and *Emile*. That is why individuals and peoples had to be made "docile"—i.e., passive to "teaching." He never counted on altruism or good will.

Since the French Revolution each generation, each shape of mind, has taken from the *Social Contract* what it has wanted. This is the sign of its greatness. It has also led to Rousseau's having been made the butt of all kinds of accusations by his enemies, in his own time and ever since. Let us, nevertheless, reiterate our opening statement: while a man is not responsible for what others may do with his work, it is also true, as Vaughan has said, that "theories are to be judged not only by intentions, but by the consequences which may naturally be drawn from them." [22]

To many readers struggling to establish democratic institutions in the eighteenth and nineteenth centuries, the *Social Contract* seemed an inspiration for their cause. Rousseau had attacked feudal institutions, monarchy, the right of the strong. He had raised the banners of popular sovereignty and popular control of the government, of universal suffrage, of equality before the law; these ideals are written in plain letters in his great tract, even if he did not mean them all. But the founders of the American republic, while they admired these principles, turned away from Rousseau to Montesquieu and to Locke, and to their Anglo-Saxon traditions, to form an open and pluralistic society.[23] In England Burke was to rise up in eloquent wrath against the French Revolution and the man whom he considered to be the theorist of the Terror, accusing him of loosing political institutions from tradition and history in order to make them the instrument of pure will.

During the Revolutionary period and in the years that followed, the *Social Contract* was also helping to form the philosophy of authoritarianism and State supremacy in the writings of Fichte and Hegel. We must pass over these intricate matters here.[24] Joseph de Maistre, the rabid *anti-philosophe* and reactionary, read and hated the eighteenth-century writings, but borrowed from those writers who even then opposed liberal views. Like Rousseau, he demands that reason be frustrated; "it should lose itself in the national mind, so that it changes its individual existence for another, collective existence." Man, he says, "needs a strong authority in charge of his existence." [25]

The book's influence grew as the century became older and the battle of ideologies grew fiercer. The men of 1848 read and revered it. The German conservatives who loathed Rousseau loathed him as a democrat. But his anti-liberalism was congenial to them, and they too took many of their ideas from him. It may not be too much to claim that Rousseau's thought was one influence that fed the nineteenth-century precursors of Nazism, even if it had no direct influence on Nazism, and even though in many essential respects it is utterly unlike Nazism. At all events, one finds in these forerunners parallel ways of thinking, and ideas and outlooks that seem "congenial." According to one intellectual historian of Germany, R. E. Herzstein, most German theorists since Hegel have held "an organic view of society," a concept alien to Western liberalism, which conceives of society

. . . as made up of individuals with commitments to various churches, social groups, etc. This is a legacy of ancient natural law theory. Germans since Hegel have tended to view society, the State, or the nation as absolute entities, not permitting other allegiances within their own preordained spheres. The individual becomes part of a whole, not the end of government. National Socialism wished to create a *Volksgemeinschaft*, a tribal communion, as an answer to the atomized individualism of modern liberal society. . . . The individual, left to the mercies of the State, is spiritually free when consciously *serving* the . . . mission of the . . . state.[26]

Moeller van den Bruck, an outstanding pre-Nazi, wrote: "Liberalism is the expression of a society that is no longer a community. . . . Every man who no longer feels a part of the community is somehow a liberal man." [27]

Herzstein points out other ideas in the dominating current of modern German intellectual history which we have encountered in Rousseau. He writes of the typical quest for "an absolute or total principle." Our analysis of Rousseau has revealed at least one absolute principle: disorder arises from the cultural liberation of the *moi humain;* order will be restored by its sublimation into the *moi commun.* Further, German ideas since Schelling (Herzstein here quotes Georg Lukács) "have represented an irrational revolt against the idea of progress." It may be argued that Rousseau gave us the example of a rational revolt against progress—rational, at least, in appearance. The German historian Ernst Troeltsch argued that if freedom was "spiritual, inward, or national," then control of the individual by the State was not a violation of his liberty. Troeltsch finally admitted after World War I that the German intellectual tradition had erred "in turning away from Western natural law theory in favor of chaotic Romanticism." [28] But German "chaotic Romanticism" was to spawn the communal anti-individualism, the absolute control and rigid value system of Nazism; and a similar paradoxical phenomenon existed within the personality and the work of Rousseau himself. We may explain this phenomenon, in both instances, by the fact that "chaotic Romanticism" was accompanied by "the Romantic cult of the group." [29]

The basic ideas persist on both sides of the political spectrum down to the present, often in unexpected places. Thus, an early twentieth-century Russian intellectual, Vyacheslav Ivanov, decried the individualism that has made the Western world one without values, a domain of blindly struggling individuals, each concerned only with the absolute validity of his own ego. He foresaw the emergence of a new spirit—a solidarity of individuals who, choosing freely, would choose in such a way as to further the interests of the group. [30] In the United States a group of writers has in recent years been reviving the principles we have found in Rousseau. These writers have urged a shift from "individuals and classes and their mutual antagonisms" to a people united in the "Great Community," the State, which "embraces all other communities." With the mutual support of religion and government, they argue, common values and the moral authority of the community can be imposed.[31] They also urge that the majority should not be limited by minority rights, but should be absolute and unlimited; and the only legitimate restraint on the majority is self-restraint.[32] The toleration of differences, the discussion of competing ideas in the open market-place, the minimal intervention into private lives which Ernest Barker called the essence of democracy, are as disprized by such writers as they are by Rousseau.[33]

The relation of Rousseau's thought to Marxism and its heirs is particularly significant. That there are many differences is obvious. But the differences are irrelevant to the question, since many other influences gradually entered the stream of history. It has already been shown that Marx and Engels did not realize the extent of their debt to Rousseau.[34] Very much as in Rousseau's system, Marxism regards the anti-social wickedness of men as the fault of society. In both views the open, pluralistic society, which permits a relatively free play of the competitive and aggressive instincts, especially when they are expressed in the power of wealth and property (Marxism will emphasize the means of production), is a society of servitude, not of freedom. The free society is one in which all obey the single general will, *regardless of the means that are used to bring about this kind of unnatural behavior.* We have, then, only to establish the right kind of society to bring the circumstances that shape men to bear on them. They can be socialized; the self-interest and general interest can be made to coincide.[35] Marx and Engels attributed war between men to economic factors.[36] Rousseau had a wider view, which not only included the economic factor, but went beyond it and did not depend upon the panacea of ending private property. In this he was both less advanced than the early Marxists and more advanced. Both systems of thought conceive of politics as including all of life, rather than only one sphere of it. The enemy, in both, is egocentricity, the individual's attachment to his own advantage. The problem is to "free" the will by releasing it from natural self-centeredness, to dissolve the attachment to individual liberties, to make the collectivity the center of the true self and its locus of self-realization.[37] Both "are essentially opposed to liberalism, that is, to the concept that places liberties in a domain outside of the collectivity and protected against it." Instead of "this social defeatism," they seek to weld the destiny of each to that of all, and consequently admire the complete integration of ancient city-states into a "beautiful totality." [38]

The totalitarian societies operating today under the aegis of Marxism-Leninism are in some ways the type of society Rousseau had in mind, although—and it must be emphasized—there is not one of them he would not have condemned and spurned for many different reasons. There are no absolute or complete identities in history. I am not, then, identifying Rousseau with what he would have disapproved of, but only with those elements of other theories that are closely similar to his and may even, ultimately or in fact, have been inspired by his. What is of significance for the purposes of this study is that such partial identities do exist.

What Lenin added to Marx was, above all, the idea that a small, elite group of leaders must take charge of the inchoate and ineffectual longings of the masses and guide them in the use of power; only the guides can, by propaganda and coercion, make them realize their own true wishes. All the forces of the State must be mobilized for this purpose of creating an egalitarian society, one which requires conformity and control of people's natural tendencies to seek a better life for themselves at the expense of others and of the collectivity. Nothing is above or beyond politics. Egalitarianism is necessary to collectivism, and control is necessary for egalitarianism. The Soviet *"mir,"* or village, was intended "not to find a consensus: it was to locate the collective will and activate the collective authority." [39] The individual and his conscience are considered a negative element.

Parliamentary government, the Marxist-Leninist agrees, is a travesty of genuine democracy in which the will of the people directly prevails and is decided by public opinion expressed through the decisions of the party, censorship boards, and the like (that is, by those who *mold* public opinion). And it is true, we must confess, that the general will may often be more directly and faithfully realized in a collectivist-leadership plan than in a parliament of deputies. That fact will not, however, make such a society open or pluralistic, one in which free self-expression and self-development are fostered.

The relation between Rousseau's political thought and the Communist totalitarian outlook has received renewed emphasis by Marxist scholars of our day. According to one of these scholars, G. Della Volpe, this relation is particularly significant in the current struggle of socialist democracy against liberalism. Rousseau precedes Communism in the desire to integrate the natural independent man into the social body by transmuting him into a social man, or citizen. Marx, in fact, quotes approvingly Rousseau's passage in the *Social Contract* (II, 7) about changing human nature. Engels credits Rousseau with following "a system of ideas almost exactly identical with that of Marx in *Capital*." Actually, declares Della Volpe, Rousseau's socialism was utopian, not scientific, as is the Marxist-Leninist doctrine. But Rousseau's distinction between two kinds of inequality, and his resolving of them in a rational society, are entirely similar to the first, or socialist, stage of Communism: to each according to his ability, or contribution. And at this stage, Lenin, like Rousseau, holds that the principal gain will be the termination of "the exploitation of man by man." Moreover, Rousseau deserves credit for breaking the Natural Law (*droit naturel*) tradition by replacing it with a sovereign (unlimited) general will.[40]

Another Marxist critic, Guy Besse, is even more insistent.[41] Rousseau and Marx are one in understanding that "it is mad to seek happiness in the struggle against others, in domination and power; it can only be found in the reconciliation of men." The whole problem for both is to make social existence a human existence; but Rousseau offers only juridical speculation, while

Marx has a "scientific" philosophy of historical materialism and a program of class struggle. One of Rousseau's great merits is to have grasped the fact that property is the source of inequality, and to have realized the danger of an aristocracy of wealth succeeding an aristocracy of birth. He denied that property is a natural right, insisting that it is, rather, one defined by society, which can restrict it as far as the general interest requires. "Rousseau aspires to authentic democracy, democracy founded on the economic equality of citizens." More exactly, he aspired to a republic of small proprietors like the one sought by the *sans-culottes* in 1794. Nevertheless, Besse criticizes Rousseau for reserving a measure of independence, of individual life, after the citizen's civic responsibilities are carried out, for allowing him some private happiness instead of making him a completely social being. Yet Rousseau realized, Besse admits, like Marx and his followers, that it is necessary to make men to whom the common good is dearer than their own. Emphasizing Rousseau's point that public service is the principal concern of citizens (III, 15), Besse lauds his attack on parliamentary government, which "evaporates the popular will" and is contrary to true democracy —a theme which Lenin was to emphasize. Of course Rousseau is an absolutist, he writes; but the absolutism is that of "the people master in its own house." And naturally, he continues, this is displeasing both to reactionaries like de Maistre and to liberals like Benjamin Constant. Here Besse defends Rousseau's collectivist theory as identical with that of Communism and opposed to bourgeois liberalism—a philosophy of conflict and exploitation.

> It would suffice to bring in Babeuf in order to measure the gap separating democracy from liberalism. . . . Between Rousseau, the social philosopher, and Rousseau, the defender of the individual, there is no opposition, for they are both enemies of *individualism*, which thrives only in the jungle. . . . The heirs of Rousseau are Marx and Lenin.[42]

With a typical Marxist reversal, Besse argues that liberals have no confidence in the people, that is, in their ability to govern themselves, while Rousseau and Lenin did!

It is true that Rousseau, too, wanted a society in which men would stop devouring each other—a community or *Gemeinschaft*, not a jungle. The most fundamental resemblance between Marxist thought and Rousseau's is that the egalitarian community presupposes that each citizen overcomes in his heart his egoistic instincts and places the community above himself. Man is free only if he wills what he should will for the good of all. In Marxism and Marxist-type societies this sentiment is focused on property; for Rousseau it is more general and spiritual. The corollary, in both cases, is the "formation" and control of the citizen. A transformation of attitudes and motivations must be wrought, in order to prepare the population for life in a social unit. While both have a common doctrine of alienation and corruption, and a scheme for overcoming them in a new society, Rousseau, better than the early Marxists, realized the depth and pervasiveness of the aggressive instincts. This is visible in his emphasis on the moral, more than on the economic, aspects in regard to both competition and alienation—a view that leads him, as Plamenatz points out, to the conviction that the State must be the superior moral and reasonable being.[43] This view explains his relative pessimism. Whereas for Marx the stage of dictatorial control (by the proletariat) was to give way to an administration based on universal morality, Rousseau more realistically could foresee no State without the force of the State. He, too, longed for a society in which all men would have dignity; but he did not, could not understand that the controls he wanted to set in motion would rob men of dignity, as well as of liberty. It is possible that Rousseau had the illusion that all power could be surrendered to the State, and that democratic control would be an effective safeguard against its abuse. But he himself suggests the mechanisms by which it can be abused, and he provides no protection except *a priori* convictions and a shadowy plebiscite. Even if one acknowledges the exploitative character of the existing society, it is difficult to deny the oppression that it would take to remove its causes completely, or the fallacy of the view that the people do not suffer any oppression in a monistic collectivism, because whatever is done is done by the people (or, in reality, in the name of the people). Let us never doubt that Rousseau was for the ultimate good of the individual; but he confused its promotion through collective action with its sacrifice to collectivism. We must agree with Thomas Jefferson that "the republican is the only form of government which is not eternally at open or secret war with the rights of mankind."

The *Social Contract* was never intended to be a blueprint for action, but only an ideal model; however, this does not alter its inherent utopian character.

Rousseau's political influence was destined to be powerful in still another respect—the rise of nationalism. Bertrand de Jouvenel has emphasized this influence, while denying that Rousseau himself was a nationalist.[44] I am inclined to disagree on the latter point. Rousseau derides cosmopolitanism, lauds the autarchic city-state, exalts patriotism, and cultivates xenophobia. Patriotism and humanity, he declares in the first of the *Lettres écrites de la Montagne*, are incompatible virtues; "the Legislator who wants both will have neither." In *Emile* he declares that "every patriot is harsh toward foreigners; they are only men, they are nothing in his eyes." The lines that follow express his approval of this attitude. He wants small republics, because the feelings of unity, of belonging, of patriotism are dissolved in the larger nation into factions and group interests. He idealizes the State as "including all the values of national civilization." [45] This is not to say, as fanatical adversaries of Rousseau have done, that he was responsible for nationalism any more than he was for the French Revolution, the Reign of Terror, or Romanticism. All of these would have come about had Rousseau never lived. His influence, however, cannot be denied. "Even those who rose up to assail his doctrines fell to a large extent under his potent spell; and the intense emotional energy which he diffused appears indestructible, being perpetually reembodied in new forms." [46]

Beyond the realm of historical figures and their acts lies the realm of constructive imagination, which was Rousseau's own. Here the analogues bring out, even more sharply, significant common modes of thought. Within our own generation, three important utopias or anti-utopias have been written in the Anglo-Saxon world: Aldous Huxley's *Brave New World* (1932); B. F. Skinner's *Walden Two* (1948); and George Orwell's *Nineteen Eighty-Four* (1949). They were written because their authors became appalled or, in Skinner's case, attracted by the new potentialities of power over men. With the ever-mounting, dramatic, revolutionary triumphs of all sorts of technologies, two facts became apparent to these deeply reflective and imaginative writers: first, that there was no way of calling a halt to this revolutionary progress; second, that every conquest of power over nature is ultimately a conquest of power over men. In a foreseeable future, it seemed, man's destiny would be removed from the realm of natural determinism and historical contingency and placed entirely within the control of the wielders of power. For there is little likelihood, it must be admitted, that available power will remain unused. From these considerations arose the sweet vision of utopia or the despairing nightmare of anti-utopia.

Utopias have generally been written in the novelistic form, and Rousseau also wrote a utopian (or anti-utopian?) novel, *La Nouvelle Héloïse*. But this similarity is of course trivial. Plato's *Republic* is a philosophical dialogue, and the *Social Contract* and the *Project of a Constitution for Corsica* are treatises.

The first significant resemblance between Rousseau and the three twentieth-century writers is the fact that he (alone among the earlier writers of utopias) relies on a new theory and methodology of human control that is essentially identical with their concepts. To be sure, not all of the earlier ideal communities were primitivistic or optimistic pictures of the triumph of man's natural goodness in the proper environment. Some, like Plato's and Morelly's, envision a totalitarian type of collectivity or closed social structure. But Rousseau alone developed the theory that the wielders of political power must capture men's minds, wills, and emotions, and also the essential techniques for doing so.[47] Although there is also overt coercion, both in his work and in the modern ones, in varying degrees, they all go beyond coercion. Our three modern utopias, then, aim their main effort at the goal which, according to Rousseau's repeated statements, was precisely his own. The idea was one of the great original creations of his genius, although it has not been recognized as such. It had roots in Helvétius and the new psychology of his time. But it was Rousseau's distinction to have been uniquely aware of unused possibilities of power over men, and to have drawn from that awareness in a series of works daring, revolutionary schemes for a new and better society. That his ideas would not be grasped in his own time, he himself, as we have noted, knew well.

The second similarity underlies the very dissimilar institutions which each of the writers creates. Institutions are not ends in themselves. They may be considered either in terms of the end they are designed to serve—which in this case is in large part the control I have just described, though the ultimate use of control may differ considerably—or else they may be considered in terms of the attitudes that inform them. These attitudes concern inter-personal relations within the polity; they are based on an attitude toward men, or on a view of man in his existential dimensions, psychological and social. It is in this context, rather than in regard to the historically conditioned accident of the institutions themselves, that we may speak of archetypes: both an archetype of the "authoritarian mind," as psychologists and sociologists have determined it since World War II; and a model of the totalitarian society which that mind tends to conceive, almost as if it lay within it as an innate structure. Here, then, there is no question of any influence on the part of Rousseau. It is rather a matter of similarities, analogues, and identities.

At the opening of Huxley's *Brave New World* is a quotation from Berdiaeff. "Utopias appear [today] far more realizable than was formerly believed." The time will come, it continues, when some "will dream of ways of avoiding utopias and of returning to a non-utopian society, less perfect and freer." Berdiaeff and Huxley were among the first to realize that utopia may be the most terrible, the most dehumanizing of human dreams. It is, except in the naïve fancy of primitivists, antithetical to the liberal spirit of contradiction, challenge, and growth.

Like Rousseau, Huxley declares that "the really revolutionary revolution is to be achieved not in the external world, but in the souls and flesh of human beings." [48] In order to achieve order and stability, the governors of the brave new world "carry out, by scientific means, the ultimate, personal, really revolutionary revolution." [49] Like Rousseau in *La Nouvelle Héloïse*, Huxley sees that "a really efficient totalitarian State" is one in which the managers (Huxley's term) control a population that does not "have to be coerced, because they love their servitude" [50]—just as Rousseau's Corsicans do. Education, propaganda, and censorship must be supplemented by childhood conditioning of the total behavioral pattern—the precise assignment of individuals to places in the social and economic hierarchy. [51]

The motto of Huxley's "Conditioning Center" is "Community, Identity, Stability." [52] General or abstract ideas are forbidden in *Brave New World*, since they lead to discontent. How Rousseau would have loved the genetic control, which produces *the certainty of physical laws* in human affairs! " 'We decant our babies as socialized human beings' "—i.e., as future workers or future World controllers. [53] Each must fit his pre-set role. (We remember Rousseau's refusal to educate or develop the intellect of the workers in *La Nouvelle Héloïse*, similar also to Huxley's "you couldn't have lower-caste people wasting the Community's time over books." [54]) And the Controller says: " 'That is the secret of happiness and virtue—liking what you've *got* to do. All conditioning aims at that: making people like their inescapable social destiny.' " [55] Rousseau said the people must not be able to imagine that there is a better condition than theirs. In both plans, the essential point is that there must be no feeling of sacrifice, only one of necessity.

Huxley is behind Rousseau in using only simple Pavlovian conditioning, whereas Rousseau, in *La Nouvelle Héloïse* and *Emile*, anticipates Skinner by his method of operant conditioning —that is, the creation of voluntary or apparently voluntary behavior that is self-reinforcing through inevitable or "mechanical" reward and punishment. But all three agree that " 'moral education . . . ought never, in any circumstances, to be rational,'" and that conditioning must continue until "'the child's mind *is* these suggestions.'"[56] Echoing almost exactly Rousseau's theory of the fatal split in men between the demands of nature and culture, the Controller criticizes the "old" world because it "didn't allow them to be sane, virtuous and happy," inasmuch as they were subject to "prohibitions they were not conditioned to obey."[57] Consequently, individual and social stability were impossible. People could do as their own wills dictated, but this was the freedom "'to be inefficient and miserable.'"[58]

In *Brave New World* people are discouraged from being alone. They must be kept occupied, with no leisure to think. Doing things "in private" is looked down upon. They are expected to seek amusement in public and together. There are "Community Sings and Solidarity Services."

> Ford, we are twelve; oh, make us one,
> Like drops within the Social River.[59]

There is no literature, only socially directed propaganda. In fact, there is nothing to write about.

Bernard Marx does not respond properly to conditioning: "'I'd rather be myself. Myself and nasty.'"[60] Wolmar got rid of such misfits fast. Saint-Preux had to give up being himself, in order to stay within the utopian domain. When Marx asserts that he wants to be "'more on my own, not so completely a part of something else,'" Lenina replies, "'How can you talk like that about not wanting to be a part of the social body? After all, everyone works for everyone else.'"[61] (The sacrifice is mutual, and what one gives up, he gets back in reciprocal sacrifice.) She insists that she is free—free to be happy. But Marx considers her idea of freedom as being "'enslaved by . . . conditioning.'" His reply strikes to the heart of the matter: "'But wouldn't you like to be free to be happy in some other way, Lenina? In your own way, for example; not in everybody else's way.'"[62] No; for her, "'when the individual feels [i.e., as an individual], the community reels.'"[63] This is one of the many slogans or catechized phrases with which the people have been conditioned, and Marx points out that they have been made to remain children where feeling and desire are concerned. He wants to know what passion is, and to be an adult.

Marx is accused of being "an enemy of society," a subverter of order, because of his heretical views on sports and sex life. " 'No offense is so heinous as unorthodoxy of behavior. . . . it strikes at society itself.' " [64] Enlargement of knowledge or intensification of consciousness is forbidden. We learn that books which the censors judge dangerous to the social order may not be published. Whether something is "social" or "antisocial" is the standard of judgment. The object is a "nice, tame" (i.e., "docile") people. " 'You can't make tragedies without social instability. The world's stable now. People are happy; they get what they want, and *they never want what they can't get*.' " [65]

John, another protester, declares, " 'I'd rather be unhappy than have the sort of false, lying happiness you were having here.' " [66] Indeed, we may say that the underlying theme of Huxley's book is the right to be unhappy, the right to live one's own way and take the consequences.

The new people are unable to understand what liberty was. " 'That's the price we have to pay for stability' " (i.e., order, harmony).[67] The choice is between liberty and happiness. Temptation, passion, and misery have been eliminated by the Controllers of society. In this way the people are completely "socialized." In respect to stability *Brave New World* differs from the other two modern utopias and is closer to Rousseau's thinking. Technological progress is not allowed. " 'We don't want to change. Every change is a menace to stability.' " [68] Science is considered disruptive and subversive. " 'It isn't only art that's incompatible with happiness; it's also science. Science is dangerous; we have to keep it most carefully chained and muzzled.' " [69]

" 'Happiness,' " says Mustapha Mond, the World Controller, " 'is a much harder master, if one isn't conditioned to accept it unquestioningly, than truth.' " [70] Believing something is a matter of being conditioned to believe it.[71] In *Brave New World*, as in

La Nouvelle Héloïse, the characters are constantly told, are constantly made to think they are happy. But they do not really *feel* happy. So in *Brave New World* they are given a supplement of happiness pills, which Wolmar unfortunately did not possess.

To have happiness it is necessary to control truth. " 'One can't have something for nothing. Happiness has got to be paid for.' " [72] And it must be paid for, Mond adds, quoting Cardinal Newman, by dependence. " 'Independence was not made for man—it is an unnatural state.' " [73] (For Rousseau, it was the natural state, which had to be eliminated in order to have the social state. The ultimate sense is identical, that of a stage that must be surpassed.) When John protests that Mond's people may be happy, but they are degraded, Mustapha replies that such a judgment depends on standards and postulates: in *Brave New World* the people experience no unpleasantness, no self-denial. John might have countered that the new society is based on *denial,* socially controlled, hidden from consciousness (as in Rousseau), and that the available satisfactions are limited and prescribed. Denial rests on basic principles: " 'There's no such thing as a divided allegiance; you're so conditioned that you can't help doing what you ought to do.' " [74] This, of course, is exactly Rousseau's theory of unity, his methodology of child-rearing, and his plan for the formation of citizens. John, however, is not to be convinced. " 'What you need is something *with* tears for a change. . . . I want poetry, I want real danger, I want freedom, I want goodness, I want sin.' " [75] He might have added, conflict. " 'In fact,' " replies Mustapha Mond, " 'you're claiming the right to be unhappy, . . . to have too little to eat, . . . to live in constant apprehension . . . [and] be tortured by unspeakable pains. . . .' " John's final reply is " 'I claim them all.' " [76] What he really is claiming is the right to be himself, the self of the *moi humain,* not that of the *moi commun.* This has a higher value, in his mind, than happiness, order, the general welfare, or the community. He is the anarchistic "natural man" in the organic society, the lover of love, the Saint-Preux whom Rousseau found it necessary either to restructure or to eliminate. [77]

George Orwell's *Nineteen Eighty-Four*, like *Brave New World*, is an anti-utopian utopia. In Orwell's totalitarian society there is greater emphasis on overt control through terror than in any of the other three societies we are considering; the main reliance in these latter is on conditioning and indoctrination. Yet it is fairly obvious that a system which relies to some extent, as Rousseau's does, on constant surveillance and intrusion on privacy, or a maximal limitation of privacy, would be bound to produce a fair amount of apprehension, if not outright terror. The figure of Orwell's "Big Brother," in many ways like Wolmar but more remote and yet more oppressive, intrudes blatantly on the consciousness. It is difficult to speculate whether Rousseau would have been attracted by the idea of continuous surveillance by television. Although he uses spying, informing, and censorship in at least four works, he places greatest weight on *la main cachée*. He would unquestionably have been revolted by the idea of children turning in their parents to authorities, or by the callous cruelty, fomenting of hatred, and sadism in *Nineteen Eighty-Four*. But while there is no possible comparison on this score, the basic idea of denying to individuals the refuge of privacy is identical, and Rousseau's board of censors, with its specific functions of controlling "opinions" and "*moeurs*" (IV, 7), is in essence equivalent to Orwell's "Thought Police." Although the "Ministry of Truth," which controls news, entertainment, education, and the arts, has no exact counterpart in Rousseau's institutions, the purposes of indoctrination and thought guidance are served in other ways.

Rousseau's tendency to use words with meanings of his own leads already to the creation of an Aesopian language, such as *Nineteen Eighty-Four* exploits systematically in its "doublethink" ("Freedom is Slavery," "Ignorance is Strength"). In Rousseau's own "Newspeak" docility is liberty (if consented to or induced and not forced), the artifices of Emile's tutor are "nature's way," the unhappiness of Clarens is "happiness," and its duplicities are "transparency" ("each shows himself to all such as he is"— whereas no one does). "Doublethink"—"to be conscious of complete truthfulness while telling carefully constructed lies"—is surely Wolmar's way of proceeding and that of Emile's tutor. "Doublethink"—"to hold simultaneously two opinions which cancel[led] out, knowing them to be contradictory and believing in both of them," [78]—is precisely illustrated by the paradox of being both "free and docile." "To repudiate morality while laying claim to it" is not unknown in Wolmar's conduct, or in the tutor's (recall the dishonest footraces) in *Emile*.[79] When it is explained in *Nineteen Eighty-Four* that "the Party rejects and vilifies every principle for which the Socialist movement originally stood, and it chooses to do this in the name of Socialism," [80] are we not justified in placing these tactics alongside those of Rousseau, who abolishes freedom in its basic meaning of the sanctity of the individual and does so in the name of freedom? Likewise, we detect a similarity of thinking in comparing his censorial board, which is the "voice of the people" (as he in effect says, creating the illusion that it is benevolent), and the "Ministry of Love," which assures order in its own unloving ways.

The common people are distrusted. The society of *Nineteen Eighty-Four* has its elite classes of rulers and managers who exploit the "proles," though not in the much more prudent, benevolent fashion of *La Nouvelle Héloïse*. It is fruitless to detail the vast differences in political institutions: Orwell had the Nazi and Communist regimes in mind. The significant point is that of identity: all political or "group interest" associations are eliminated. There is no freedom of speech, press, or assembly in either realm. "There will be no literature, no art, no science"— that is, except that which is directed by the State toward its chosen ends.[81]

As was the case with Wolmar (and Julie), the people are conditioned to love and adore Big Brother, with the nuance of respect for power. Community hikes and spontaneous demonstrations are carefully organized. Children are conditioned to set emotional reactions, which have the predictability of physical laws. And, as foreshadowed in the *Social Contract* and the "Lettre à M. de Beaumont," "Thoughtcrime" comes into prominent existence in the world of *Nineteen Eighty-Four*.

Let us consider the conditioning and control patterns a little more closely. Lies and deceit are one cornerstone. "Information," instruction, and entertainment are manipulated for the State's purposes.[82] Recreation is reduced to a minimum, and the ascetic life is eulogized; physical exercise is important. Orwell, to be sure, imagines techniques far beyond those Rousseau would have attempted, such as "Newspeak." Nevertheless, the purpose of that language—"to narrow the range of thought"—is similar in kind, if not in degree, to what we see in the *Project of a Constitution for Corsica*.[83] Winston's (the hero's) feeling that the man to whom he is listening is "not a real human being but some kind of dummy" recalls the uneasy feeling that some of Saint-Preux's statements, or Emile's, give us.[84] Sex is feared and repressed. A "Junior Anti-Sex League" promotes "cleanmind-edness." The repression of sexual activity and the restriction of marriages among Party members is on a different plane from the similar control among the servants at Clarens, but the aims are identical: to displace the pleasure drives from their egocentric focus and to prevent "loyalties which it [i.e., the Party, or rulers] might not be able to control." [85] Therefore the members' sex drives are damped down "by careful early conditioning, by games and cold water, . . . by lectures, parades, songs, slogans, and martial music." [86] Emile is spared the second group of these techniques in the control of his sexuality, but they are put to work for other social purposes, as in *Considerations on the Government of Poland*. Recreations are all communal, and as in *Brave New World* a taste for solitude is considered dangerous individualism.[87]

While Rousseau places greater emphasis, perhaps, on the conditioning process than on the inquisitorial process, the latter does exist both in *La Nouvelle Héloïse* and in *Emile*, as well as in the provisions for surveillance of citizens. Could not Orwell's description of the "scientist of today" as a "mixture of psychologist and inquisitor, studying with extraordinary minuteness the meaning of facial expressions, gestures, and tones of voice" [88] be easily applied to Wolmar, *"the living eye,"* and to the ever-observant, ever-prying tutor? But the leaders of *Nineteen Eighty-Four* also realize that the problem "is educational. . . . It is a problem of continuously molding the consciousness." [89] Elaborate mental training is undergone in childhood. "Private emotions" are conditioned out, so that all emotion is focused on the State. Reflection is bypassed; the right-thinking citizen will know, "without taking thought, what is the true belief or the desirable emotion." [90] How coincidental, too, that one purpose of the conditioning is, just as in Wolmar's system, to control memory! [91] As for refractory individuals, " 'We do not merely destroy our enemies; we *change* them. . . . We capture [the enemy's] inner mind, we *reshape* him. . . . We bring him over to our side . . . genuinely, heart and soul.' " [92] This is precisely what Wolmar did with Saint-Preux.

The ideal of the society in *Nineteen Eighty-Four* is "a nation of warriors and fanatics, marching forward in perfect unity, all thinking the same thoughts. . . ." [93] While the State claims to have liberated the common people from bondage, they are really considered to be "natural inferiors who must be kept in subjection"—"like animals," Orwell adds, in contrast to Rousseau's thought, "like children." [94] Another significant analogy is that in both imaginary societies the leaders take care not to instruct the masses in the philosophy underlying the political and social system; it is enough that they be instilled with patriotism and loyalty.[95] These loyalties replace individual relationships.[96] This aspect of *Nineteen Eighty-Four* makes us think particularly of Wolmar's domain, but it is present in Rousseau's later political treatises. In writing for Corsica Rousseau might well have said, "a hierarchical society was only possible on a basis of poverty and ignorance," except that his hierarchy is dissimulated.[97] "It had long been realized," writes Orwell, "that the only secure basis for oligarchy is collectivism." [98]

Control of minds, wills, and emotions is as important, then, in *Nineteen Eighty-Four* as in Rousseau's ideal world, and even more ruthlessly pursued. " 'We create human nature,' " says O'Brien; [99] Rousseau "forms" citizens. In Orwell's novel as in Huxley's the rebellious individual is defeated. (In *La Nouvelle Héloïse*, a far more profound psychological work, Wolmar, the "guide," is defeated at the end: he began too late.) Orwell's

rebellious Julia affirms: " 'They can make you say anything . . . but they can't make you believe it. They can't
get inside you.' " [100] This is also true of Wolmar's relationship
with his Julie, as he finally learns—to quote the words of Orwell's Winston: "The inner heart, whose workings were mysteri-
ous even to yourself, remained impregnable." [101] But Winston
will discover that *he* is mistaken.

The test to which Saint-Preux is submitted with Laura is
something like Winston's testing by O'Brien: both men are
required to go against their real convictions and substitute another judgment for their own, as in the *Social Contract*. O'Brien
tells Winston that this is done to cure him and make him
sane—i.e., to make possible his reintegration. These are also
Wolmar's motives.

Winston learns, from a book he comes upon, that by comparison with his society "all the tyrannies of the past were half-
hearted and inefficient." In past ages "the ruling groups were
always infected to some extent by liberal ideas, and were
content . . . to regard only the overt act, and to be uninterested
in what their subjects were thinking." [102] In other words, there
was always some pluralism, some dissent, some lack of surrender
to a unanimous will. And this was so partly because there was no
way to keep the "citizens under constant surveillance," and
partly because the leaders did not know how to "manipulate
public opinion" so as to establish "not only complete obedience
to the will of the State [i.e., in actions], but complete uniformity
of opinion." [103] If we eliminate from the above sequence of
thoughts and quotations two words, "tyrannies" and "liberal,"
which (for different reasons) are inappropriate, everything else
might easily have been written by Rousseau, and would have
been subscribed to by him.

Revolt is impossible in *Nineteen Eighty-Four*, not only because "there is no way in which discontent can become articu-
late," but because the people have no possibilities of comparison
with other ways of life. [104] They are cut off, like the Corsicans,
both from the past and from other countries. The fact that
leadership is not hereditary, but rises from the ranks, neutralizes

opposition. More positively, the image of the "semi-divine leader" (cf. Rousseau's description of the Legislator) is cultivated. Knowledge, wisdom, happiness, and virtue come from following his inspiration.[105]

The rulers must wield power because man is what he is. "Men in the mass were frail, cowardly creatures who could not endure liberty or face the truth." The resulting political philosophy therefore postulates that it became necessary for them to be "systematically deceived by others who were stronger than themselves." The "choice for mankind lay between freedom and happiness"; and, "for the great bulk of mankind, happiness was better." [106]

This *was* Rousseau's philosophy; but, by a twist of Orwell's ironic genius, it turns out that this is *not* the real philosophy of *Nineteen Eighty-Four*, after all. According to Orwell, to use power in Rousseau's fashion, in order to bring about a paradise, a just and happy society, is self-delusion. The real object of power is power. " 'Power is power over human beings. Over the body —but, above all, over the mind.' " [107] So it was, I believe, consciously or more probably unconsciously, for Rousseau, tormented and rejected by men and women all his life. That is why he chose the prophetic vocation and dreamed all his dream worlds. In them, godlike, he controls men and women and shapes them as he wills, even as Orwell puts it: " 'Power is in tearing human minds to pieces and putting them together again in new shapes of your own choosing.' " [108] But his conscience was secure; for his dreams had no self-serving or sadistic ends. He would have used power to be a savior; he loved Man (if not men), and was showing them the *only* way—*his* way—to happiness. Man must, in O'Brien's words, be " 'saved from himself.' " [109]

Walden Two is the serious imagining of one of America's leading modern behaviorists, who has been interested in the prediction and control of behavior. Very much like Rousseau (although the *institutions* are entirely different), he creates a society of equality, happiness, and justice, one in which freedom is apparently preserved, even while everything is "guided" by a system of partly unseen controls. As Frazier—the Wolmar of *Walden Two,* a genius or godlike figure who manipulates the others—puts it, " 'We enjoy seeming to be free' " [110]—a statement which epitomizes Rousseau's worlds. In the societies of both authors men are "free" and "docile." Skinner, like Rousseau, is acutely conscious of man's aggressive egoism in society. " 'Each of us is engaged in a pitched battle with the rest of mankind.' " [111] If previous utopias have failed, it is because they were planned to allow men's natural goodness to assert itself. " 'What more can you ask for as an explanation of failure?' " [112] The government must " 'accept the responsibility for building the sort of behavior needed for a happy State.' " [113] Both rely on conditioning and indoctrination, and to a lesser extent on incentives, while they exclude the "technological" methods of control envisioned by Huxley and Orwell. To their properly conditioned citizens co-operative, rather than selfishly competitive, living is "natural." In both societies men have been "made over" into social beings. *Walden Two* is the least exploitative of the four, but the goal of efficiency is as important there as in the others. [114] Skinner's *apparent* belief, like Rousseau's, is that a badly organized society is responsible for what is wrong with people. The *real,* though tacit, assumption, however, is that it is *people* who are wrong for *society.* That is why the main thrust in all these works goes beyond the creation of new institutions to the remaking of people. The reorganization of society is really determined by this main preoccupation. " 'In the long run, *man is determined by the State.'* " [115]

Like Rousseau, Frazier finds that " 'there are a lot of things about the way we're all living now that are completely insane,' " and so he invents a rational society. [116] Not forgetting that rational plans and human nature are antithetical, he realizes that complete control over men is necessary, and that it can be acquired only by remaking them. " 'Nothing short of that will produce a *permanent* social structure.' " [117] Both Rousseau and

Skinner are convinced that reform is utterly futile: "Political action [is] of no use in building a better world"; instead, " 'you must operate on a different level entirely.' " [118] In fact, " 'nothing short of the complete revision of a culture would suffice.' " [119] The programs are revolutionary, in Huxley's—or Rousseau's— sense of the word. " 'We can now deal with human behavior in accordance with simple scientific principles.' " [120] This was Rousseau's grand scheme in *La morale sensitive:* if only "we knew how to force the animal economy to favor the moral order which it upsets so often!" [121] We can, says Frazier, " 'change human behavior. . . . We can *make* men adequate for group behavior.' " [122] We remember Rousseau's statement: *"Il faut former des hommes, former des citoyens."* [123]

Frazier, too, is impelled to build " 'a co-operative society,' " one in which men can live together without fighting and get what they need without hurting each other. [124] His group will be small, isolated, and almost autarchic—possessing the three qualities desired by Rousseau. Life in Walden Two is simple, without luxury, without unnecessary professions. Theoretically, all men are equal; but inevitably there are those who guide and manage, and those who are guided and managed. There is no leisure class; all must do physical labor—as in the *Project of a Constitution for Corsica.* At this initial stage the workers choose their activities; in another generation, however, they will not be free to select their jobs: " 'our educational system will see to that.' " [125] (Again we have that interesting, indeed sinister, use of the word "education," and, as in the other utopias, the ultimate disposing of the lives of others.)

In this utopia, *égalité* and *fraternité* (if not *liberté*), and the Golden Age have all come true. [126] There are no troubles, no boredom, no fatigue. The competitive spirit has been excised, " 'thanks to a special bit of cultural engineering.' " [127] Individuals " 'are *seldom compared.'* " [128] People have only unselfish motives. [129] There is the usual revulsion against the world of books. Although the inmates are free to write, one wonders what there is to write about in paradise, in a world without aggressive and competitive drives, without ethical or political judgments. Music and art, on the other hand, are encouraged, doubtless on the assumption that they do not lead to intellectual independence.

The whole society of *Walden Two* rests on a system of denaturing and restructuring men, largely by operant conditioning and habituation. This is called, variously, "human engineering," "behavioral engineering," "cultural engineering," "social engineering." Society, reasons Frazier, " 'attacks early, when the individual is helpless. It enslaves him almost before he has tasted freedom.' " But it does a bad job, because it fails to induce him to behave in the way that is best for the group.[130] This is now the job of Frazier-Wolmar, the behavioral engineer. He will " 'shape the behavior of the members of a group so that they will function smoothly for the benefit of all.' "[131]

The behaviorist tends to diminish the importance of heredity; Frazier admits it cannot be overcome. One feels his regret, his implied preference for Helvétius' view, but then, with this statement heredity is forgotten and he does pretty much as he wants. Coercion is avoided. " 'We don't use force. All we need is adequate behavioral engineering.' "[132] Exactly like Rousseau, Frazier says that through coercion we can control a person's acts, but not his desires to behave in certain ways. And unless the latter is accomplished, " 'We haven't really altered his potential behavior at all.' "[133] Difficult with adults (as we saw in the case of Saint-Preux), conditioning is easy with children. We know, comments Frazier, that behavior is determined by the seeking of pleasure and the avoidance of pain. " 'If it's in our power to create any of the situations he likes or to remove any situation he doesn't like, we can control his behavior. . . . As a result, the probability that he will behave that way again goes up.' "[134] Frazier's procedure, which is precisely like that of Emile's tutor, is to " 'set up certain behavioral processes which will lead the individual to design his own good conduct.' " But control " 'always rests . . . in the hands of society.' "[135] Here, too, overt punishment is eschewed, as the child is made receptive to the impersonal necessity of things.[136] Each child is watched carefully to see how he reacts. Eventually, but gradually, control is transferred to the child himself (after he has been conditioned to the proper reflexive reactions) and to other members of the group.

Marriage has been reduced to a physical relationship (to avoid rivalry and aggression?). Indeed, it is noteworthy that in all three modern utopias there is a deep underlying fear of love between man and woman—as there was in Rousseau's. We are assured that the psychic dimension of sexuality is not really important and that sexual aggressiveness " 'is no more *natural* than quarrelsomeness.' " [137] The "science of behavior" replaces the parent-child relationship, exactly as in *Emile*.[138] In fact, the whole pattern of relationships between the sexes, like the individuals themselves, has been "restructured." [139] In general, the sexual drive has (somehow!) been greatly abated in Walden Two. We remember Emile when we read that adolescent boys in Walden Two never find " 'sex amusing or secretly exciting,' " that in fact, they are scarcely interested.[140]

Shall we be surprised if the society of *Walden Two* also operates on the principle of duplicity, or *la main cachée*? Or if we learn that everything "seemed wholly casual, wholly haphazard," whereas it really is all planned in "a comprehensive, almost Machiavellian design"? [141] Here, too, "everyone seemed to be enjoying extraordinary freedom, while the efficacy of the whole is preserved." [142] Again, we find the idea that, if people are made to *want* to do unpleasant work, they will no longer find it unpleasant.

> We can achieve a sort of control under which the controlled, though they are following a code much more scrupulously than was ever the case under the old system, nevertheless *feel free*. They are doing what they want to do. . . . By a careful cultural design, we control not the final behavior, but the *inclination* to behave—the motives, the desires, the wishes. The curious thing is that in that case the question of freedom never arises. . . . [Men] never strike against forces that make them *want* to act the way they do.[143]

In *Walden Two* the society is "free," because there is no forceful restraint—only hidden control. In fact, " 'we increase the feeling of freedom,' " adds Frazier. " 'Our members are practically al-

ways doing what they want to do—what they "choose" to do—
but we see to it that they want to do precisely the things which
are best for themselves and the community. Their behavior is determined, yet they are free.' " [144]

In these passages we have a remarkable phenomenon, surely
—not only an exact duplication of certain important aspects of
Rousseau's thinking (capturing of wills, hidden control, and
especially the paradox of "freedom and docility"), but almost, in
the last quotation, duplication of his words. The response to all
this duplicity is given by Castle, Frazier's adversary in the dialogue: " 'I can't believe you can really get freedom and spontaneity through a system of tyrannical control.' " [145] Furthermore,
although an illusion of privacy is carefully fostered and one can
be alone, both public and private interpersonal conduct is under
constant surveillance by psychologists.

The citizens of Walden Two vote, too, but only after being
instructed by a "Political Manager" in what their interests
(which are " 'all alike' ") are. [146] This is quite familiar—the
"guide" and the vote as a ritual consecration of unanimity and an
act of commitment (perhaps also as part of the illusion of freedom). Elsewhere we are told that voting has a point to it only in
a small meeting, " 'especially on a yes-or-no question.' " [147]
Throughout *Walden Two* runs distrust of the people as incapable and unworthy of having a real voice in deciding who is to
govern them, and how. [148] They are children, to be led and
trained. " 'The only thing that matters is one's day-to-day happiness and a secure future.' " [149] Moreover, we are told, there is no
"propaganda" in Frazier's society: " 'Walden II must be *naturally* satisfying' "! [150]

We are also told that there is no guide or leader. Actually,
Frazier is the master puppeteer behind the scenes. Along with
him is a group of hidden Planners. " 'We deliberately conceal
the planning and managerial machinery.' " [151] Frazier laughs at
questions about such things as the dignity and integrity of the
individual. Castle accuses him of being " 'an artist in power,
whose greatest art is to conceal art.' " [152] This is precisely what
Rousseau has said about the Legislator.

In his mind Frazier compares himself to God: " 'I look upon my work, and behold, it is good.' " [153] But he is more powerful and successful, he thinks, than God. He is forced finally to admit all this. " 'Of course I'm not indifferent to power! And I like to play God. . . . These are my children. . . . I love them.' " [154] Frazier, or Wolmar-Rousseau—it is pretty much the same.

The result of all this, claims Frazier, is a uniformly pleasant social existence, amazing economic efficiency, complete devotion to the community, and readiness to sacrifice for it. In each mind, one law is written: " 'We must always think of the whole group.' " [155] Just as Rousseau had demanded, no one thinks of himself except as part of the group. Individuals think not of personal triumph over others, but only of " 'triumph over nature and over oneself.' " [156] There is not the slightest desire for domination. How could it be otherwise, when the citizens have been deeply instilled with a " 'social conscience' "—the conscience of the *moi commun?* [157] People, instead of engaging in a wild chase for pleasure, are content with satisfying their needs.

While there is not quite a "civil religion" in Walden Two, Frazier has " 'borrowed some of the practices of organized religion—to inspire group loyalty and strengthen the observance of the Code.' " [158]

Castle points out to Frazier that he has substituted artful compulsion for intelligence and initiative; no spontaneous change of course is possible. To this Frazier replies: " 'What the plan does is to keep intelligence on the right track, for the good of society rather than of the intelligent individual.' " [159] There is only one right way.[160] When cornered, Frazier is forced to admit to an *idée fixe*, that of controlling human behavior.[161]

In our democracies, claims Frazier, " 'it's not the will of the people, . . . it's the will of the majority. . . . My heart goes out to the everlasting minority.' " [162] He does not consider the fact that in liberal societies the right of the majority over minorities (or over individuals) is not unlimited. In his society unanimity is so engineered that no minority is possible—just as Rousseau would have it. There are no rights of dissent or opposition, though protest, at least, is allowed. *Laissez-faire* democracy must be disposed of—a goal justified by the equality and the just society that will result.

Frazier rails against "power politics," gliding over the fact that his molding of men is power in its most absolute (and to many, its most obnoxious) form. He is against "propaganda," but all for manipulation of opinion. For both Skinner and Rousseau the latter technique is basic. And how remarkably like Rousseau's way of thinking is a statement like this: " 'The Russians are still a long way from a culture in which people behave as they *want* to behave, for their mutual good.' " [163] What is here assumed is a "real will" of the people, a "true self," identical with the *volonté générale* and the *moi commun*. Skinner, too, wants to " 'build the Superorganism,' " and to " 'increase the natural power of the community by leaps and bounds.' " [164]

Walden Two is not a static society, Frazier asserts. The sciences of behavior march on. Greater perfection may be expected in the design of personalities, in the control of temperaments and motivations. Again drawing close to Helvétius' type of behaviorism, he predicts that behavioral control will make people mathematicians or musicians, even if they are born without any ability. [165]

One of the defects of *Walden Two* is the uneasy feeling it gives us of disposing very lightly of deep-seated drives, aggressions, and antagonisms. There is a convenient and absolute suspension of all human forces and differentiae that would disrupt Frazier's perfect harmony. This is one fault of which Rousseau cannot be accused. In *La Nouvelle Héloïse,* for instance, we see resistances and relapses in the socialization process. Skinner's work is also quite vague; a few principles and general examples are only superficially touched upon. Rousseau, on the other hand, describes precise situations and the experiences of individuals who are in them. Skinner never asks how we can be sure that power will be used for the general welfare; he assumes the leaders will never be corrupted by power. [166] Rousseau is aware of this problem, and his doctrine of popular sovereignty does provide an ultimate safeguard against deviation of power for the ends of those who wield it.

Like *Brave New World, Walden Two* creates a pall of homogeneous happiness; no one is frustrated, no one is sad, no one weeps. In this state of blissful euphoria, it is difficult to recognize the subjects as human beings. Is such a state really good for human beings, as Skinner assumes? Even if he could " 'arrange a world in which conflicts do not occur,' " he would deprive us of our deep human need for discontent.[167] Surely one of his subjects, too, will cry out for the right to suffer, if that is the price of making his own destiny and his own self. This complete sense of belonging, of existing in no other dimension—is it justified on the grounds that the inner and outer divisions have been ended? Do we have to pay too high a price to be remade into social beings? No wonder a feeling of repulsion lingers on long after we have escaped from the closed island of *Walden Two*. Like the other societies we have described, it is something of a nightmare, and the thought of drifting back into it keeps us from sleeping.[168]

A significant attitude common to our four utopian systems is aversion to the past and to the idea of historical continuity. In these both revolutionary and rationalistic political systems there is a desire to abolish the past and start anew.[169] Thus, while most of the eighteenth-century *philosophes,* working within the historical context, sought reform and renewal, our utopians scorn reform and consider all of history a long and useless mistake, in which nothing praiseworthy is to be found. Unguided experience is inevitably fatal. Societies have been the "mess" they have always been because there was no Frazier-Wolmar to guide them. We must, then, wipe the slate clean—at least in the minds which our new society will comprise. The lucky citizens of all of these new societies are conditioned to live only in the present. In *Brave New World* the slogan is "Was and will make me ill. I take a gramme and only am." [170] In *Nineteen Eighty-Four* no written records—historical or otherwise—are kept, except as propaganda, for the past would be a barrier to conditioning. "The past had not only been altered, it had been destroyed. . . . History has stopped. Nothing exists except an endless present in which the Party is always right." [171] This is what, on an individual basis, Wolmar had tried to do with Saint-Preux and Julie; it is tacitly assumed in the *Social Contract.*

In none of the other works is hatred of history so savagely and repeatedly expressed as in *Walden Two.* " 'Why don't we just start all over again the right way?' " [172] The book is filled with scorn for history and historical scholarship. Children are cut off from the past. " 'We discourage any sense of history. . . . We don't teach history.' " [173] " 'I have little interest,' " declares Frazier, " 'in conclusions drawn from history.' " [174] The study of history is " 'an honorable snooze.' " [175] The reason given for this aversion is that history is not "scientific"—that is, it does not lead to *predictive laws.* [176] Skinner, like Rousseau, desires and requires human behavior to be reduced to predictable (i.e., manageable) reactions to stimuli. [177]

Beyond the scorn for history, and associated with it, is scorn for philosophy and "rational justification," and for all intellectual pursuits other than the scientific. One of the interlocutors (Burris) is aroused when Castle suggests that Frazier needs a good course in the humanities. Only " 'experimental test' " is valid, " 'experimentation, not reason.' " [178]

Several observations about this attitude seem appropriate at this point. In the first place, Skinner's book is one long "rational justification." In the second place, the *ends* in Walden Two are *rational* decisions, known in advance. There is never any experimenting with them, or any questioning of them. In fact, it is on the basis of *history* that they are assumed to be valid! The " 'Why don't we just start all over again the right way?' " is, as Burke makes plain, the epitome of rationalism in its most fanatical form. Mankind must make a choice, we are told, between freedom and happiness. But, as we have already asked, is it certain that the kind of homogenized happiness described here is more valid, more valuable, than freedom? Is living in harmony the highest good? (The same objections apply, of course, to Rousseau.) In the third place, Skinner takes "scientific" and "unscientific" to be magic words, automatically establishing human truth and falsehood and doing away with all difficulties. It is obvious that no humanist wrote this book: the reduction of "human truth" to predictive laws and reactions is, precisely, destructive of the human. In the fourth place, the "humanities," to which he has such a violent aversion, lead away from absolutes, and are necessarily concerned with individuals primarily and with individual differentiae. They consider individual experience most real, and individuals the center of value. Therefore they are inimical to his tyranny of happiness-efficiency. Skinner undoubtedly senses that the scientific spirit does not lead to political rebellion, while philosophy, history, and literature are considered essential to a "liberal" education because they tend to free the human mind and spirit and offer alternatives to monistic ends and values. If Skinner had been a humanist, he would surely have known the increment of wisdom that comes from a perspective on ourselves as we view ourselves in the light of what has gone before, and from the insights into what men are, have been and done, and can do. He might not, for instance, have denied *homo politicus*. He might have realized that memory of the past—individual and cultural—is specifically and distinctively human. But, as we have seen, he cannot really escape history and frequently calls on it to support his own dream. The truth is that we can learn more about human beings from history than from Skinner.

The dream is that of all utopias, the dream man has long caressed of complete mastery over his own destiny. It is Skinner's dream, it is Rousseau's. Can it be attained? *History* shows us that it is folly to predict limits to human ingenuity and power. But there is also another question. Is the price likely to be an ironic peripeteia, as in tragedy? The complete mastery—will it be autonomy or a complete loss of mastery? The price of triumph over man and the universe may turn out to be the dehumanization of men. Our four utopias all point in this direction. Huxley saw it most clearly. Rousseau, it would seem, was forced to this end despite himself, perhaps without realizing it, as he worked out the destinies of his characters in *La Nouvelle Héloïse* in situations that embody the norms, methods, and goals common to all four.[179]

Notes

[1] For a more complete description and some interesting pages on the formation of the "Rousseau legend," see L. Trénard's informative article "La Diffusion du *Contrat social* (1762–1832)," in *Etudes sur le "Contrat social,"* pp. 425–58; and J. Godechot, *"Le Contrat social* et la Révolution occidentale de 1762 à 1789," in *ibid.*, pp. 393–405.

[2] J. Dehaussy, "La Dialectique de la souveraine liberté dans le *Contrat social,"* p. 140.

[3] *Jugement sur la polysynodie de l'Abbé de Saint-Pierre*, in *Oeuvres,* Hachette edition, V, 348–49. G. H. Sabine has remarked: "The virtues of loyalty and patriotism, which Rousseau chiefly admired, and the glory of finding happiness in the welfare of the group need have no special reference to democracy. It is hard to say whether Rousseau belonged more truly to Jacobin republicanism or to a conservative reaction." (*A History of Political Theory*, p. 579.)

Derathé comments: "Rousseau's politics are static. Our author neither sees nor feels the necessity of modifying or changing legislation by adapting it to the transformations of society." ("Les Rapports de l'exécutif et du législatif," p. 166). It would be more exact to say that for Rousseau the transformations are, if possible, to be avoided, and by every possible means. When we are in Utopia, there is no place to go. Rousseau dreaded change and admired permanence.

[4] See E. Champion, *Jean-Jacques Rousseau et la Révolution française* (Paris, 1909).

[5] See G. H. MacNeil, "The Anti-Revolutionary Rousseau," *American Historical Review*, LVIII (1953), 808–23.

[6] "Adresse d'un citoyen très actif" (MS in Bibliothèque Nationale, Paris, France), n.d., p. 12.

[7] A. Vitry, *Jean-Jacques Rousseau à l'Assemblée Nationale* (Paris, 1789), pp. 38, 41, 50.

[8] C. F. Lenormant, *Jean-Jacques Rousseau, aristocrate* (Paris, 1790), p. 5.

[9] In P. Gudin, *Supplément au "Contrat social"* (Paris, 1791), p. 194.

[10] *Ibid.* Sade, incidentally, called Moses, Lycurgus, and Numa (Rousseau's three heroes) "thought-tyrants."

[11] A. Soboul, "Classes populaires et Rousseauisme sous la Révolution," *Annales historiques de la Révolution française*, XXXIV (1962), 421–38 *passim*.

[12] *Ibid.*

[13] See G. H. MacNeil, "The Cult of Rousseau in the French Revolu-

tion," *Journal of the History of Ideas,* VI (1945), 197–212; and H. Peyre, "The Influence of Eighteenth Century Ideas on the French Revolution," *Journal of the History of Ideas,* X (1949), 63–87. Billaud-Varenne reported the decrees of the Committee of April 20, 1794: "You must entirely refashion a people that you desire to make free—destroy its prejudices, change its habits, limit its needs, eradicate its vices, purify its desires." (Quoted in H. J. Tozer, trans., *The Social Contract,* p. 94.) The analogy with Mao's "cultural revolution" is inescapable. Sparta and the ancient republics were objects of eulogy during the Terror.

[14] A. Soboul, "J.-J. Rousseau et le Jacobinisme," in *Etudes sur le "Contrat social,"* pp. 405–24.

[15] J. Van Eerde and A. Hubbard, "The Christian Religion in the *Grande Encyclopédie* and in *The Great Soviet Encyclopedia,*" in *Saggi filosofici* (Turin), XIV (1964), 21 n.

[16] J. A. Leith, *The Idea of Art as Propaganda in France* (Toronto, 1965), *passim.*

[17] *Emile,* p. 303.

[18] I. Fetscher, "Rousseau's Concepts of Freedom," p. 55.

[19] C. Mazauric, "Le Rousseauisme de Babeuf," p. 439.

[20] *Ibid.,* p. 459.

[21] *Ibid.,* pp. 462–63.

[22] C. E. Vaughan, ed., *Political Writings,* I, 53.

[23] Rousseau's influence in America is not yet clear. We are awaiting Paul Spurlin's study of this subject.

[24] See G. H. Sabine, *A History of Political Theory,* pp. 594–95; G. Vlachos, "L'Influence de Rousseau sur la conception du *Contrat social* chez Kant et Fichte," in *Etudes sur le "Contrat social,"* pp. 459–80; and H. Marcuse, *Reason and Revolution* (London, 1941), pp. 201–5. Among other ideas, J. G. Fichte declares that a new education must produce "strict necessity in the decisions of the will, the opposite being impossible. Such a will can henceforth be relied on with confidence and certainty." (*Addresses* [Chicago: Open Court, 1922], p. 20.) Like Rousseau, Hegel thought the individual will can never *of itself* will the general interest; always ego-centered, it does not contain that universality which would give common ground to both the particular and the general interest. If the individual is to attain freedom, his liberation must come about against his will. What Hegel calls the "civil society" (existing societies) cannot achieve unity or freedom because of its intrinsic contradictions. These ideals can be achieved only by the State (a superior entity that materializes the moral and rational order), whose task is to bring about the perfect unity of the individual and the universal. The individual conscience must be taught not to take individualistic attitudes, but to focus on what it has in common with others. A dialectical synthesis must be brought about to

end the dilemma of choice between the individual and the collective whole.

[25] *The Works of Joseph de Maistre,* trans. J. Lively (New York, 1965), p. 109.

[26] R. E. Herzstein, "German Intellectuals and German Reality, 1789–1933," *Arts and Sciences,* LXVII, No. 22 (May 29, 1967), pp. 37–38.

[27] Quoted in F. Stern, *The Politics of Cultural Despair* (Berkeley, 1961), pp. 51, 259, 277–78.

[28] The foregoing quotations are from Herzstein, "German Intellectuals and German Reality, 1789–1933," pp. 38–39.

[29] The analogy, though valid, is strictly limited by differences of personality and historical conditioning. We must emphasize that Rousseau would have been revolted by Nazism's nihilism and sadistic cruelty.

[30] In this instance (as in many others I do not mention) direct attribution is probable but not certain. No one can measure Rousseau's contribution to the general fund of ideas that have filtered through the modern mind. Nor can anyone evaluate the fact that Fidel Castro was an ardent student of the *Social Contract,* or that it was cited by Eichmann's defense attorney.

[31] S. De Grazia, *The Political Community: A Study of Anomie* (Chicago, 1948).

[32] W. Kendall, *John Locke and the Doctrine of Majority Rule* (Urbana, 1940); "Prolegomena to Any Future Work on Majority Rule," *Journal of Politics,* XII (1950).

[33] E. Barker, *Reflections On Government* (London, 1942), pp. 26, 175, 196.

[34] G. Della Volpe, "Critique marxiste de Rousseau," in *Etudes sur le "Contrat social,"* pp. 503–14. Engels, however, in *Anti-Dühring,* marveled at Rousseau's anticipation of Marx.

[35] G. Besse, "Marx, Engels et le XVIIIᵉ siècle français," in *Studies on Voltaire and the Eighteenth Century,* XXIV (1963), 164.

[36] *Ibid.,* pp. 168–69.

[37] See R. de Lacharrière, "Rousseau et le socialisme," in *Etudes sur le "Contrat social,"* p. 525. This is an important and lucid article.

[38] *Ibid.,* pp. 516–17.

[39] J. Van Eerde and A. Hubbard, "The Christian Religion in the *Grande Encyclopédie* and in *The Great Soviet Encyclopedia,*" p. 21.

[40] G. Della Volpe, "Du *Discours sur l'inégalité* à *l'Etat et la Révolution,*" *Europe,* No. 391–92 (1961), pp. 181–88. See also R. de Lacharrière, "Rousseau et le socialisme." Both B. Gagnebin and M. Launay also affirm that modern "socialism" (i.e., Communism) "issued in part from the theories of Rousseau." (Review of *Oeuvres complètes,* Vol. III [Pléiade edition], in *AJJR,* XXXVI [1963–65], 408–9.)

[41] See "De Rousseau au Communisme," pp. 167–80.

[42] *Ibid.*, p. 177.

[43] *Man and Society, Political and Social Theory*, I, 371–73, 408–16.

[44] B. de Jouvenel, "Rousseau évolutionniste pessimiste," in *Rousseau et la philosophie politique* (Paris, 1965), pp. 1–20.

[45] G. H. Sabine, *A History of Political Theory*, p. 594.

[46] H. J. Tozer, trans., *The Social Contract*, p. 81.

[47] Of course the technical developments of modern science (drugs, television, genetic control), which figure prominently in the twentieth-century utopias, lay outside of his scope. But I am inclined to think, from all we have seen, that he might have incorporated some of them, had they been available to him, into the arsenal of weapons of control which he puts into the hands of his shadowy "guides" or "leaders."

[48] Foreword to *Brave New World* (New York: Harper and Row, Publishers, Incorporated, 1950), p. xxiv.

[49] *Ibid.*, p. xxv.

[50] *Ibid.*, p. xxvii.

[51] Huxley uses two other techniques not to be found in Rousseau: the distribution of happiness drugs and the genetic standardization of "the human product." Contrary to Rousseau, Huxley envisions complete sexual permissiveness or anarchy (which is strictly enforced), as a compensation for the loss of other freedoms and a preventative of personal loyalties.

[52] *Brave New World*, p. 6.

[53] *Ibid.*, p. 14.

[54] *Ibid.*, p. 24.

[55] *Ibid.*, p. 17.

[56] *Ibid.*, pp. 29, 32.

[57] *Ibid.*, p. 47.

[58] *Ibid.*, p. 54.

[59] *Ibid.*, p. 95.

[60] *Ibid.*, p. 105.

[61] *Ibid.*, p. 106.

[62] *Ibid.*, p. 107.

[63] *Ibid.*, p. 110.

[64] *Ibid.*, p. 176.

[65] *Ibid.*, p. 263. Emile's tutor says: "You promise to be docile, and I promise to use this docility only to make you the happiest of men." (*Emile*, p. 406.)

[66] *Brave New World*, p. 213.

[67] *Ibid.*, p. 264.

[68] *Ibid.*, p. 269.

[69] *Ibid.*, p. 270.

[70] *Ibid.*, p. 272.

[71] *Ibid.*, p. 282.

[72] *Ibid.*, p. 274.
[73] *Ibid.*, p. 279.
[74] *Ibid.*, p. 285.
[75] *Ibid.*, p. 287.
[76] *Ibid.*, p. 288.

[77] Professor Gregor Sebba (in a private communication) suggests that the leader of the Brave New World has very much the same intellectual constitution as Rousseau's Legislator, whom only his ultimate success distinguishes from the fraud. Dr. Sebba suggests that it would be illuminating to compare the treatment of the betrayer of Rousseau's civic religion with those leaders of the Brave New World who are becoming affected [infected?] by the arts and ideas—a problem which also worried Rousseau, who knew that with the printing press ideas cannot be kept out indefinitely.

[78] G. Orwell, *Nineteen Eighty-Four* (New York, 1949), p. 36. Elsewhere Orwell describes "doublethink" as the use of "conscious deception while retaining the firmness of purpose that goes with complete honesty." (*Ibid.*, p. 215.) This description applies to Rousseau's tutor.

[79] *Ibid.*, p. 36. We scarcely need add that it was not unknown in Rousseau's own conduct, as in his apology for abandoning his children, or certain episodes of the "affair at the Hermitage."

[80] *Ibid.*, p. 217.
[81] *Ibid.*, p. 270.
[82] *Ibid.*, pp. 43–44.
[83] *Ibid.*, p. 53.

[84] *Ibid.*, p. 55. Thus when Winston calls his wife "the human sound track," we think, for instance, of Emile's closing words.

[85] *Ibid.*, p. 65.
[86] *Ibid.*, p. 68.
[87] *Ibid.*, p. 81.
[88] *Ibid.*, p. 194.
[89] *Ibid.*, p. 209.
[90] *Ibid.*, p. 212.
[91] *Ibid.*, p. 252.
[92] *Ibid.*, pp. 256, 258.
[93] *Ibid.*, p. 74.
[94] *Ibid.*, p. 71.

[95] *Ibid.*, and p. 157: "The world-view of the Party imposed itself most successfully on people incapable of understanding it."

[96] *Ibid.*, p. 166.

[97] *Ibid.*, p. 191. Unlike Rousseau, Orwell realizes that there is no return to an agricultural society.

[98] *Ibid.*, p. 207.
[99] *Ibid.*, p. 272.

[100] *Ibid.,* p. 167.
[101] *Ibid.,* p. 168.
[102] *Ibid.,* p. 206.
[103] *Ibid.,* pp. 206–7.
[104] *Ibid.,* pp. 208, 214.
[105] *Ibid.,* pp. 198, 209.
[106] *Ibid.,* p. 265 (for all the quotations in this paragraph).
[107] *Ibid.,* pp. 266, 267.
[108] *Ibid.,* p. 270.
[109] *Ibid.,* p. 271.
[110] *Walden Two* (New York, 1948), p. 68.
[111] *Ibid.,* p. 85. Also: Competitiveness is " 'incompatible with the good of all mankind.' " (pp. 247–48.)
[112] *Ibid.,* p. 129. Liberal democracy is " 'based on a scientifically invalid conception of man.' " (p. 227.) In Skinner's vocabulary "scientific" is a "loaded" word that includes the implication "true."
[113] *Ibid.,* p. 137. After all, what people want is security and freedom from responsibility. (pp. 138–39.)
[114] Modern economic technology, as in the other modern utopias, is fully utilized.
[115] *Ibid.,* p. 227. Rousseau's belief is identical.
[116] *Ibid.,* p. 3.
[117] *Ibid.,* p. 163. (Italics added.) As we shall later note, history is surpassed and abolished.
[118] *Ibid.,* pp. 9, 161.
[119] *Ibid.,* p. 260.
[120] *Ibid.,* p. 163.
[121] *Confessions,* in *Oeuvres,* Pléiade edition, p. 409.
[122] *Walden Two,* p. 163.
[123] Frazier later says: " 'The potency of behavioral engineering can scarcely be overestimated. . . . We could teach our children to be satisfied with a very limited and rigorous existence.' " (*Ibid.,* p. 172.)
[124] *Ibid.,* pp. 84, 4. Cf. the second *Discourse.*
[125] *Ibid.,* p. 48.
[126] *Ibid.,* pp. 74–75.
[127] *Ibid.,* p. 73.
[128] *Ibid.,* p. 104. (Italics added.) Rousseau judges the competitive instincts to be highly useful, when re-educated and directed toward the communal interests. Frazier, however, does use emulation.
[129] *Ibid.,* p. 200.
[130] *Ibid.,* p. 85.
[131] *Ibid.,* p. 145.
[132] *Ibid.,* p. 134. There are rules, however, such as not talking to outsiders about the Community, not gossiping, not giving thanks or

expressing sympathy. Some might consider these practices dehumanizing, but Skinner *wants* to "denature" man.

[133] *Ibid.,* p. 217.

[134] *Ibid.,* p. 216.

[135] *Ibid.,* p. 86.

[136] A toss of the coin determines which are the lucky children who may eat and which must wait.

[137] *Walden Two,* p. 109.

[138] *Ibid.,* p. 117. Unlike Skinner, however, Rousseau was a strong defender of the family. Either it did not occur to him that the absorption of the individual into the collective whole might conflict with the *volonté particulière* of a lesser whole and with loyalty to it, or, more likely, he preferred not to confront the problem.

[139] *Ibid.,* p. 119.

[140] *Ibid.,* p. 188.

[141] *Ibid.,* p. 95.

[142] *Ibid.,* p. 96.

[143] *Ibid.,* pp. 218–19. (Italics added.)

[144] *Ibid.,* p. 247.

[145] *Ibid.,* p. 105. Deception is used also in dealing with the outside world. (*Ibid.,* p. 167.)

[146] *Ibid.,* p. 164.

[147] *Ibid.,* p. 221.

[148] *Ibid.,* pp. 219–25.

[149] *Ibid.,* p. 225.

[150] *Ibid.,* p. 175.

[151] *Ibid.,* p. 196.

[152] *Ibid.,* p. 210.

[153] *Ibid.,* p. 246.

[154] *Ibid.,* pp. 249–50.

[155] *Ibid.,* p. 132.

[156] *Ibid.,* p. 92.

[157] *Ibid.,* p. 124.

[158] *Ibid.,* p. 166. At the meetings psychologists are the priests!

[159] *Ibid.,* p. 212.

[160] *Ibid.,* p. 214. He also makes the unwarranted assumption that people are as controlled in present societies as in his. Later on, Castle shows that regimentation, though " 'pretty cleverly concealed,' " is " 'regimentation just the same.' " Frazier's answer is, again, that we are all regimented. (pp. 256–57.)

[161] *Ibid.,* p. 240.

[162] *Ibid.,* p. 223.

[163] *Ibid.,* p. 230.

[164] *Ibid.,* p. 244.

[165] *Ibid.,* pp. 243–44.

[166] He touches once on the question, but his answer is both sophistical and a *petitio principii.* (*Ibid.,* pp. 226–27.)

[167] *Ibid.,* p. 133.

[168] A distinguished biologist, René Dubos, declares that the desire "to provide man with a sheltered environment in which he is protected as completely as possible from traumatic experiences" is dangerous, "because of the fact that many important traits of man's nature cannot develop normally, or remain in a healthy state, without constant stimulation and challenge. . . . While emotional neutrality minimizes social conflicts, the consequences of an excessively sheltered life are certainly unfavorable in the long run." ("Science and Man's Nature," *The Graduate Journal* [Austin], VII [1965], 57–58.) Personal happiness, love and freedom, the desire for adventure and change, for individual experience and variety of experiences—these are inherent and healthful drives.

[169] This statement must be qualified for Rousseau. It is true for his ideal system. It is not true for the existing societies (Corsica, Poland) to which he applies it, or for corrupted societies which are irredeemable. In regard to the latter, he is extremely conservative and opposed to change.

[170] *Brave New World,* p. 104. The "gramme" refers to "soma," the happiness pill.

[171] *Nineteen Eighty-Four,* p. 106.

[172] *Walden Two,* p. 4.

[173] *Ibid.,* pp. 196, 198.

[174] *Ibid.,* p. 102.

[175] *Ibid.,* p. 257.

[176] *Ibid.,* p. 199. In other words, since it does not use scientific techniques, history is only falsehood.

[177] Ironically, Frazier not infrequently finds it useful to refer to history to make a point, but takes the curse off it when he does so: " 'I'm not a historian'—Frazier laughed explosively—'quite the contrary.' " (*Ibid.,* p. 222.) He does quote the history of science as predictive.

[178] *Ibid.,* pp. 144, 145. If Skinner had been less scornful, he might not have made the naïve and antiquated error of arguing against individual and political freedom by denying freedom of will.

[179] It would not be difficult to go beyond the genre of utopian fiction and find interesting similarities, of more than casual character, between Rousseau's thought and modern analyses of authoritarian institutions. Those who are familiar with *La Nouvelle Héloïse* will find the following description of the archetypal totalitarian institution, by Erving Goffman, most striking:

> First, there are the *house rules,* a relatively . . . formal set of prescriptions and proscriptions which lay out the main requirements of inmate conduct. These regulations spell out the austere round of life in which

the inmate will operate. . . . *Second,* against the stark background, a small number of clearly defined *rewards or privileges* are held out in exchange for obedience . . . in action and spirit. . . . House rules and privileges provide the functional requirements of the third element in the privilege system: *punishments.* These are designated as the consequence of breaking the rules. One set of these punishments consists of the temporary or permanent withdrawal of privileges or abrogation of the right to try to earn them. In general, the punishments meted out in total institutions are of an order more severe than anything encountered by the inmate in his home world. . . . One mode of adaptation to the setting of a total institution is that of *conversion.* The inmate appears to take over completely the official or staff view of himself and tries to act out the role of the perfect inmate [Saint-Preux]. . . . Every total institution . . . seems to develop . . . a set of institutionalized practices through which staff and inmates come together closely enough so that each may have an image of the other that is somewhat favorable. . . . Instead of differences between the two levels, we will then find that unity, solidarity and joint commitment to the institution are expressed. In form, these institutionalized get-togethers are characterized by a release from the formalities and task orientation that govern inmate-staff contacts and by a softening of the usual chain of command. . . . these activities represent "role releases." . . . A somewhat different type of institutional ceremony is found in the *annual party* (sometimes held more than once a year) at which staff and inmates "mix" through standard forms of sociability, such as commensalism, party games or dancing. At such times, staff and inmates will have the license to "take liberties" across the caste line. . . . Often a high-ranking officer attends as a symbol of management and (it is hoped) of the whole establishment. He dresses well, is moved by the occasion, and gives smiles. . . . his interaction with inmates will take a special benign form; inmates are likely to show embarrassment and respect, and he is likely to display an avuncular interest in them. . . . A final note should be added about these institutional ceremonies. They tend to occur with well-spaced periodicity and to give rise to some social excitement. All the groupings in the establishment join in and have a place regardless of rank or position, but a place that expresses this position. . . .

(From M. R. Stein, A. J. Vidich, and D. M. White, eds., *Identity and Anxiety: Survival of the Person in a Mass Society* [Glencoe, 1960], pp. 456–76. Copyright © 1960 by The Free Press, a Corporation. Reprinted by permission of The Macmillan Company.)

4. Conclusion

Our discussion of influences and analogues will not have been idle if it can lead us to a general conclusion. Just as psychologists and sociologists have arrived at an empirically grounded model of the authoritarian personality, I think we may, without too much risk, speak of a model or archetype of the totalitarian society. Such a society incarnates the authoritarian's attitude toward men and the world. Moreover, if we accept these two models—of the authoritarian personality and the totalitarian society—it will be manifest, I feel, from a consideration of Rousseau's character and thought, that he presents a classic example of both.

From the endless variety of institutions in the various totalitarian societies of the past and the present—these are historical contingencies—four basic points may be derived that constitute the archetype.

First, there is the charismatic "guide" or "leader." Superior to the others, his voice is the voice of the general will, or the voice of the people. He knows their will, and "informs" them of it. He gives them their laws, controls or manages (secretly, as far as possible) their opinions and way of living. He treats the people like children, and they love and/or respect and fear him. Often he tends to assume a semi-divine, or superhuman image: consider Moses, Lycurgus, Numa; Wolmar, Emile's tutor, the anonymous leaders and lawgivers in the *Social Contract* and *Project of a Constitution for Corsica;* and, different though they are in character, Hitler, Stalin, Mao Tse-Tung.[1] *Brave New World* has its World Controller, *Nineteen Eighty-Four* its Big Brother, and *Walden Two* its Frazier, the all-wise scientist-leader embodying the mythos of our own time. Rousseau's ideal communities need such a figure at their inception; in none of these communities, nor in any of the others mentioned, is any clear provision made for this figure's succession, but the spirit of the institutions has its own momentum and persistence, its own requirements. In a total body, in which the parts have lost their autonomy, somewhere there must be a brain, a prime mover, whether his role is to establish the society or to keep it going. Apparently, there must also be someone who is the magnet and receptacle into which drain the affections of the parts—loyalty, love, fear, respect, confidence.

Second, there is an ideal of Community. It expresses itself in a more or less fictitious idea of equality—equality principally in the sense that all give devoted, unlimited sacrifice to the collective Whole and are part of its body. Sometimes, but not necessarily, a fictitious ideal of equality in wealth or in status is created —that is, a classless society. But nearly always the idea of "equal" or "classless" has the sense that exploitation by selfish group interests and egoistic individuals is (theoretically) eliminated; anything required by the State is for the good of all, and so is not exploitation.

Third is the precept and goal of unanimity. As there is only one right way, there can be only one will. All those who are not in agreement with this will are in error, and, if they persist, are criminal and must surrender or be crushed. This unanimity is, in turn, a condition for harmony. All, being parts of the collective "body," work in different ways, in an organic society, toward the common end. That is why neither Wolmar's treatment of his servants and workers nor the biological or psychological preparation for subaltern roles in more recent works is "exploitation." The Community, Collectivity, or State, embodying the real will of all, cannot exploit.[2]

Finally, there are the numerous techniques, applied individually or *en masse,* to mobilize and control the minds, wills, and emotions of the people. For their own good the people, wickedly selfish or irresponsible and child-like, must be the subjects of such a process. All would accept Rousseau's dictum: "He who dares to undertake to found a people must feel himself able to change, so to speak, human nature." The basic methods are the same, except that modern technology offers wider, more refined, and perhaps eventually more complete techniques of control. The reading of history, as well as of political utopias, shows us that once this process is started, it tends to become all-pervasive, and theoretical restrictions become meaningless.[3] As far as possible, the people are to remain unaware of the processes of control. They think they are being told the truth, they are made to think they are free: at least this is the intent of those who are actually in control of power.

This model also answers the rather idle question of whether we can describe an eighteenth-century political philosophy as "totalitarian." The fact that the word did not exist does not prevent that which it describes from having existed, prior to the word, any more than it does the man whose mind and personality expressed that philosophy. For I again say that without the man and specifically his personality type the philosophy could not have existed. Rousseau had virtually all the characteristics of what we now describe as the "authoritarian personality."[4] Because he needed to reassure himself, and to show others that he was not an inferior being, he put on the messianic robes. Going off, as he describes it, into the realm of fantasy that was always more real and more precious to him than reality, he locked himself in his own world, a private utopian world, in which by an ego-defensive projection he identified himself with the leaders of ideal fictitious structures. About his projections he felt, and expressed, dogmatic certainty. There was only one way to redemption—the way he was showing to mankind. He had the truth.

Deep in his mind lay the unending and unfulfilled dream of going back, of recapturing innocence and the happiness of beginnings. When he and Mme. de Warens went to Les Charmettes, he recalls, "Oh, Maman, I said to that dear one, kissing her and flooding her with tears of tenderness and joy, this is the place of happiness and innocence."[5] In his utopian world a kind of innocence is recaptured. By inducing reflexive virtue, by shaping people's minds and emotions into inner unity and harmony, the necessity of doubt and choice, and therefore conflict, is eliminated. Equality and happiness are regained by the complete sublimation of natural independence and the elimination of the partial dependence of our societies. Men compete no longer to hurt each other, but only to show their devotion and sacrifice for the Whole of which they feel themselves equal and fraternal parts. Unity and harmony prevail among men and within each man. Society, Rousseau was sure, had deformed men. Society, he dreamed, could re-form them. The fall and the redemption. And he was the savior, showing the way.

Rousseau's personality was complex. He was an "anarchist," or at least an outsider, in his own society. He was also a revolutionary, a Christ-like Legislator (in his fantasies), an authoritarian (in his thinking). All these aspects are closely related and not subject to dissociation. Thus the anarchist dreams of a society to which he can truly belong, and that society requires a complete revolution; the revolution involves concepts that are typical of the way of thinking of the authoritarian personality—that is, both "submission to the yoke" (a favorite phrase of Rousseau's)—and the benevolent molding of others by a supreme figure, or guide, into whom he projects himself.

This is not to say that for Rousseau, personally, the political solution was the only possible one. For him there was also the possibility of rejecting society, even the one of his own creation, and retreating into an autarchic isolation. In *Emile* he considers it for a moment, and in the *Rêveries du promeneur solitaire* he surrenders to it. But his surrender was reluctant, a last resort, and certainly it was not what he could suggest as a general solution.

Sometimes it is claimed that Rousseau was an individualist, that he respected the sacredness of individuality. After our examination, in the preceding chapters, of his thought as expressed in several of his works, one might be tempted to oppose this claim outright. But it is, in fact, a half-truth. His *own* individuality is sacred. Constantly he exalts it, makes himself the center of the world, a witness to the generations and judge of mankind, God's scourge and minister. He *does* praise the independence of natural man, but states that it is worthless outside the state of nature; and he *does* urge independence from "opinion"—but only in our existing false societies and, even then, only for men, not women. In the organic society he devises, the "controllers" of opinion strive for unanimity.[6] To write that it is easier to conceive of Rousseau's turning his back to society and stalking out into the woods than submitting to control is to fail utterly to understand the intricacies of his personality, especially its dynamics of dependence and independence.

Too often critics have been led astray by Rousseau's ambiguity of language and the duplicity of the situations he creates. *La Nouvelle Héloïse* is not, as we read, the realm of happiness, but that of unhappiness. *Emile* is not, as we read, an education for freedom, but a masterpiece of human engineering in which the definition of freedom is unhesitating, reflexive conformity to pre-set values and modes of behavior.[7] The *Social Contract* is not the outline of a free society, but the blueprint for a freely regimented society. Let us not forget that in Rousseau's State free inquiry and discussion are to be suppressed in the name of freedom, or that equality is a goal which justifies a vast system of oppression and violation of the individual mind and soul—a system which alone can ensure the apparent equality. Nowhere does Rousseau allow men a significant measure of freedom to create their own destiny, to be really self-determining—not in *Emile,* not in *La Nouvelle Héloïse,* not in the political writings. The people will be sovereign; but their destiny is decided by the leadership (clearly implied in the *Social Contract* and stipulated in the later writings), which controls opinion, education, surveillance, and other pressures. Rousseau had a psychological fixation on illusion and deception, on *la main cachée.* It is the *illusion* of self-determination that is fostered, never the reality. We must always come back to Rousseau's great symbol of Julie's garden in *La Nouvelle Héloïse,* which epitomizes all his work. The whole antithesis between Rousseau and the liberal *philosophes* is also epitomized in the contrast between Julie's garden and Candide's garden. The latter is an enterprise of freely co-operating individuals; they grumble and are far from the utopian city of El Dorado. But they have learned from experience that this is the best they can do in the world of men as they are, and so, out of enlightened self-interest and with limited ends in mind, they work together with a decent measure of fraternity and good will. They never pretend to establish an ideal society, unity, and harmony, or to solve all the problems. Julie's garden, in contrast, is a utopian, self-sufficient enclosure, in whose limited sphere unlimited perfection is attained. Nothing in her garden is forcefully or overtly coerced; everything is, so to speak, "conditioned" and "guided" by the gardener's "hidden hand." Everything seems free (i.e., natural), but it is all illusion.

Everything entitles us to interpret the *Social Contract* as reflecting the same ideas and methods we find in the other works. That is why we have tried to view Rousseau's system and his society as a whole, embracing all his writings. This is how he conceived them; this is what he means when he speaks of the unity of his work.

Professor John Plamenatz is the dupe of none of Rousseau's artifices. Why can we not follow him, then, when in the brilliant essay in which he fights so hard to "save" Rousseau for the side of the angels he asserts that all Rousseau meant was that ultimately people would willingly put the public interest first, and that the rest is just a method of education to bring them to this point? [8] First, the argument smacks too much of the Marxist utopian assurance that after "a certain point" government will wither away. Second, what lies before that point of willingness, the process of "education," is repugnant and unacceptable. Third, the process is not one that is capable of being limited. Common sense and history both confirm this, and there is nothing in Rousseau's texts to indicate that he thought otherwise. On the contrary, the evidence is ample that he envisaged a continuing indoctrination, control, and conditioning, and a continuing vigilance over the citizens—all to be in the hands of the State.

The reason is clear, and we see it throughout: Rousseau had confidence neither in men nor in enlightenment (which he above all avoids), but only in guidance. That is why I have suggested that his polity might properly be called a "guided democracy." The great error in interpreting the *Social Contract* has been to think that he counts on laws to govern men. But he himself repeatedly denied this, and placed greatest emphasis on "education," censorship, surveillance and denunciation, control of "opinion," and inculcation of emotions and ideas—the whole hidden apparatus.

When freedom becomes the synonym of docility, the meaning of the word is perverted, and we are speaking the Aesopian language of the totalitarian. Rousseau always considers the masses as children and treats them as such. They need guides and moral guardians, like Moses and Lycurgus, who have the skill and the charisma required to "form people" and to control them by capturing their wills. That control must be perpetuated, or harmony and order will be overturned by the *natural* force of the *moi humain*. Rousseau expresses this aim too often and too consistently for there to be room for doubt; and his aim involves a degree of control that is not consonant with liberty, as we understand that word. Rousseau does not think it difficult for the skillful manipulator, who understands the mechanisms of human behavior and reactions, to fool and to guide people.[9] Voting is a ceremony, a rite. After the pressures which are applied from childhood have formed the citizen, he conceivably may be allowed to be autonomous—that is, assuming that the additional pressures to which he is constantly subjected in *Project of a Constitution for Corsica* and *Considerations on the Government of Poland* are removed. But then, like Emile, he will be allowed "autonomy" only because his will has been captured, because he has been reshaped in the desired mold, so that, thinking the right thoughts and experiencing the right emotions, he will respond, when he receives "guidance," with a precommitment to the *moi commun*. Rousseau's citizen is free only in the sense that, having been "formed," he has been compelled, unknowingly, to will this aim "freely."

Yet Rousseau constantly speaks of "liberty," or freedom, and we must know what he means by that word. His sincerity about this idea cannot be doubted. We may feel that he is unscrupulous in his methods of guidance, but he is absolutely committed to the kind of liberty he preaches. First we must understand what liberty does *not* mean, in his conception. It does not mean a government in which we express our will through representatives, a government of checks and balances, or a counterpoise or compromise of conflicting wills and interests. It does not mean inalienable rights, constitutionally specified or traditionally sacred, beyond the reach of the majority or a so-called general will. It does mean, first, independence of the city-state from foreign oppression, interference, and influence—in other words, something approaching autarchy. And he often uses the word in this sense only, when others have interpreted it according to their own meaning. Second, it signifies independence of the individual from the will or power of any other individual or group. Third, as the price for this independence, it means the individual's total dependence on, or willing obedience and submission to, the "impersonal, inflexible yoke" of the general will (the analogue of natural necessity), as expressed in law,[10] or as that will is understood and executed by the officers of government.[11] "Freedom," to Rousseau, always means willing obedience to "necessity" (physical, moral, political), and complete independence in all other regards.[12] Liberty, expressed in Rousseau's vocabulary, is the fact of being *liberated* from the lower *moi humain* to be uplifted into the *moi commun*.[13]

This whole system reduces liberty to something formal or mechanical. It deprives individuals of inner freedom. It is remarkable that a number of scholars still try to present a system of social constraint as if it were a system of liberty. To suppose that an original commitment to the rule of the majority or general will carries with it an unlimited promise of absolute intellectual, emotional, and volitional submission, regardless of what those who formulate the general will do or require and regardless of one's own convictions—this is to turn the meaning of liberty topsy-turvy. Such "liberty," permitting of little or no sphere reserved to the "human self," can only be a pretext for absolute control, as it is in all totalitarian societies. When dissent is silenced, approval is assured. A liberal society is one that respects individual freedom of conscience and recognizes the legitimacy of loyalty to something that transcends political authority. Why should the minority of conscientious objectors, asks McAdam, believe that the majority are always right? Must we assume that dissent from the so-called general will is a matter of egoism and passion? May it not be in the name of justice and conscience, of something above the law? But Rousseau will not let there be anything above the law, which creates and defines the right; and for him the individual conscience can never be above the collective conscience of the general will. Although liberty is regarded by him as man's moral right, it "can be expressed only collectively as a sovereign right." [14] But as Constant said, despotic power is evil in itself, regardless of who wields it. "A maximization of political liberty, in Rousseau's sense, does not entail a maximization of personal liberty." [15] That is why he speaks of "austere democracy" and of "the yoke of liberty." [16]

Like the general will, Rousseau's liberty is an abstract, quasi-mystical element; it is not rooted in concrete individual experience. It is the freedom not of the *moi humain* but of the self, conditioned to experience itself, as Rousseau states, only as a part of the *moi commun*. Considered from the viewpoint of the secret control which Rousseau demands, freedom is an induced illusion, like that of Spinoza's falling stone, or even a semi-hysteria. Hegel, who had read his Rousseau well, wrote in the *Philosophy of History* that "the history of the world is the disciplining of the uncontrolled *natural* will, bringing it into obedience to a universal principle and conferring *subjective* freedom." [17] That is why the substitution of Rousseau's definition of liberty for the traditional definition "requires by its very essence the denaturing of men." [18] The law is his "universal principle." However, to obey only the law (even if it were only the law that was to be obeyed) is not, as I have said, a sufficient condition of freedom, since laws may be so coercive as to destroy freedom in any meaningful sense. Liberty depends on the number and kind of laws that have to be obeyed, not on mere obedience to legitimate authority. To say that every law makes us free is a doctrinaire abstraction.

Nor is equality before the law, as Rousseau maintains, an adequate condition of freedom, although it is a necessary one. Equality, wrote Hegel, does not let us distinguish between equality of treatment and equality of mistreatment. In theory, equality and slavery are not exclusive—especially if the master is the State. No dependence, no matter how complete, can, in Rousseau's view, affect or diminish an individual's liberty, because the general will is his true will and it is impersonal and equal for all.

In the liberal view there is no will that is held to be, by definition, everybody's; a plurality of wills is recognized and even encouraged. But for Rousseau, as Gilliard has pointed out, it is not for individuals to judge the State or its laws.[19] He has freed the State from the traditional limits of the Natural Law school and replaced them by the complete submission of the minority to the general will, which has been "discovered" by the voting process. For him "true" will is opposed to the private will, which is not aimed at the general welfare. Impersonal dependence on the Whole, participation, equality in the application of laws: these, for Rousseau, are the sole and sufficient conditions of a free society.

The simple fact is that nothing could be more inimical to the society Rousseau desired than the freedom of pluralism; in its presence the remaking and "denaturing" of man would be impossible. Because human nature is what it is, a truly "co-operative," collective, or organic society can never be a free society. Rousseau's thesis is that the citizen can be at once a free individual and a member of a society whose exclusive goal is the common good, and from which variant individual and group interests are eliminated by the "educational," supervisory, and animating techniques he proposes. In our view, the two parts of the proposition are mutually exclusive.[20]

Rousseau did not ignore the evidence of human behavior or the testimony of history. Unlike the anarchists of the eighteenth and nineteenth centuries, he never thought that men would be good once corrupt institutions were eliminated; he knew that men had made those institutions. That is why all his societies are characterized by rigid discipline and regulation of the individual by those who rule. Rousseau never entertains the Christian idea that men can love each other, or place others above themselves. Instead, he has the genius to realize that each ego can be made to identify itself emotionally with a relatively impersonal group or institution—as we know individuals do with athletic teams, schools, or nations. In this way ego-centeredness is overcome by projecting the ego into a fictitious relation of identity with something that is not really itself—even to the point of sacrificing one's life.

Rousseau's constant ideal is "order." Order, to be sure, is an essential condition of political liberty and individual freedom. But there are many kinds of order. The question is whether Rousseau's order is designed to promote individual liberty, as many commentators maintain, or to force the individual to think of himself only as part of the organic whole, as Rousseau himself distinctly states. His attitude is quite clear: man, the only disorderly element, must be reduced to the order that prevails elsewhere in nature (or in God's world, if one prefers). Referring to Emile, P. Burgelin writes, "Doesn't he see that the whole trouble comes from the fact that our freedom disturbs the order?" [21] For Rousseau this truth is equally applicable to society. With freedom the competitive, acquisitive, aggressive tendencies immediately come into play. Now if the source of evil in society is freedom, then obviously the remedy lies in its suppression or control. That is the purpose of the collective State and of the action of the Legislator-Pedagogue. Rousseau knew that the socialization of man could not be accomplished without conditioning, coercion, and the repression of individual independence or rights. The unity he sought could not be created or maintained voluntarily or in an open, pluralistic society. But the *feeling* of freedom is a necessary ruse to mask control and a way of obtaining willing consent. It is necessary if we are to remake men into the *docile* components of the *moi commun*.[22] Unless men act "freely," the whole process will fail.

"Docile," in its etymological sense, means that a subject can be easily taught or guided. It is difficult not to think that for Rousseau it means that what the leader (*"chef"* or *"guide"*) says is good will be approved and what he says is bad will be disapproved. This duplicity is inherent in Rousseau's thinking from beginning to end. In the *Social Contract* the stratagem is participation, but the freedom is juggled away by the total character of the participation and by the grip of censorship and the guide. The individual exists, at best, only as a mathematical unit in making the collective will; beyond that, he must be a part of it, as far as it extends. Absolute conformity becomes the definition of liberty; nonconformity is treason to liberty and justifies "force" being brought into play. No nuances, degrees, or alternatives are admissible.

While Rousseau emphasizes participation to the practical exclusion of safeguards, the liberal view emphasizes the safeguards. If Rousseau had not been able to count on the indoctrination mechanisms of the State, we may be sure that he would never have admitted the idea of popular suffrage, for he had no confidence in the people. How attractive it sounds when Rousseau says that liberty is "obeying a law that we prescribe to ourselves," until we realize that it is no longer the existential self of which he is talking but a transcendent self, and that the self we feel to be ours no longer has any status. How typical are the father's words to Sophie: "The husband who suits you should be of your choosing and not ours. But it is for us to judge whether you are not mistaken about his suitability, and whether, without realizing it, you are not doing something other than what you want." [23] Similarly, Rousseau would agree with d'Holbach, who declares in his *Ethocratie* that freedom is "the right to do for your own happiness or interest whatever is not contrary to the happiness or interest of others"; [24] but for Rousseau the determination of what constitutes the "happiness or interest of others" is removed entirely from the untrustworthy individual and given to the State.

Rousseau's political theory in the *Social Contract* has as its object to show how a civil society can be created without depriving its members of their liberty. The contracting party must feel as free as before. As we have seen, he tries to accomplish this by changing the meaning of "liberty," relating it to a new, artificial will or self (*le moi commun*). But the "liberty" in Rousseau's new terms remains as absolute as ever—even more absolute, since it no longer has recognizable limits. For liberal writers, such as Locke, authority is accepted as a frank limit to individual liberty and is not proposed as the new meaning of liberty. A part is kept, a part is given up. Even in Rousseau's own time, Elie Luzac, in a refutation of the *Social Contract*, denied the validity of his explanation that, if one participates in the formation of the general will, by virtue of that participation the general will and his own are necessarily identical.

> Whoever undertakes a commitment gives up a part of his liberty, because he limits his will by new obligations. Consequently, instead of speaking of an association *by which each, uniting with all, still obeys only himself, and remains as free as before,* you should have aimed at an association in which *each* loses as little freedom as possible.[25]

For Rousseau, the transmuted notion of liberty produced a new and total liberty. The word must, in his scheme, acquire a meaning that will allow the reconditioning of human beings and the elimination of individual independence. And so, through the two elements of participation and equality, any obligation that is imposed becomes an act of freedom, one that requires the individual to be free.

In Rousseau's State there will be an ever-increasing invasion of the private sphere (a *sine qua non* of liberty) by the public. This is inevitable in all societies of the type. In the politics of collectivism privacy is sacrificed to the group. The person is unimportant and disregarded; only "the people" count.[26] As P. Grosclaude has remarked, it is impossible in Rousseau's system to fix a limit to the public domain. There is bound to be "a continuing process of absorption of individual souls by the State; gradually the thought of the Man-Citizen becomes annexed, confiscated, drowned in a sort of collective soul, fashioned by the State."[27] The *Project of a Constitution for Corsica* bears witness to this. Any significant limitation would mean the continuance of natural independence. Logic, human nature, and history all show that the supposed "limitation" to "total" alienation, which we have discussed, is meaningless. Even in the more general *Social Contract*, we encounter a statement such as this one: "The better the State is constituted, the more do public affairs supersede private ones in the minds of the Citizens. There are even many fewer private matters. . . ." (IV, 15.) In a perfect State, men "have only one will," and that will is "directed toward the general welfare." Sexual puritanism, obscurantism, and condemnation of luxury all fit into the pattern. Professor Plamenatz suggests that in Rousseau's State there will be little restraint by laws, because passions are weak. He does not stop to ask how passions are made weak, and this is the essential point which refutes the first statement. Yet, he goes on to admit that a man is free not only when he is in conformity with the moral will, but "to the extent that he can live as seems good to him" and according to his own values and aspirations; otherwise men must become somebody else that they do not wish to be.[28]

If there is to be but one will, the antithesis of liberty and authority must be completely abolished; and this is precisely what the theory does. In a liberal society that antithesis can only be attenuated and compromised, never resolved. As Hume wrote, neither liberty nor authority can absolutely prevail; but "the authority which confines liberty can never and perhaps ought never in any constitution become quite entire and uncontrollable."[29] The authority of a magistrate, he adds, "can never subvert other opinions equally rooted with that of [the magistrate's] title to dominion." Rousseau's society denies the second condition and controverts the first. Before him, Montesquieu had written that in democracies "the people's power has been confused with the people's freedom."[30] And long before him, Aristotle had warned that extreme democracy is a "collective tyranny," in which the people are a single composite autocrat. Such a system, in which "whatever the majority decides must be the perfect embodiment of justice," leads to the leader or demagogue, whose power "rests on the universal sovereignty of the people, who lend him a ready ear and thus enable him to control the voting." [31]

In such a society the very nature of moral value is bound to change. That is why, despite all that has been said to the contrary, it is meaningless to call Rousseau's scheme one for an "ethical State," except in the sense that his State becomes *de facto* the source and arbiter of moral value. To inculcate virtue is his goal; but that word now acquires a specific and unique point of reference. As d'Entrèves puts it, "meta-state" values are excluded. [32] Virtue, like all else, will take on a political coloration and coalesce, as in the Robespierrian regime, with patriotism. It will signify to overcome the ego-centered instinct and to live for the collective Whole, the nation and its will.

Rousseau's phrase, "he will be forced to be free," has probably inspired more agitation than any other. There is something repugnant about it. Pierre Naville, in a contemporary refutation, called Rousseau's phrase "a nice antithesis" and asserted that force destroys freedom. [33] We have seen that Rousseau's idea goes beyond the concept of participation alluded to in the passage quoted from Luzac. It involves the rational concept of freedom as compelled obedience to an "ought," rather than to desire (desire may also be to adhere to an obligation). J. Plamenatz has astutely remarked that Rousseau "draws our attention to something peculiar to the sense of duty." [34] In obeying the law we may be thwarted, but we feel free because it is the law. Nevertheless, even if we accept this idea, it does not solve the problem of who really determines the "ought" that one is free in obeying. And, as Sabine has pointed out, to say that coercion is really not coercion is "a paradox of the worst sort. . . . In other words, coercion is not really coercion because when a man individually wants something different from what the social order gives him, he is merely capricious and does not rightly know his own good or his own desires." In this fashion "liberty" becomes the name

> . . . for a sentiment with which even attacks on liberty wish to be baptized. . . . What was almost inevitably implied was that a man whose moral convictions are against those commonly held in his

community . . . ought to be suppressed. . . . Forcing a man to be free is a euphemism for making him blindly obedient to the mass or the strongest part. Robespierre made the inevitable application when he said of the Jacobins, "Our will is the general will." [35]

The liberal society and Rousseau's society are antipodal. Thucydides reports Diodotus as having said, "In fine, it is impossible to prevent, and only great simplicity can hope to prevent human nature from doing what it has once set its mind upon, by force of law or by any other deterrent force whatsoever." [36] Rousseau's purpose was to outflank this assertion, by reaching to the mind itself and to the heart. He said it many times, and nowhere more forthrightly than in "Political Economy."

All eighteenth-century political writers derived their systems from a theory of human nature. Most held that we must adhere to that nature, direct it but not violate it. To violate it, Diderot said, is useless and vain, productive of conflict only. Many thought that the task was to discover "natural" laws of government, grounded in human nature and relations, in Natural Law and natural rights, or in the laws of economics. Rousseau, like other utopians with a collectivist bent, broke with the natural. The social order, he wrote in *Emile,* is exactly the opposite of the natural order. The original human nature had been lost in a semi-mythical past, and the existing one was an intolerable disaster. The only human nature he could accept was one yet to be realized. He thought, as Marx was to think later, that history is a transformation of human nature; but he did not have Marx's religious faith that a utopian future was built into history.

Rousseau's purpose and hope were expressed most clearly by himself, some half-dozen years later, in a letter to the Physiocrat the Marquis de Mirabeau (26 July 1767). The great problem in politics, he writes, is "to find a form of government in which laws are above men." Comparing it to the quadrature of the circle, he admits that it may well have no solution. Should it not, he continues,

my opinion is that we must go to the opposite extreme, and put men as far above laws as possible; I should like the despot to be god. In a word, I see no tolerable middle ground between the most austere democracy and the most perfect Hobbism; for the conflict between men and laws, which puts a continual internal war in the State, is the worst of all political states.[37]

Order and harmony are, as ever, the *desiderata;* discipline and control of men (preferably in an "austere democracy"), the means.[38]

The contrast between Rousseau's political philosophy and that of the contemporary *philosophes* who were in the liberal tradition, such as Montesquieu, Voltaire, and Diderot, is only too evident. Whereas Rousseau had no confidence in an unconditioned, unguided people, Montesquieu wrote: "The people are admirably suited to choose those to whom they are to confide some part of their authority." [39] Diderot also declared the people capable of choosing "the most honest and best instructed man" as their representative.[40] Both believed in representative government and in what we call liberties and rights. For all these writers, the individual, rather than the community, the nation, or the State, is the seat of value. In his *Observations sur l'instruction aux députés,* Diderot declared: "The right of opposition seems to me, in a society of men, a natural, inalienable and sacred right." Without liberty, the individual is not a man. And Diderot did not mean "liberty" in Rousseau's sense: he meant that individuals, and the interest groups they form, do not lose all their validity, or their independence, in society. While Duclos, like Rousseau, thought that mores, rather than laws, shape a nation, he, like the other reformers, did not think of taking possession of men's consciences and trusted in laws (perhaps too naïvely) to control men's behavior in an adequate, but not complete, fashion.

Like Diderot and other writers of his time, Rousseau understood the problem as a conflict between man's nature as an ego and as a social being, or between the individual and society. This antithesis, together with the problem of the rational anarchist or nihilist, was present in the minds of both men. A part of Rousseau's purpose was to prove Diderot wrong and to solve the dilemma. Not for him was the *laissez-faire* philosophy of the Physiocrats, who believed that egoistic forces would work themselves out to a natural harmony. He clearly rejects Diderot's constant refusal to subordinate the individual's interests to those of the State. He had naught but scorn for the liberal alternative many proposed, to regulate competing egoisms by rules of fair play, by a better legislation and government, by enlightening men, or even, as in Montesquieu, by using egoistic motives. He could not have understood the liberal view as Adam Ferguson expressed it: "Liberty is maintained by the continuing difference and opposition of numbers, not by their concurring zeal. . . . In free States, therefore, the wisest laws express that medium and composition which contending parties have forced one another to adopt." [41] His mentality was unable to tolerate the idea that dissent from sanctioned opinion is vital to the general welfare, that diversity is socially desirable, or that the minority have inalienable rights. For him, the test of political institutions was their restoration of unity.

Rousseau was deeply impressed by the miserable condition of the French peasants and by the parasitic luxury of the aristocrats. He felt and recognized the "class struggle," although he never clearly formulated it, as he observed a wealthy, cultivated minority exploiting the many. Despite the rise of the middle classes, there was enough truth in this picture to enable us to understand his wrath at the injustice of the social system, his longing for a different world. [42] Rousseau was burdened, writes Vaughan, with "the sense that oppression is abroad upon the earth, that the weak are everywhere sacrificed to the strong, that the forms of justice are universally employed to maintain and perpetuate injustice." That is why justice is to be secured "only when the individual will has been totally 'surrendered' or 'annihilated,' and its place taken by that of the community at large." [43] For him there was only one way—to put an end to the competition and contention, to control not only men's acts but their wills, so that they could live in a true society. He did not—indeed, could not —imagine that the total State can be a harsher exploiter and oppressor than individuals or groups, because in his abstract thinking the Whole could not exploit itself or wish to injure itself, and the State could have no interest other than that of its citizens. We see this in the regime of *La Nouvelle Héloïse*, where the exploitation is supposed to be a benevolent part of a happy collectivity. Since the condition of "equality" seemed to him an adequate safeguard, he did not imagine that all can be equally miserable and enslaved, and their lot far worse than in the societies he condemned, in which exploitation and oppression were more or less limited and inefficient.

As J. Plamenatz has so well expressed it, "Rousseau puts his mind to a problem which the Stoics ignored: What is the social and political order in which men do not acquire the needs and passions which prevent their being happy?" [44] The order which "would do for all what Emile's tutor does for his pupil" will perforce follow the same patterns of absolute control, modified for different conditions. To prevent the members from having needs they cannot satisfy, or which would cause them to make demands on others that others would be unwilling to meet, equality of a kind must be enforced. A way of life must be imposed that will make the members think that appeasing their appetites and aspirations is not the manner of life that will really satisfy them; that if certain *desiderata* are beyond their immediate power, they should not make it their purpose (as Diderot's Rameau or Sade's characters did) to acquire that power at the expense of others. Like most eighteenth-century writers, Rousseau was acutely conscious of the fact that men would do this if they were left to follow their nature.[45] He was right in supposing that men (except in some organic societies of primitive peoples) have always lived by exploiting others. This trait is natural to them, and distinguishes them as a species. Rousseau conceived a society of equal submission to the *moi commun*, incarnated in the State, so that exploitation would be no longer possible. This would be the true triumph of culture over nature. But to accomplish this end, is it not necessary, as Rousseau said it was, to "capture wills," to make men do willingly what is demanded of them, to develop "docility"? In order to make them want to be free, in accordance with this predetermined definition of liberty (which makes any other freedom an unfreedom), it is first necessary to deprive them of their liberty. "We must subject men to make them free." This control of needs and desires again controverts the supposition that Rousseau looked forward, even in theory, to an ultimate reliance on self-discipline—he could not, at least, unless and until the individual could be brought to a point where his actions would be necessary reactions, as in the case of Emile. Again we see why, in Rousseau's mind, freedom and order are antithetical, why "behavioral engineering" is required to overcome (or prevent) the false order—which is a real disorder—of existing societies.

The words "liberty" and "free" have been a doctrinal part of the vocabulary of both totalitarians and their adversaries. Almost all ideologies have hoisted these banners, and yet each one has given those words a different meaning. Rousseau, like the later Marxists, felt that only a revolutionary approach, purging present societies of their injustices, could assure real liberty, even though personal, political, and intellectual liberties had to be sacrificed to assure the total force of the general will. He leads us ultimately to the self-defeating paradox that a "free" society cannot tolerate free individuals; if the latter are not carefully nurtured, supervised, and controlled, they will destroy the former.

It is obvious, incidentally, that if men are prevented from having needs and desires beyond what it is decided that they should have, happiness is also determined from without the sentient individual. This was indeed Rousseau's expressed preference for "public" happiness over private. It is difficult not to imagine the same pall of conformity we saw in the modern utopias extending over his ideal realms.

The city of the social contract is a recapturing of the state of nature in the sense that no individual will be in the power of others, that there will be no search for domination, no war among men—the ideals for which Marxism was also to strive. Impersonal dependency on the Whole, like that on nature, is free of the taint of the aggressive individual ego. But in all positive respects, the city is unlike the state of nature, which cannot therefore be considered as a model for it. The contract is a new beginning.[46] The true model, in Rousseau's thought, is not nature, but Julie's garden.

The eighteenth-century Enlightenment is often thought of as a simple, unified movement leading to liberal democracy. This is a historical simplification, indeed, a falsification. To understand the historical reality we must see the place of antithetical tendencies, such as moralism and nihilism, authoritarianism and anarchism, competing in the same era. The elements of liberal democracy are present in many eighteenth-century writers; but the idea of totalitarian democracy also had its roots in the period.

The liberal stream of thought which the Enlightenment passed on to the future wanted to protect the plurality of interests while regulating their interplay. For Rousseau, whether in Wolmar's domain or in the society of the contract, there could be only one interest; and the collectivity had to be a monolith. Only in this way could the great questions of the time be answered: How is the sacrifice of personal good to be justified? How are men to be led to make the sacrifice? How is such a demand to be reconciled with the theory that the only motive of behavior is self-interest? To which we may add: How is one to justify a condition in which man, born free, is in chains? This was the question Rousseau had set out to answer at the beginning of the *Social Contract*.

It is not inappropriate to quote here de Tocqueville's words about the menace of oppression—a type of oppression different from anything there had been in the world before—that hangs over a democracy. He speaks of an absolute, protective power:

> It gladly works for their happiness, but wants to be sole agent and judge thereof. It provides for their security, foresees and supplies their necessities, facilitates their pleasures, manages their principal concerns, directs their industry, makes rules for their testaments. . . . It does not break men's will, but softens, bends and guides it. . . . It hardens, enervates, stifles, and stultifies so much that in the end each nation is no more than a flock of timid and hardworking animals with the government as its shepherd.[47]

The concept of freedom varies from one culture to another, according to the peculiar historical experience of each. One might add that it varies between two types of individuals, according to personality and intellectual outlook. Rousseau's case supports this view. Certainly, what he wanted and designed seemed to him to be freedom, and in some societies it would be so considered. We must, when we call it authoritarian and oppressive, be perfectly clear that we are speaking from the viewpoint of our own society, one that cultivates pluralism and openness and considers the individual human being to be the locus of value.

Rousseau loved mankind, if not men. He looked around him and dreamed of a better life than the one he saw. He felt the enmity among men, understood the increasing materialism that had taken possession of the world. He knew that civilization had embarked on a perilous course in which men might become mere objects, losing the subjective realm of their existence, their inner selves. He was the first to feel the problem of human unhappiness in modern society, the alienation, injustice, and moral corruption. With his passion for abstract justice, he wanted to end the exploitation of man by man. Never, in his political speculation, did he seek refuge in God, or escape in mechanical or historical determinism. He thought only—when he did not retreat into himself—of regenerating man, of regenerating society. Because he wanted to reverse the prevailing ethos of each against all, of acquisitiveness and egocentricity versus community, he felt that mere reform was a futile delusion, a trap that ends in our being made a part of "the system." A social order founded on exploitation, ruthless competition, and hypocrisy cannot be reformed; it can only be eliminated. It never occurred to him that the monolithic State, in the name of all, for the good of all could exploit and crush individuals. "Under an appearance of euphoria a sly, implacable order is installed." [48] He was going to show men how to be happy. History testifies that this idealism recurs, and that in every instance it succumbs to the force of power, or the power of force. The idealists are liquidated first.

Rousseau's "new order" was only a dream, a speculation. But, he felt, unless the course of society could be halted—and that meant changing man's whole world and man himself—there was no hope for the future. It is obvious that many still believe that he was right, and I do not pretend to have proved that he was not. Certainly, "warfare" among individuals and self-interested power groups, all seizing what they can at the expense of others and of society as a whole, exists, more or less, in all open societies. This may be the price for living in society—especially in individual-centered societies—without being social in the sense that certain animals are and that Rousseau would have liked us to be—that is, able to react *socially* with the certainty of physical laws. Should we pay this price? It may be that Rousseau's ideals —a passionate devotion to social justice and to the sense of community, the responsibility to contribute to the welfare of the collective—outweigh all other considerations. But I am more inclined to think that absolutes and human reality are incompatible, and that the only way to put an end to evil, injustice, inequality, and aggression is to make an end to mankind—which does not discharge us, however, from the duty of continually resisting wrongs. However that may be, we can make such a judgment only if we understand objectively the kind of society Rousseau wanted, and if we do not delude ourselves about its character or pretend that it was in any way like our own.

Michael Oakeshott has said that "human life . . . appears generally . . . as a predicament. . . . Every masterpiece of political philosophy springs from a new vision of the predicament, each is the glimpse of a deliverance or the suggestion of a remedy." In this essay, I have tried to suggest that as we look over the span of Rousseau's writings, his messianic dream of a millennial deliverance is a nightmare far worse than the reality he so properly condemned. The modern behaviorist who affirms that it is possible to condition people to like anything or to act according to any desired pattern, so that there is only one predictable reaction to any stimulus, has been anticipated with clarity and precise detail, in principle and method, by Rousseau. Such is the extraordinary modernity of his thought. But even if this can be done, we in a free, pluralistic society are not willing to allow society or government to exercise this power. We sense that the obtaining of such specific predictable responses that might give to moral laws the necessity of physical laws would be inseparable from the dehumanization of man. What is human are not specific responses, but flexibility, creativity or spontaneity, the imagination of new possibles, and judgment according to our values. This is what Rousseau feared and wanted to control or bypass.[49] He was willing to give to government the power to do to men all it deemed necessary as the only way of achieving a true society. And it is for this reason, more than any other, that I consider him a totalitarian. What matters, after all, is what happens to the individual.

Notes

[1] I obviously do not mean to imply that Rousseau would have liked the Führer, or that his hero figures resemble him. I am referring to *roles,* not to the way in which specific individuals enact them.

[2] The admission, in *Nineteen Eighty-Four,* that the wielders of power do exploit is only the disabused view, expressed *in camera,* of those who have learned the realities beyond the utopian dream.

[3] Rousseau perhaps never conceived of a secret police, as such. But when we consider his censors who, supposedly the declarers of public opinion, actually control thoughts and behavior; his surveillance, spying, and delation; his proposal to judge thoughts from behavior; his injunction to the Legislator to control secretly the people's opinions—taking all these proposals into consideration, how far are we from the idea of a secret police?

[4] Among these are subjective certainty, a conspiratorial outlook, ethnocentrism and nationalism (Rousseau dreams of walled-in domains and is hostile to outsiders and fearful of their influence), admiration of strong men and military virtues, distinction of groups of inferior people, rigidity and absoluteness, refusal to compromise in ideology or action, separation of men and women, latent homosexuality, a feeling of the world as hostile, a fear of complex, transient relationships, and an aversion to complex, nuanced explanations.

[5] *Confessions,* p. 224.

[6] See my article, "Rousseau et l'opinion.' "

[7] Once again, all education involves pre-set values and modes of behavior; but we do not define freedom as conformity to them—not even reflective conformity.

[8] J. Plamenatz, *Man and Society, Political and Social Theory*, I.

[9] An analogical statement is made by the guide, Wolmar, about Saint-Preux: "He is spirited, but weak and easy to subjugate. I make use of this advantage by tricking his imagination." (*La Nouvelle Héloïse*, Part IV, Letter XIV, p. 494.)

[10] "It is because of the laws that he does not obey men." (*Lettres écrites de la Montagne*, Lettre VIII, in *Oeuvres*, Pléiade edition, III, 842; also 492.)

[11] "As long as the government acts only for the public good, it is impossible for it to offend liberty, because then it is only carrying out the general will, and nobody can call himself enslaved when he obeys only his own will." (Fragment, in *Oeuvres*, Pléiade edition, III, 484.) It is obvious that in these circumstances, the government is the judge of the public good and the general will, and that it imposes the identification expressed at the end. Another will and judgment becomes ours, so that we cannot dispute it or disobey it. In an earlier work Rousseau had expressed a different view: "the pretext of the public good is always the most dangerous scourge of the people." (See "Political Economy," in *Political Writings*, I, 254.) Either his thinking evolved, or he had the example of existing States in mind.

[12] In *La Nouvelle Héloïse* and *Emile* it is the same relation of dependence and willing submission to the guide or superior person—doing what *he* knows we ought to do.

[13] As S. Cotta puts it, "The fact nonetheless remains that this legal liberty [as contrasted with the state of nature] can be obtained only by the strictest submission and obedience to the general will, by the sacrifice of all personal aspirations and opinions." Liberty is the "deliverance from servitude to egoistic individualism," freedom from error. "One no longer has the right to be wrong." Both a sphere of individual autonomy and the right to one's own opinions put the *self* above the *whole* and are principles of disorder. Liberty is "servile conformity." Rousseau, concludes Cotta, wants "a mechanical, static and not a dialectical harmony," not the "responsible, creative freedom of the self" or the "autonomy of the human person." ("Théorie religieuse et théorie politique chez Rousseau," pp. 186–89.)

[14] J. I. McAdam, "Rousseau and the Friends of Despotism," p. 41.

[15] *Ibid.*

[16] If the general will is truly arrived at by counting votes, writes Bronowski, we need only fear the tyranny of the majority. "If, however, the general will is an abstract 'justice,' then the shadow of Robespierre and his 'reign of virtue' looms upon the threshold of history. And this is exactly what happened." (*The Western Intellectual Tradition*, p. 302.)

[17] Italics added.

[18] J. Dehaussy, "La Dialectique de la souveraine liberté dans le *Contrat*

social," p. 131. J. N. Shklar remarks that freedom for Rousseau was not "a matter of doing as one pleases, but of *not* being compelled, either from within or without, to do what one does *not* wish to do." ("Rousseau's Images of Authority," p. 931.) The point overlooked in this statement is that it is the *wish* that Rousseau's strategy is designed to control, and control absolutely.

[19] F. Gilliard, "Etat de nature et liberté dans la pensée de Jean-Jacques Rousseau," in *Etudes sur le "Contrat social,"* pp. 112, 117.

[20] See J. C. Herold, "The Solitary Wanderer," pp. 95–102.

[21] P. Burgelin, "The Second Education of Emile," *Yale French Studies,* No. 28, p. 108. Elsewhere, in a beautiful passage, Burgelin develops the theme that Rousseau's problem was to reconcile order and existence, or reason and feeling. (*La Philosophie,* p. 572.) The solution is unity and harmony, within the individual and in the collective society.

[22] We recall one of Rousseau's statements in *Emile:* "Let him always think he is the master, but always be his master. There is no subjection so perfect as that which keeps the appearance of liberty; in this way we capture the will itself. . . . Of course he must always do what he wants, but he must want only what you want him to do." (*Emile,* p. 121.)

[23] *Emile,* p. 508.

[24] P. H. T. d'Holbach, *Ethocratie ou le gouvernement fondé sur la morale* (Amsterdam, 1776), p. 20.

[25] E. Luzac, *Lettre d'un anonyme à M. Jean-Jacques Rousseau* (Paris, 1766), quoted in R. Derathé, "Les Réfutations du *Contrat social* au XVIII° siècle," *AJJR,* XXXII (1950–52), 44.

[26] In liberal societies there is a large, well-defined private sphere from which government authority is excluded, and which is jealously protected. Sabine has observed that Rousseau "originated the romantic cult of the group, and this was the fundamental difference between his social philosophy and the individualism from [*sic*] which he revolted. . . . Rousseau's philosophy emphasized the aggrandizement of the group, the satisfaction of participation and the cultivation of the non-rational." (*A History of Political Theory,* p. 592.) This does not account for *Emile,* in which Rousseau infuses his own longing for independence *vis à vis* existing societies.

[27] P. Grosclaude, Commentary in *Jean-Jacques Rousseau et son oeuvre,* p. 263. Also P. Burgelin: "The police pry into private life. Social man never belongs to himself; his whole life is public, and the problem of government is not so much to direct actions by discipline as to envelop the individual, to penetrate him with habits, to arouse desires, and so to know him completely as the tutor does the child." Rousseau likes small towns, "where the citizen's house is of glass," and women, by their gossip, "perform the role of censors." (*La Philosophie,* p. 559.)

[28] J. Plamenatz, *Man and Society, Political and Social Theory,* I, 390,

416. The contrary view, that freedom is not the free will of an individual, but the "rational will," an absolute, is reformulated by Hegel in his *Lectures on the History of Philosophy* (London, 1955), III, 402. Consider also the following statement by R. N. Fano, a social scientist:

> Whereas the enforcement of social norms may be essential to the effective operation of society, it is practically impossible to establish social norms that are reasonable for all people in all situations. Some deviations from social norms are to be expected and tolerated. Furthermore, they are essential to social experimentation and therefore to social progress. Privacy is the mechanism that enables society to ignore deviations it regards as permissible while still upholding social norms and punishing flagrant violations of them. It is also the mechanism that permits the gradual evolution of social norms. . . . In a sense privacy decouples the individual from the rest of society. It is a social function needed to keep his thoughts and actions from being distorted by society's reaction to them.

(Review of A. F. Westin, *Privacy and Freedom*, in *The Scientific American*, Vol. 218 [May, 1968], p. 150.)

[29] Hume, "Of the Origin of Government," in *Hume's Moral and Political Philosophy*, ed. H. D. Aiken (New York, 1948), pp. 313–14.

[30] *De l'Esprit des lois*, Book XI, Chapter 2.

[31] *Aristotle's Politics and the Athenian Constitution*, p. 109. The criticism often levelled against Rousseau since the eighteenth century, that his system would lead to a tyranny of the majority, is valid only if we remember that it is a tightly controlled majority, with the real directive power in the hands of one or a few. The accusation that he favored an individualistic anarchy springs, needless to say, from a total misunderstanding of his thought.

[32] In *Rousseau et la philosophie politique*, pp. 254–55.

[33] P. Naville, *Examen du Contrat Social de Jean-Jacques Rousseau. . . , AJJR*, XXII (1933), 61.

[34] J. Plamenatz, "Ce qui ne signifie pas autre chose, sinon qu'on le forcera d'être libre," in *Rousseau et la science politique, Annales de philosophie politique*, No. 5, pp. 150–51.

[35] G. H. Sabine, *A History of Political Theory*, pp. 590–91. Robespierre said, "The government of the Revolution is the despotism of liberty against tyranny." We are reminded of Rousseau's "inflexible yoke of liberty."

[36] *History of the Peloponnesian War*, p. 204.

[37] In *Correspondance générale*, XVII, 157.

[38] A year later, Rousseau wrote to his friend du Peyrou that the king must be master first, and then just; it would be better the other way, "but that is beyond the reach of mankind." (*Correspondance générale*, XIX, 23.)

P. Burgelin, in his masterful study *La Philosophie de l'existence de*

Jean-Jacques Rousseau, argues that Rousseau's despotism is only theoretical. (p. 560.) I should say that it is his liberty that is theoretical, and that the despotism is built into his institutions and his maxims of government. Burgelin also claims that Rousseau's "absolute despotism" is justified because it is exercised in the name of reason (p. 563), which (we infer from other pages) is a reflection of the divine order, or also the immanence of God in our conscience. Thus if we do not separate order in man from order in the State, "informing on others is the accusation brought by our own heart before the tribunal of our conscience." (p. 564.) However, despotism, exercised in the name of reason or of conscience, is still despotism; and on the practical or political level, as Rousseau knew, reason is never pure or unalloyed by will, and laws are rarely "approved in every conscience." (p. 541.) Are they any the less "inflexible and insuperable"? For Burgelin, this is the "price of human dignity." One wonders where is the dignity of Saint-Preux and Emile, both "infantilized," or of the Corsicans.

It is important to realize that in the *Social Contract,* as in the *Discourses,* Rousseau slides with deceptive ease from the abstract or theoretical plane to the political or historical plane, keeping the best of both worlds for his cause. When Rousseau says that obedience to "the law one has prescribed to himself is freedom," with all the meanings we have already examined, or when Burgelin concludes that it ends alienation and restores man to himself, we are on a philosophical plane, dealing with an ideal conception of man. We are on the plane of politics or experience when Burgelin quotes: "if you want laws to be obeyed, see to it . . . that for men to do what they should, it is enough for it to occur to them that they should do it" (p. 557), and when he admits that Rousseau's thought "leads him to minimize the individual person in order that it become more and more fused into the social body." (p. 552.)

[39] *De l'Esprit des lois,* Book II, Chapter 27.

[40] *Observations sur la confection des lois,* ed. P. Ledieu (Paris, 1921), Article 18.

[41] A. Ferguson, *An Essay on the History of Civil Society,* 1766, quoted by D. Thomson in "The Dream of Unanimity," *Fortnightly Review,* New Series, CLXXIII (1953), 79–80.

[42] We can, of course, similarly understand the reactions in the nineteenth century of French and German socialists or communists, who saw in the wake of the French Revolution only the substitution of a more cruel and efficient set of masters. Rousseau was as hostile to the nascent "capitalism" as to the expiring feudalism. The rising bourgeois liberalism was based on egocentric individualism, while for Rousseau the revolutionary idea of popular sovereignty was a way of conserving "a retrograde traditional economic and social condition." (I. Fetscher, *Rousseaus politische Philosophie* [Neuwied, 1960], reviewed in *Studi francesi,* No.

25.) His desired rural autarchy was more adaptable to control and to the collectivist idea.

[43] C. E. Vaughan, ed., *Political Writings*, I, 53–54; see also 56–57.

[44] J. Plamenatz, "Ce qui ne signifie pas autre chose, sinon qu'on le forcera d'être libre," p. 146.

[45] L. G. Crocker, *Age of Crisis* (Baltimore, 1959), Chapter 11.

[46] "Man depends immediately on law instead of on nature." (J. Starobinski, "Du *Discours sur l'inégalité* au *Contrat social*," in *Etudes sur le "Contrat social*," pp. 108–9.) Nature, however, is utilized, as in the cultivation of intense rivalry for distinction on the basis of zeal in the public service.

[47] *Oeuvres, papiers et correspondance* (Paris, 1952), Vol. 1, Part 2, pp. 324–25.

[48] R. Mauzi, *L'Idée du bonheur au XVIIIᵉ siècle*, p. 622.

[49] His purpose is "to set up automatons who will make of immediate [reflexive] life a life of virtue." (J. Starobinski, *Jean-Jacques Rousseau, la transparence et l'obstacle* [Paris, 1957], p. 266.)

Bibliography

"Adresse d'un citoyen très actif." Unpublished manuscript in Bibliothèque Nationale, Paris, France. No date.

Aristotle. *Aristotle's Politics and the Athenian Constitution*, edited and translated by J. Warrington. London, 1959.

Barker, Ernest. *Reflections on Government*. London, 1942.

Barth, H. "Volonté générale, volonté particulière," in *Rousseau et la philosophie politique*. Paris, 1965, pp. 35–50.

Bauclair, P. L. de. *Anti-Contrat Social*. La Haye, 1765.

Besse, Guy. "De Rousseau au Communisme," *Europe* (Paris), No. 391–92 (1961), pp. 167–80.

———. "Marx, Engels et le XVIIIᵉ siècle français," in *Studies on Voltaire and the Eighteenth Century* (Geneva), XXIV (1963), 155–70.

Bourguin, Maurice. "Les Deux tendances de Rousseau," *Revue de métaphysique et de morale* (Paris), XX (1912), 353–69.

Bronowski, J., and B. Mazlish. *The Western Intellectual Tradition*. New York, 1960.

Broome, J. H. *Rousseau. A Study of His Thought*. New York, 1963.

Burgelin, P. *La Philosophie de l'existence de Jean-Jacques Rousseau*. Paris, 1952.

———. "The Second Education of Emile," *Yale French Studies* (New Haven), No. 28 (1961–62), pp. 106–11.

Casini, Paolo. "Rousseau e Diderot," *Rivista Critica di Storia della Filosofia*. Florence, 1964, pp. 240–70.

Cassirer, Ernst. *The Question of Jean-Jacques Rousseau*. New York, 1954.

Cattaneo, M. A. *Le Dottrine politiche di Montesquieu e di Rousseau*. Milan, 1964.

Champion, E. J.-J. *Rousseau et la Révolution française*. Paris, 1909.

Cobban, A. *In Search of Humanity*. New York, 1960.

Constant, Benjamin. *Principes de politique,* in *Oeuvres,* édition de la Pléiade. Paris, 1957.
———. Review of Paul L. Léon, *L'Idée de volonté générale chez J.-J. Rousseau et ses antécédents historiques, Annales de la Société Jean-Jacques Rousseau* (Geneva), XXV (1936), 287–92.
Cotta, S. "L'Idée de parti dans la philosophie de Montesquieu," *Actes du Congres Montesquieu.* Bordeaux, 1956.
———. "La Position du problème de la politique chez Rousseau," in *Etudes sur le "Contrat social" de Jean-Jacques Rousseau.* Paris, 1965, pp. 177–90.
———. "Théorie religieuse et théorie politique chez Rousseau," in *Rousseau et la philosophie politique.* Paris, 1965, pp. 171–94.
Crocker, L. G. *An Age of Crisis. Man and World in Eighteenth Century French Thought.* Baltimore, 1959.
———. *Jean-Jacques Rousseau: The Quest* (1712–1758). New York, 1968.
———. "Julie, ou la nouvelle duplicité," *Annales de la Société Jean-Jacques Rousseau* (Geneva), XXXVI (1963–65), 105–52.
———. *Nature and Culture. Ethical Thought in the French Enlightenment.* Baltimore, 1963.
———. "The Priority of Justice or Law," *Yale French Studies* (New Haven), No. 28 (1962), pp. 34–42.
———. "Rousseau et la voie du totalitarianisme," in *Rousseau et la philosophie politique.* Paris, 1965, pp. 99–136.
———. "Rousseau et 'l'opinion,'" *Studies on Voltaire and the Eighteenth Century* (Geneva), LV (1967), 395–415.
De Grazia, S. *The Political Community: A Study of Anomie.* Chicago, 1948.
Dehaussy, J. "La Dialectique de la souveraine liberté dans le *Contrat social,*" in *Etudes sur le "Contrat social" de Jean-Jacques Rousseau.* Paris, 1964, pp. 119–41.
Della Volpe, G. "Critique marxiste de Rousseau," in *Etudes sur le "Contrat social" de Jean-Jacques Rousseau.* Paris, 1964, pp. 503–14.
———. "Du *Discours sur l'inégalité* à *L'Etat et la Révolution,*" *Europe* (Paris), No. 391–92 (1961), pp. 151–88.
Derathé, R. "Les Rapports de l'exécutif et du législatif chez Jean-Jacques Rousseau," in *Rousseau et la philosophie politique.* Paris, 1965, pp. 153–69.
———. "Les Réfutations du *Contrat social* au XVIII° siècle," *Annales de la Société Jean-Jacques Rousseau* (Geneva), XXXII (1950–52), 7–54.
———. "La Religion civile selon Rousseau," *ibid.,* XXXV (1959–62), 161–70.
———. Review of R. de Lacharrière, *Etudes sur la théorie démocra-*

tique: Spinoza, Rousseau, Hegel, Marx, in *ibid.*, XXXVI (1963–65), 356–58.

————. *Rousseau et la science politique de son temps.* Paris, 1950.

Diderot, D. *Observations sur l'instruction de S. M. I. aux députés pour la confection des lois*, ed. P. Ledieu. Paris, 1921.

————. *Plan d'une université*, in *Oeuvres*, Vol. III, ed. Assézat and Tourneux. Paris, 1875.

————. *Réfutation d'Helvétius*, in *ibid.*, Vol. II.

Dubos, René. "Science and Man's Nature," *The Graduate Journal* (Austin), VII (1965), 45–67.

Durkheim, Emile. *Montesquieu and Rousseau: Forerunners of Sociology.* Ann Arbor, 1960.

Ehrard, Jacques. *L'Idée de nature en France pendant la première moitié du XVIIIᵉ siècle.* Paris, 1963.

Eisenmann, Charles. "La Cité de Jean-Jacques Rousseau," in *Etudes sur le "Contrat social" de Jean-Jacques Rousseau.* Paris, 1964, pp. 191–201.

Fano, R. N. Review of A. F. Westin, *Privacy and Freedom*, in *The Scientific American* (New York), Vol. 218 (May, 1968).

Ferguson, A. *An Essay on the History of Civil Society* (7th edition). Edinburgh, 1814.

Fetscher, I. "Rousseau's Concepts of Freedom in the Light of His Philosophy of History," *Nomos* (New York), IV (1962), 29–56.

————. *Rousseaus politische Philosophie.* Neuwied, 1960.

Fichte, J. G. *Addresses.* Chicago, 1922.

Francis, Madeleine. "Les Réminiscenses spinozistes dans le *Contrat social* de Jean-Jacques Rousseau," *Revue philosophique* (Paris), Vol. 141 (1951), pp. 61–84.

Gilliard, F. "Etat de nature et liberté dans la pensée de Jean-Jacques Rousseau," in *Etudes sur le "Contrat social" de Jean-Jacques Rousseau.* Paris, 1964, pp. 111–18.

Godechot, J. "Le *Contrat social* et la Révolution occidentale de 1762 à 1789," in *Etudes sur le "Contrat social" de Jean-Jacques Rousseau.* Paris, 1964, pp. 393–405.

Gossman, Lionel. "Rousseau's Idealism," *Romanic Review* (New York), LVII (1961), 173–82.

Gouhier, Henri. "La Religion du Vicaire Savoyard dans la cité du *Contrat social*," in *Etudes sur le "Contrat social" de Jean-Jacques Rousseau.* Paris, 1964, pp. 263–75.

Green, T. H. *Works.* 3 vol. London, 1893.

Grosclaude, Paul. Commentary in *Jean-Jacques Rousseau et son oeuvre*, Actes et Colloques. Paris, 1963.

Gudin, Paul-Philippe. *Supplément au "Contrat social."* Paris, 1791.

Hegel, F. *Lectures on the History of Philosophy*. London, 1955.
Hempel, Wido. Review of Otto Vossler, *Rousseaus Freiheitslehre*, in *Annales de la Société Jean-Jacques Rousseau* (Geneva), XXXVI (1963–65), 311–20.
Herold, J. C. "The Solitary Wanderer," *Horizon* (New York), VI (1964), 95–102.
Herzstein, R. E. "German Intellectuals and German Reality, 1789–1933," *Arts and Sciences* (New York University Bulletin), Vol. LXVII, No. 22 (May 29, 1967), pp. 33–39.
Hocking. W. E. *Man and the State*. New Haven, 1926.
d'Holbach, P. H. T., baron. *Ethocratie ou le gouvernement fondé sur la morale*. Amsterdam, 1776.
———. *La morale universelle*. 3 vols. Paris, 1820.
Hume, D. "Of the Origin of Government," in *Hume's Moral and Political Philosophy*, ed. H. D. Aiken. New York, 1948, pp. 311–14.
Huxley, Aldous. *Brave New World*. New York, 1950.
Jouvenel, B. de. "Rousseau évolutionniste et pessimiste," in *Rousseau et la philosophie politique*. Paris, 1965, pp. 1–20.
Kendall, Willmore. *John Locke and the Doctrine of Majority Rule*. Urbana, 1940.
———. "Prolegomena to Any Future Work on Majority Rule," *Journal of Politics* (Gainesville), XII (1950), 694–713.
Lacharrière, R. de. "Rousseau et le socialisme," *Etudes sur le "Contrat social" de Jean-Jacques Rousseau*. Paris, 1964, pp. 515–35.
Langer, Susanne. *Philosophy in a New Key*. Cambridge, 1942.
Launay, Michel. Review of J.-J. Rousseau, *Oeuvres complètes* in *Annales de la Société Jean-Jacques Rousseau* (Geneva), XXXVI (1963–65), 406–19.
———. "Rousseau au Collège de France," *Europe* (Paris), No. 405–6 (1963), pp. 334–354.
Leigh, R. A. "Liberté et autorité dans le *Contrat social*," in *Jean-Jacques Rousseau et son oeuvre*, Actes et Colloques. Paris, 1963, pp. 249–64.
Leith, J. A. *The Idea of Art as Propaganda in France*. Toronto, 1965.
Lenormant, Ch.-Francois. *Jean-Jacques Rousseau, aristocrate*. Paris, 1790.
Ludwig, Emil. *Conversations with Mussolini*. Boston, 1933.
Luzac, Elie. *Lettre d'un anonyme à M. Jean-Jacques Rousseau*. Paris, 1766.
McAdam, J. I. "Rousseau and the Friends of Despotism," *Ethics* (Chicago), LXXIV (1963), 34–43.
MacNeil, G. H. "The Anti-Revolutionary Rousseau," *American Historical Review* (New York), LVIII (1953), 808–23.

————. "The Cult of Rousseau in the French Revolution," *Journal of the History of Ideas* (New York), VI (1945), 197–212.

Maistre, J. de. *The Works of Joseph de Maistre*. Translated by J. Lively. New York, 1965.

Marcuse, H. *Reason and Revolution*. London, 1941.

Mauzi, Robert. *L'Idée du bonheur au XVIIIe siècle*. Paris. 1960.

Mazauric, C. "Le Rousseauisme de Babeuf," *Annales historiques de la Révolution française* (Paris), XXXIV (1962), 439–64.

Meister, J. H. *De la morale naturelle*, London, 1788.

Mercier, L. S. *L'an deux mille quatre cent quarante*. 3 vols. Paris, 1786.

Meyer, Paul. "The Individual and Society in Rousseau's *Emile*," *Modern Language Quarterly* (Seattle), XIX (1958), 99–114.

Montesquieu. *De l'Esprit des lois*, ed. Jean Brethe de la Gressaye. 4 vols. Paris, 1950–61.

[Naville, Pierre.] *Examen du Contrat Social de Jean-Jacques Rousseau avec des remarques pour servir d'antidote à quelques principes*, in *Annales de la Société Jean-Jacques Rousseau* (Geneva), XXII (1933), 9–151.

Neumann, F. *The Democratic and the Authoritarian State*. Glencoe, 1957.

Orwell, George. *Nineteen Eighty-Four*. New York, 1949.

Peyre, H. "The Influence of Eighteenth Century Ideas on the French Revolution," *Journal of the History of Ideas* (New York), X (1949), 63–87.

Plamenatz, John. "Ce qui ne signifie pas autre chose, sinon qu'on le forcera d'être libre," in *Rousseau et la science politique, Annales de philosophie politique* (Paris), No. 5 (1965), pp. 137–52.

————. *Man and Society, Political and Social Theory*. 2 vols. New York, 1963.

Plato. *The Republic*, in *The Dialogues of Plato*. Translated by B. Jowett. 2 vols. New York, 1937.

Polin, Raymond. "Le Sens de l'égalité et de l'inégalité chez Jean-Jacques Rousseau," in *Etudes sur le "Contrat social" de Jean-Jacques Rousseau*. Paris, 1964, pp. 143–64.

Ritter, E. "Direct Democracy and Totalitarianism," *Diogenes* (New York), No. 7 (1954), pp. 59–67.

Rousseau, Jean-Jacques. *Correspondance*, ed. R. A. Leigh. Geneva, 1965 *et seq.*

————. *Correspondance générale*, ed. Dufour-Plan. 20 vols. Paris, 1924–34.

————. *Discours sur les sciences et les arts*, ed. George R. Havens. New York, 1946.

————. *Du Contrat social*, ed. M. Halbwachs. Paris, 1962.

————. *Emile*, ed. F. and P. Richard. Paris, 1951.

————. *Julie, ou la Nouvelle Héloïse,* ed. D. Mornet. 4 vols. Paris, 1925.

————. *Julie, ou la Nouvelle Héloïse,* ed. R. Pomeau. Paris, 1960.

————. *Oeuvres,* ed. Ch. Lahure. 13 vols. Paris: Librairie Hachette, 1865.

————. *Oeuvres,* ed. B. Gagnebin and M. Raymond. 3 vols. Paris: Gallimard (Bibliothèque de la Pléiade), 1959 (Vol. I), 1961 (Vol. II), 1964 (Vol. III).

————. *Political Writings,* ed. C. E. Vaughan. 2 vols. Cambridge, 1915.

————. *Politics and the Arts. Letter to M. d'Alembert on the Theatre.* Translated with notes and an introduction by Allan Bloom. Glencoe, 1960.

————. *The Social Contract.* Translated by H. J. Tozer. London, 1895.

Sabine, G. H. *A History of Political Theory* (revised edition). New York, 1950.

Schinz, A. *Etat présent des travaux sur Jean-Jacques Rousseau.* New York, 1941.

Shklar, J. N. "Rousseau's Images of Authority," *American Political Science Review* (Menasha), LVIII (1964), 919–32.

Skinner, B. F. *Walden Two.* New York, 1948.

Soboul, A. "Classes populaires et Rousseauisme sous la Révolution," *Annales historiques de la Révolution française* (Paris), XXXIV (1962), 421–38.

————. "J.-J. Rousseau et le Jacobinisme," in *Etudes sur le "Contrat social" de Jean-Jacques Rousseau.* Paris, 1964, pp. 405–24.

Spink, J. S. *Jean-Jacques Rousseau et Genève.* Paris, 1934.

Spinoza, B. de. *Writings on Political Philosophy,* ed. A. G. A. Balz. New York, 1937.

Starobinski, J. "Du *Discours sur l'inégalité* au *Contrat social,*" in *Etudes sur le "Contrat social" de Jean-Jacques Rousseau.* Paris, 1964, pp. 97–110.

————. *Jean-Jacques Rousseau, la transparence et l'obstacle.* Paris, 1957.

Stein, M. R., A. J. Vidich, and D. M. White (eds.). *Identity and Anxiety: Survival of the Person in a Mass Society.* Glencoe, 1960.

Stern, F. *The Politics of Cultural Despair.* Berkeley, 1961.

Talmon, J. L. *The Rise of Totalitarian Democracy.* Boston, 1952.

Thomson, D. "The Dream of Unanimity," *Fortnightly Review* (London), New Series, CLXXIII (1953), 75–80.

Thucydides. *History of the Peloponnesian War.* Translated by R. Crawley. New York, 1950.

Tönnies, Ferdinand. *Community and Society.* East Lansing, 1957.

Trenard, L. "La Diffusion du *Contrat social* (1762–1832)," in *Etudes sur le "Contrat social" de Jean-Jacques Rousseau*. Paris, 1964, pp. 425–58.

Van Eerde, J., and A. Hubbard. "The Christian Religion in the *Grande Encyclopédie* and in *The Great Soviet Encyclopedia*," *Saggi filosofici* (Turin), XIV (1964), 5–22.

Vattel, E. de. *Le droit des gens*. 3 vols. Washington, D. C., 1916.

Vitry, Aubert de. *Jean-Jacques Rousseau à l'Assemblée Nationale*. Paris, 1789.

Vlachos, G. "L'Influence de Rousseau sur la conception du *Contrat social* chez Kant et Fichte," in *Etudes sur le "Contrat social" de Jean-Jacques Rousseau*. Paris, 1964, pp. 459–80.

Voltaire. *Correspondance*, ed. T. Besterman. Geneva, Vol. 57 (1960), pp. 213–14.

Weiss, Peter. *The Persecution and Assassination of Jean-Paul Marat as Performed by the Inmates of the Asylum of Charenton under the Direction of the Marquis de Sade*. New York, 1965.

Wollaston, W. *The Religion of Nature Delineated*. London, 1726.

Wright, E. H. *The Meaning of Rousseau*. London, 1929.